ELEMENTS OF

Literature

INTRODUCTORY COURSE

The Holt Reader
An Interactive WorkText

Instruction in Reading Literature and Informational Materials

Standardized Test Practice

HOLT, RINEHART AND WINSTON

A Harcourt Education Company

Austin • Orlando • Chicago • New York • Toronto • London • San Diego

CREDITS

Supervisory Editors: Juliana Koenig, Fannie Safier

Managing Editor: Mike Topp

Administrative Managing Editor: Michael Neibergall

Senior Product Manager: Don Wulbrecht

Editors: Susan Kent Cakars, Quraysh Ali Lansana, Crystal Wirth, Michael Zakhar

Copyediting Supervisor: Mary Malone

Senior Copyeditor: Elizabeth Dickson

Copyeditors: Christine Altgelt, Joel Bourgeois, Emily Force, Julie A. Hill, Julia Thomas Hu, Jennifer Kirkland, Millicent Ondras, Dennis Scharnberg

Project Administration: Elizabeth LaManna

Editorial Support: Bret Isaacs, Brian Kachmar, Erik Netcher

Editorial Permissions: Kimberly Feden, Carrie Jones, David Smith

Design: Bruce Bond, *Design Director, Book Design*

Electronic Publishing: Nanda Patel, JoAnn Stringer, *Project Coordinators;* Sally Dewhirst, *Quality Control Team Leader;* Angela Priddy, Barry Bishop, Becky Golden-Harrell, Ellen Rees, *Quality Control;* Juan Baquera, *Electronic Publishing Technology Services Team Leader;* Christopher Lucas, *Team Leader;* Lana Kaupp, Kim Orne, Susan Savkov, *Senior Production Artists;* Ellen Kennedy, Patricia Zepeda, *Production Artists;* Heather Jernt, *Electronic Publishing Supervisor;* Robert Franklin, *Electronic Publishing Director*

Production/Manufacturing: Belinda Barbosa Lopez, Michael Roche, *Senior Production Coordinators;* Carol Trammel, *Production Manager;* Beth Prevelige, *Senior Production Manager*

Contents

PART 2 Reading Informational Materials

PART 3 Standardized Test Practice

Literature

Informational Materials

Skills Contents

Reading Skills for Informational Texts

To the Student

A Book for You

Imagine this. A book full of stories you want to read and informational articles that are really interesting. Make it a book that actually tells you to write in it, circling, underlining, jotting down responses. Fill it with graphic organizers that encourage you to think a different way. Make it a size that's easy to carry around. That's *The Holt Reader: An Interactive WorkText*—a book created especially for you.

The Holt Reader: An Interactive WorkText is designed to accompany *Elements of Literature*. Like *Elements of Literature,* it's designed to help you interact with the literature and informational materials you read. The chart below shows you what's in your book and how the book is organized.

PART 1 Reading Literature	PART 2 Reading Informational Materials	PART 3 Standardized Test Practice
Literary selections from *Elements of Literature*	Informational texts topically or thematically linked to literary selections	Standardized test practice of literature and informational reading

Learning to Read Literary and Informational Materials

When you read informational materials like a social studies textbook or a newspaper article, you usually read to get the facts. You read mainly to get information that is stated directly on the page. When you read literature, you need to go beyond understanding what the words mean and getting the facts straight. You need to read between the lines of a poem or story to discover the writer's meaning. No matter what kind of reading you do—literary or informational—*The Holt Reader: An Interactive WorkText* will help you practice the skills and strategies you need to become an active and successful reader.

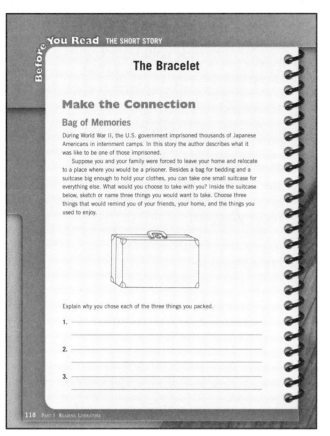

Setting the Stage: Before You Read

In Part 1, the Before-You-Read activity helps you make a personal connection with the selection you are about to read. It helps you sharpen your awareness of what you already know by asking you to think and write about a topic before you read. The more you know about the topic of a text, of course, the easier it is to understand the text. Sometimes this page will provide background information you need to know before you read the text.

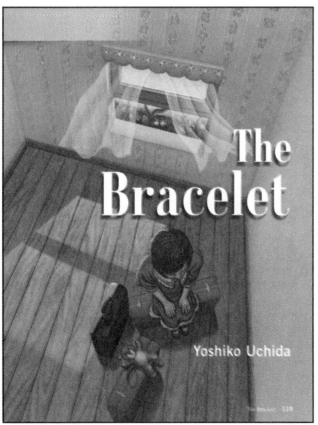

Interactive Selections from *Elements of Literature*

The literary selections in Part 1 are many of the same selections that appear in *Elements of Literature,* Introductory Course. The selections are reprinted in a single column and in larger type to give you the room you need to mark up the text.

IDENTIFY
Who is this story's narrator? Circle her name.

IDENTIFY
A figure of speech is a comparison between two seemingly unlike things. Underline the figure of speech that the author uses to describe her empty house. Tell whether it's a metaphor (a comparison that says that one thing *is* another) or a simile (a comparison that says one thing is *like* another).

INTERPRET
Re-read lines 18–37. Based on the details in these lines, make a generalization about the way Japanese Americans were treated during World War II.

WORDS TO OWN
evacuated (ē·vak′yōō-āt′ìd) v.: removed from the area.
interned (in-turnd′) v.: confined; jailed.
aliens (āl′yənz) n.: people who are not U.S. citizens.

"Mama, is it time to go?"

I hadn't planned to cry, but the tears came suddenly, and I wiped them away with the back of my hand. I didn't want my older sister to see me crying.

"It's almost time, Ruri," my mother said gently. Her face was filled with a kind of sadness I had never seen before.

I looked around at my empty room. The clothes that Mama always told me to hang up in the closet, the junk piled on my dresser, the old rag doll I could never bear to part with—they
10 were all gone. There was nothing left in my room, and there was nothing left in the rest of the house. The rugs and furniture were gone, the pictures and drapes were down, and the closets and cupboards were empty. The house was like a gift box after the nice thing inside was gone; just a lot of nothingness.

It was almost time to leave our home, but we weren't moving to a nicer house or to a new town. It was April 21, 1942. The United States and Japan were at war, and every Japanese person on the West Coast was being evacuated by the
20 government to a concentration camp. Mama, my sister Keiko, and I were being sent from our home, and out of Berkeley, and eventually out of California.

The doorbell rang, and I ran to answer it before my sister could. I thought maybe by some miracle a messenger from the government might be standing there, tall and proper and buttoned into a uniform, come to tell us it was all a terrible mistake, that we wouldn't have to leave after all. Or maybe the messenger would have a telegram from Papa, who was interned in a prisoner-of-war camp in Montana because he had worked
30 for a Japanese business firm.

The FBI had come to pick up Papa and hundreds of other Japanese community leaders on the very day that Japanese planes had bombed Pearl Harbor. The government thought they were dangerous enemy aliens. If it weren't so sad, it would have been funny. Papa could no more be dangerous than the mayor of our city, and he was every bit as loyal to the United States. He had lived here since 1917.

When I opened the door, it wasn't a messenger from anywhere. It was my best friend, Laurie Madison, from next
40 door. She was holding a package wrapped up like a birthday present, but she wasn't wearing her party dress, and her face drooped like a wilted tulip.

"Hi," she said. "I came to say goodbye."

She thrust the present at me and told me it was something to take to camp. "It's a bracelet," she said before I could open the package. "Put it on so you won't have to pack it." She knew I didn't have one inch of space left in my suitcase. We had been instructed to take only what we could carry into camp, and Mama had told us that we could each take only two suitcases.
50 "Then how are we ever going to pack the dishes and blankets and sheets they've told us to bring with us?" Keiko worried.

"I don't really know," Mama said, and she simply began packing those big impossible things into an enormous duffel bag—along with umbrellas, boots, a kettle, hot plate, and flashlight.

"Who's going to carry that huge sack?" I asked.

But Mama didn't worry about things like that. "Someone will help us," she said. "Don't worry." So I didn't.

Laurie wanted me to open her package and put on the
60 bracelet before she left. It was a thin gold chain with a heart dangling on it. She helped me put it on, and I told her I'd never take it off, ever.

"Well, goodbye then," Laurie said awkwardly. "Come home soon."

"I will," I said, although I didn't know if I would ever get back to Berkeley again.

I watched Laurie go down the block, her long blond pigtails bouncing as she walked. I wondered who would be sitting in my desk at Lincoln Junior High now that I was gone. Laurie
70 kept turning and waving, even walking backward for a while, until she got to the corner. I didn't want to watch anymore, and I slammed the door shut.

The next time the doorbell rang, it was Mrs. Simpson, our other neighbor. She was going to drive us to the Congregational

IDENTIFY
Pause at line 49. Underline the words that tell you what Laurie gives Ruri.

INFER
Why does Laurie's gift mean a lot to Ruri? What does a heart usually symbolize, or stand for? Why does Ruri say she will never take it off?

Strategies to Guide Your Reading: Side Notes

Notes in the side column accompany each selection. They guide your interaction with the text and help you unlock meaning. Many notes ask you to circle or underline in the text itself. Others provide lines on which you can write. Here are the kinds of notes you will work with as you read the selections: identify, retell, infer, predict, interpret, evaluate, visualize, and build fluency.

Identify asks you to find information (like the name of a character or a description of the setting) that is stated directly in the text. You will often be asked to circle or underline the information in the text.

Retell asks you to restate or explain in your own words something that has just happened.

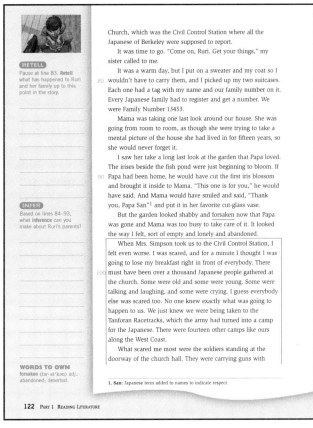

RETELL
Pause at line 83. **Retell** what has happened to Ruri and her family up to this point in the story.

INFER
Based on lines 84–93, what **inference** can you make about Ruri's parents?

WORDS TO OWN
forsaken (fɔr-sā′kən) *adj.*: abandoned; deserted.

Church, which was the Civil Control Station where all the Japanese of Berkeley were supposed to report.

It was time to go. "Come on, Ruri. Get your things," my sister called to me.

It was a warm day, but I put on a sweater and my coat so I
80 wouldn't have to carry them, and I picked up my two suitcases. Each one had a tag with my name and our family number on it. Every Japanese family had to register and get a number. We were Family Number 13453.

Mama was taking one last look around our house. She was going from room to room, as though she were trying to take a mental picture of the house she had lived in for fifteen years, so she would never forget it.

I saw her take a long last look at the garden that Papa loved. The irises beside the fish pond were just beginning to bloom. If
90 Papa had been home, he would have cut the first iris blossom and brought it inside to Mama. "This one is for you," he would have said. And Mama would have smiled and said, "Thank you, Papa San"[1] and put it in her favorite cut-glass vase.

But the garden looked shabby and forsaken now that Papa was gone and Mama was too busy to take care of it. It looked the way I felt, sort of empty and lonely and abandoned.

When Mrs. Simpson took us to the Civil Control Station, I felt even worse. I was scared, and for a minute I thought I was going to lose my breakfast right in front of everybody. There
100 must have been over a thousand Japanese people gathered at the church. Some were old and some were young. Some were talking and laughing, and some were crying. I guess everybody else was scared too. No one knew exactly what was going to happen to us. We just knew we were being taken to the Tanforan Racetracks, which the army had turned into a camp for the Japanese. There were fourteen other camps like ours along the West Coast.

What scared me most were the soldiers standing at the doorway of the church hall. They were carrying guns with

1. **San:** Japanese term added to names to indicate respect.

110 mounted bayonets. I wondered if they thought we would try to run away and whether they'd shoot us or come after us with their bayonets if we did.

A long line of buses waited to take us to camp. There were trucks, too, for our baggage. And Mama was right; some men were there to help us load our duffel bag. When it was time to board the buses, I sat with Keiko, and Mama sat behind us. The bus went down Grove Street and passed the small Japanese food store where Mama used to order her bean-curd cakes and pickled radish. The windows were all boarded up, but there was a sign
120 still hanging on the door that read, "We are loyal Americans."

The crazy thing about the whole evacuation was that we were all loyal Americans. Most of us were citizens because we had been born here. But our parents, who had come from Japan, couldn't become citizens because there was a law that prevented any Asian from becoming a citizen. Now everybody with a Japanese face was being shipped off to concentration camps.

"It's stupid," Keiko muttered as we saw the racetrack looming up beside the highway. "If there were any Japanese spies around, they'd have gone back to Japan long ago."
130 "I'll say," I agreed. My sister was in high school and she ought to know, I thought.

When the bus turned into Tanforan, there were more armed guards at the gate, and I saw barbed wire strung around the entire grounds. I felt as though I were going into a prison, but I hadn't done anything wrong.

We streamed off the buses and poured into a huge room, where doctors looked down our throats and peeled back our eyelids to see if we had any diseases. Then we were given our housing assignments. The man in charge gave Mama a slip of
140 paper. We were in Barrack 16, Apartment 40.

"Mama!" I said. "We're going to live in an apartment!" The only apartment I had ever seen was the one my piano teacher lived in. It was in an enormous building in San Francisco, with an elevator and thick-carpeted hallways. I thought how

BUILD FLUENCY
Read the boxed passage out loud. Try to use a voice that shows how scared Ruri feels. When you read the passage carefully, you'll notice other feelings too. For instance, Ruri's amazed to see how many Japanese people have gathered. See if your voice can capture all of Ruri's different feelings.

INTERPRET
Pause at line 126. Were the Japanese Americans evacuated because they were disloyal or because they were Japanese? Give reasons for your answer.

Infer asks you to make an **inference,** or an educated guess. You make inferences on the basis of clues writers give you and on experiences from your own life. When you make an inference, you read between the lines to figure out what the writer suggests but does not say directly.

Predict asks you to figure out what will happen next. Making predictions as you read helps you think about and understand what you are reading. To make predictions, look for clues that the writer gives you. Connect those clues with other things you've read, as well as your own experience. You'll probably find yourself adjusting predictions as you read.

Interpret asks you to explain the meaning of something. When you make an interpretation of a character, for example, you look at what the character says or does, and then you think about what the character's words and actions mean. You ask yourself why the character said those words and did those things. Your answer is the interpretation. Interpretations help you get at the main idea of a selection, the discovery about life you take away from it.

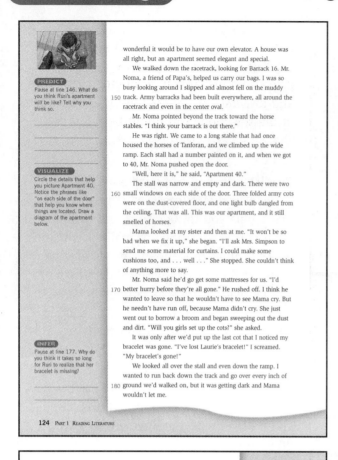

PREDICT
Pause at line 146. What do you think Ruri's apartment will be like? Tell why you think so.

VISUALIZE
Circle the details that help you picture Apartment 40. Notice the phrases like "on each side of the door" that help you know where things are located. Draw a diagram of the apartment below.

INFER
Pause at line 177. Why do you think it takes so long for Ruri to realize that her bracelet is missing?

wonderful it would be to have our own elevator. A house was all right, but an apartment seemed elegant and special.

We walked down the racetrack, looking for Barrack 16. Mr. Noma, a friend of Papa's, helped us carry our bags. I was so 150 busy looking around I slipped and almost fell on the muddy track. Army barracks had been built everywhere, all around the racetrack and even in the center oval.

Mr. Noma pointed beyond the track toward the horse stables. "I think your barrack is out there."

He was right. We came to a long stable that had once housed the horses of Tanforan, and we climbed up the wide ramp. Each stall had a number painted on it, and when we got to 40, Mr. Noma pushed open the door.

"Well, here it is," he said, "Apartment 40."

160 The stall was narrow and empty and dark. There were two small windows on each side of the door. Three folded army cots were on the dust-covered floor, and one light bulb dangled from the ceiling. That was all. This was our apartment, and it still smelled of horses.

Mama looked at my sister and then at me. "It won't be so bad when we fix it up," she began. "I'll ask Mrs. Simpson to send me some material for curtains. I could make some cushions too, and . . . well . . ." She stopped. She couldn't think of anything more to say.

Mr. Noma said he'd go get some mattresses for us. "I'd 170 better hurry before they're all gone." He rushed off. I think he wanted to leave so that he wouldn't have to see Mama cry. But he needn't have run off, because Mama didn't cry. She just went out to borrow a broom and began sweeping out the dust and dirt. "Will you girls set up the cots?" she asked.

It was only after we'd put up the last cot that I noticed my bracelet was gone. "I've lost Laurie's bracelet!" I screamed. "My bracelet's gone!"

We looked all over the stall and even down the ramp. I wanted to run back down the track and go over every inch of 180 ground we'd walked on, but it was getting dark and Mama wouldn't let me.

124 PART 1 READING LITERATURE

I thought of what I'd promised Laurie. I wasn't ever going to take the bracelet off, not even when I went to take a shower. And now I had lost it on my very first day in camp. I wanted to cry.

I kept looking for it all the time we were in Tanforan. I didn't stop looking until the day we were sent to another camp, called Topaz, in the middle of a desert in Utah. And then I gave up.

But Mama told me never mind. She said I didn't need a 190 bracelet to remember Laurie, just as I didn't need anything to remember Papa or our home in Berkeley or all the people and things we loved and had left behind.

"Those are things we can carry in our hearts and take with us no matter where we are sent," she said.

And I guess she was right. I've never forgotten Laurie, even now.

INTERPRET
Circle what Mama says in lines 193-194. She suggests the story's theme, the main idea or special message that the author is saying about life. State the theme in your own words.

EVALUATE
Yoshiko Uchida said that she wrote about the internment of Japanese Americans so that nothing like that would ever happen in the United States again. In a war situation, where people fear a group whose members look like the enemy, would recalling this story—and other stories and movies like it—do any good? What seems most unjust to you about what happens to Ruri? Give reasons for your answer.

THE BRACELET 125

Evaluate asks you to form opinions about what you read. For example, you might see the following note at the end of a story: "How satisfying is the ending of this story? Give two reasons for your answer."

Visualize asks you to picture the characters, settings, and events being described in a selection. As you read, look for details that help you make a mental picture. Think of visualizing as making your own mental movie of a selection.

Build Fluency asks you to read a poem or passages from a story. It lets you practice phrasing, expression, and reading in meaningful chunks. Sometimes hearing text read aloud makes the text easier to understand.

Words to Own lists words for you to learn and own. These words are underlined in the selection, letting you see the words in context. The words are defined for you right there in the side column.

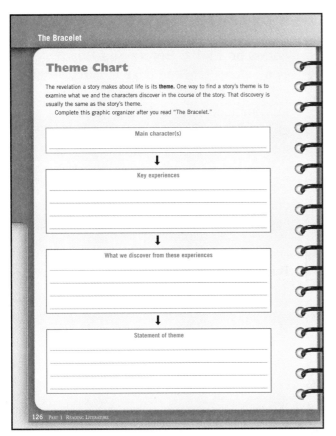

After You Read: Graphic Organizers

After each selection, **graphic organizers** give you a visual way to organize, interpret, and understand the reading or literary focus of the selection. You might be asked to chart the main events of the plot or complete a cause-and-effect chain.

The Bracelet

Theme Chart

The revelation a story makes about life is its **theme.** One way to find a story's theme is to examine what we and the characters discover in the course of the story. That discovery is usually the same as the story's theme.

Complete this graphic organizer after you read "The Bracelet."

Main character(s)

↓

Key experiences

↓

What we discover from these experiences

↓

Statement of theme

126 PART 1 READING LITERATURE

The Bracelet

Vocabulary and Comprehension

A. Match words and definitions. Write the letter of the correct definition next to each word.

Word Bank
evacuated
interned
aliens
forsaken

_____ **1.** aliens   **a.** removed from an area

_____ **2.** evacuated   **b.** imprisoned or confined

_____ **3.** forsaken   **c.** foreigners

_____ **4.** interned   **d.** abandoned; deserted

B. Choose three words from above. Use each word in a sentence.

1. _____

_____

2. _____

_____

3. _____

_____

C. Answer each question below.

1. How does Ruri describe her garden?

_____

_____

2. Why weren't Ruri's parents American citizens?

_____

_____

3. What did Apartment 40 look like?

_____

_____

THE BRACELET 127

After You Read: Vocabulary and Comprehension

Vocabulary and Comprehension worksheets at the end of literary selections check your knowledge of the Words to Own and your understanding of the selection.

PART 2 Reading Informational Materials

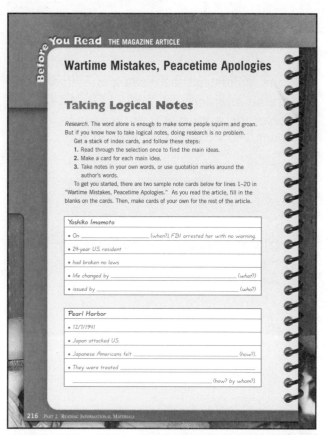

Focus on Skills: Before You Read
The Before-You-Read page in Part 2 teaches skills and strategies you'll need to read informational materials like textbooks, newspaper and magazine articles, and instructional manuals. You'll learn how to recognize text structure, find the main idea, and determine an author's perspective or point of view on these Before-You-Read pages.

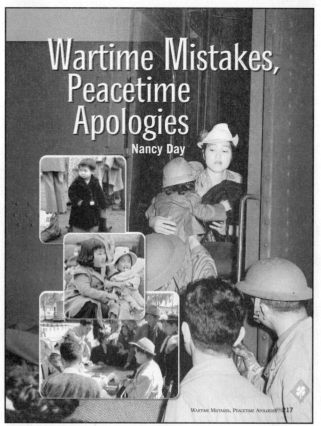

Interactive Informational Texts
The informational texts in Part 2 are linked by theme or by topic to the literature selections that appear in *Elements of Literature,* Introductory Course and *The Holt Reader: An Interactive WorkText,* Introductory Course. For example, the text you see on the example pages reproduced here comes from an informational text on internment camps for Japanese Americans during World War II. You might want to read the text after you've finished "The Bracelet," Yoshiko Uchida's moving story of a young girl's experiences in an internment camp in Montana during World War II. The informational selections are printed in a single column and in larger type to give you the room you need to mark up the text.

Strategies to Guide Your Reading: Side Notes

As in Part 1, **notes** in the side column accompany each selection. They guide your interaction with the text and help you unlock meaning. Many notes ask you to circle or underline in the text itself. Others provide lines on which you can write. Here are the kinds of notes you will work with as you read the informational materials in Part 2: identify, retell, infer, predict, interpret, evaluate, visualize, and build fluency. See pages xii–xiv for an explanation of each note.

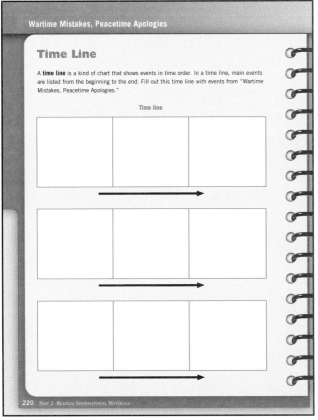

After You Read: Graphic Organizers

After each selection, a **graphic organizer** gives you a visual way to organize, interpret, and understand the selection. These organizers focus on the strategy introduced on the Before-You-Read page. You might be asked to collect supporting details that point to a main idea or to complete a comparison chart.

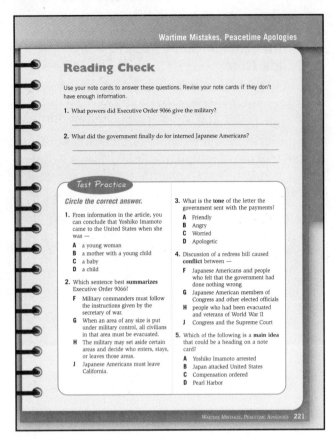

Wartime Mistakes, Peacetime Apologies

Reading Check

Use your note cards to answer these questions. Revise your note cards if they don't have enough information.

1. What powers did Executive Order 9066 give the military?

_____

2. What did the government finally do for interned Japanese Americans?

_____
_____

Test Practice

Circle the correct answer.

1. From information in the article, you can conclude that Yoshiko Imamoto came to the United States when she was —
   A a young woman
   B a mother with a young child
   C a baby
   D a child

2. Which sentence best **summarizes** Executive Order 9066?
   F Military commanders must follow the instructions given by the secretary of war.
   G When an area of any size is put under military control, all civilians in that area must be evacuated.
   H The military may set aside certain areas and decide who enters, stays, or leaves those areas.
   J Japanese Americans must leave California.

3. What is the **tone** of the letter the government sent with the payments?
   A Friendly
   B Angry
   C Worried
   D Apologetic

4. Discussion of a redress bill caused **conflict** between —
   F Japanese Americans and people who felt that the government had done nothing wrong
   G Japanese American members of Congress and other elected officials
   H people who had been evacuated and veterans of World War II
   J Congress and the Supreme Court

5. Which of the following is a **main idea** that could be a heading on a note card?
   A Yoshiko Imamoto arrested
   B Japan attacked United States
   C Compensation ordered
   D Pearl Harbor

WARTIME MISTAKES, PEACETIME APOLOGIES **221**

After You Read: Reading Check and Test Practice

Reading Check and Test Practice worksheets at the end of informational selections check your understanding of the selection with short-answer and multiple-choice questions. The multiple-choice questions are similar to the ones you'll answer on state and national standardized tests.

A Walk Through — PART 3 Standardized Test Practice

STANDARDIZED TEST PRACTICE   INFORMATIONAL MATERIALS

DIRECTIONS

Read the informational article. Then, read each question that follows on page 283 and circle the letter of the best response.

Celebrating the Quinceañera
Mara Rockliff

You stand at the back of the church between your parents and godparents, your knees shaking. You feel special, and a bit awkward, in your first formal dress and your tiara. Your honor court has walked up the aisle ahead of you: fourteen girls in pastel dresses, fourteen boys in tuxedos. With you and your escort there are fifteen couples—one for each year of your life. The long months of planning and preparation have finally ended. Your quinceañera has begun.

The quinceañera (kĕn'sā·ā·nye'rə, from the Spanish words *quince*, "fifteen," and *años*, "years") is a rite of passage celebrated by Mexicans and Mexican Americans. People believe that the tradition can be traced back to the Aztec culture, in which girls commonly married at the age of fifteen. Today a girl's quinceañera marks her coming-of-age. It means that she is ready to take on adult privileges and responsibilities.

The most important part of your quinceañera is the *misa de acción de gracias,* the thanksgiving Mass. You slowly walk up the aisle to the front of the church. You kneel, placing a bouquet of fifteen roses on the altar to thank the Virgin Mary for bringing you to this important day. A birthstone ring glitters on your finger, and a religious medal hangs from your neck, inscribed with your name and today's date—special gifts from adult relatives or friends of the family. The priest will bless your medal during the Mass.

Next comes a sermon, followed by prayers and readings from the Bible. You recite your speech, and the service ends. Then the photographer rushes over, and you pose for an endless series of photographs with your family and friends.

But the quinceañera celebration has just begun, for the fiesta is still to come. You enter to the sound of music, a traditional mariachi band or a DJ playing current hits. You dance in turn with your father, your grandfathers, your escort. You and your honor court perform a group dance that you have rehearsed. Then everyone joins in the dancing.

You're almost too excited to eat, but the food is wonderful. There's your favorite—chicken in mole sauce, made from chilies and unsweetened chocolate.

282 PART 3 STANDARDIZED TEST PRACTICE

The tables are covered with everything from tamales and corn soup to an elaborately decorated cake.

Later, as everyone watches, your father removes the flat shoes you have worn all day and replaces them with a pair of high heels. In your parents' eyes you are no longer a child. They'll treat you differently from now on, and they'll expect you to act more like an adult as well.

Among your many gifts, one stands out: the last doll. It's not a toy for you to play with, of course; it's a symbol of the childhood you're leaving behind. If you have a younger sister, you might present it to her. You look around at the people who have watched you grow up. You see tears in many eyes. The quinceañera is a tradition many centuries old, but for you it will happen only once.

---

1. A **summary** of this article would —
   A criticize aspects of the celebration
   B cover the most important points
   C discuss the quality of the writing
   D focus on one part of the article

2. In an **outline** of this article, all of these might be details under a main heading *except* —
   F girl dances with father and grandfathers
   G honor court performs dance
   H DJ or mariachi band plays music
   J what happens at the party

3. If you quoted a phrase or sentence from this article on a note card, you would put the writer's words —
   A in quotation marks
   B in capital letters
   C in parentheses
   D in a footnote

4. Which sentence best states the **main idea** of this article?
   F The food is the best part of the quinceañera.
   G The quinceañera happens only once in a girl's lifetime.
   H The quinceañera is a girl's rite of passage into adulthood.
   J Girls who celebrate their quinceañera usually do not appreciate what it represents.

5. If you were taking notes for a **summary** of this article, what event would you cite in the blank below?
   You go to thanksgiving Mass.

   _____

   Your medal is blessed.
   You give a speech.
   A Father gives you high heels.
   B You receive a symbolic doll.
   C You enjoy a wonderful feast.
   D You place roses on the altar.

CELEBRATING THE QUINCEAÑERA 283

Putting Your Skill as a Reader to the Test
The last part of this book gives you practice in reading and responding to the kinds of literary and informational selections you read in Parts 1 and 2. The selections and multiple-choice questions are similar to the ones you'll see on state and national standardized tests.

PART 1   READING LITERATURE

Just Once

Make the Connection

Football Dreams

One dream that many of us share is to hear a crowd cheering, just once, just for us. In this story, Bryan "the Moose" Crawford has that dream. The Moose has always been a team player, but, just once, he wants to carry the ball.

Here's a list of football terms used in the story. Use this list to answer the questions below. If you know nothing about football, wait till you have finished reading the story, and then answer the questions.

end zone	linebacker	fullback	quarterback
kicker	touchdown	goal	fifty-yard line
referee	five-yard line		

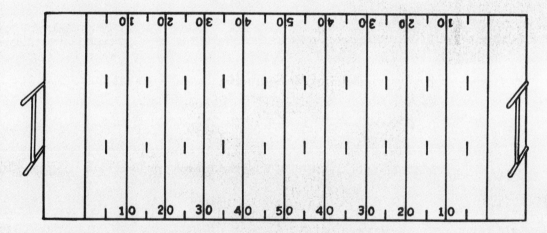

1. Underline the four words that name parts of a football field. Then, use the words to label the drawing of the football field above.

2. Which word means a football score? _____

3. List the names of four football positions.

    a. _____   c. _____

    b. _____   d. _____

4. What word means a "sports judge"? _____

JUST ONCE

Thomas J. Dygard

IDENTIFY

In lines 1–14, underline
the words that tell about
the Moose's special talents
in football. Circle the
position he plays.

_____

_____

_____

INFER

Pause at line 20. Based on
what you've read so far,
what **inferences,** guesses
based on clues in the text,
can you make about the
Moose's **character?**

_____

_____

_____

_____

_____

_____

_____

IDENTIFY

Underline where you find
out what the Moose wants
to do.

WORDS TO OWN
devastating (dev'əs·tāt'iŋ) v.
used as adj.: causing great
damage or destruction.
nurturing (nur'chər·iŋ) v.:
promoting the growth of;
nourishing.

Everybody liked the Moose. To his father and mother he was
Bryan—as in Bryan Jefferson Crawford—but to everyone at
Bedford City High he was the Moose. He was large and strong,
as you might imagine from his nickname, and he was pretty
fast on his feet—sort of nimble, you might say—considering his
size. He didn't have a pretty face but he had a quick and easy
smile—"sweet," some of the teachers called it; "nice," others said.

But on the football field, the Moose was neither sweet nor
nice. He was just strong and fast and a little bit <u>devastating</u>
10 as the left tackle of the Bedford City Bears. When the Moose
blocked somebody, he stayed blocked. When the Moose was
called on to open a hole in the line for one of the Bears'
runners, the hole more often than not resembled an open
garage door.

Now in his senior season, the Moose had twice been named
to the all-conference team and was considered a cinch for all-
state. He spent a lot of his spare time, when he wasn't in a
classroom or on the football field, reading letters from colleges
eager to have the Moose pursue higher education—and football—
20 at their institution.

But the Moose had a hang-up.

He didn't go public with his hang-up until the sixth game of
the season. But, looking back, most of his teammates agreed
that probably the Moose had been <u>nurturing</u> the hang-up
secretly for two years or more.

The Moose wanted to carry the ball.

For sure, the Moose was not the first interior lineman in the
history of football, or even the history of Bedford City High,
who banged heads up front and wore bruises like badges of
30 honor—and dreamed of racing down the field with the ball to
the end zone[1] while everybody in the bleachers screamed his
name.

But most linemen, it seems, are able to stifle the urge. The
idea may pop into their minds from time to time, but in their

---

1. **end zone:** area between the goal line and the end line (the line marking the
   boundary of the playing area) at each end of a football field.

hearts they know they can't run fast enough, they know they can't do that fancy dancing to elude tacklers, they know they aren't trained to read blocks. They know that their strengths and talents are best utilized in the line. Football is, after all, a team sport, and everyone plays the position where he most

40 helps the team. And so these linemen, or most of them, go back to banging heads without saying the first word about the dream that flickered through their minds.

Not so with the Moose.

That sixth game, when the Moose's hang-up first came into public view, had ended with the Moose truly in all his glory as the Bears' left tackle. Yes, glory—but uncheered and sort of anonymous. The Bears were trailing 21–17 and had the ball on Mitchell High's five-yard line, fourth down,[2] with time running out. The rule in such a situation is simple—the best back

50 carries the ball behind the best blocker—and it is a rule seldom violated by those in control of their faculties.[3] The Bears, of course, followed the rule. That meant Jerry Dixon running behind the Moose's blocking. With the snap of the ball, the Moose knocked down one lineman, bumped another one aside, and charged forward to flatten an approaching linebacker. Jerry did a little jig behind the Moose and then ran into the end zone, virtually untouched, to win the game.

After circling in the end zone a moment while the cheers echoed through the night, Jerry did run across and hug the

60 Moose, that's true. Jerry knew who had made the touchdown possible.

But it wasn't the Moose's name that everybody was shouting. The fans in the bleachers were cheering Jerry Dixon.

It was probably at that precise moment that the Moose decided to go public.

In the dressing room, Coach Buford Williams was making his rounds among the cheering players and came to a halt in front of the Moose. "It was your great blocking that did it," he said.

2. **fourth down:** In football the team holding the ball is allowed four downs, or attempts to carry the ball forward at least ten yards.

3. **faculties:** mental powers.

IDENTIFY

Underline, and then number, three reasons why linemen usually don't carry the ball.

RETELL

Re-read lines 44–63. Then **retell** what happens in the sixth game that leads the Moose to "go public" with what he wants.

WORDS TO OWN
anonymous (ə·nän′ə·məs) *adj.*: nameless; done by an unidentified person.

PREDICT

Pause at line 78. How do you think Coach Williams will answer the Moose?

_____

_____

_____

_____

_____

_____

_____

_____

INTERPRET

Conflict is a clash between opposing characters or forces. The Moose is on one side of the main conflict in this story. Who or what opposes him?

_____

_____

_____

_____

_____

WORDS TO OWN

tolerant (tăl′ər·ənt) *adj.*: patient; showing acceptance of others.

"I want to carry the ball," the Moose said.

70   Coach Williams was already turning away and taking a step toward the next player due an accolade[4] when his brain registered the fact that the Moose had said something strange. He was expecting the Moose to say, "Aw, gee, thanks, Coach." That was what the Moose always said when the coach issued a compliment. But the Moose had said something else. The coach turned back to the Moose, a look of disbelief on his face. "What did you say?"

"I want to carry the ball."

Coach Williams was good at quick recoveries, as any high

80 school football coach had better be. He gave a tolerant smile and a little nod and said, "You keep right on blocking, son."

This time Coach Williams made good on his turn and moved away from the Moose.

The following week's practice and the next Friday's game passed without further incident. After all, the game was a road game over at Cartwright High, thirty-five miles away. The Moose wanted to carry the ball in front of the Bedford City fans.

Then the Moose went to work.

He caught up with the coach on the way to the practice field

90 on Wednesday. "Remember," he said, leaning forward and down a little to get his face in the coach's face, "I said I want to carry the ball."

Coach Williams must have been thinking about something else because it took him a minute to look up into the Moose's face, and even then he didn't say anything.

"I meant it," the Moose said.

"Meant what?"

"I want to run the ball."

"Oh," Coach Williams said. Yes, he remembered. "Son,

100 you're a great left tackle, a great blocker. Let's leave it that way."

The Moose let the remaining days of the practice week and then the game on Friday night against Edgewood High pass

---

4. accolade (ak′ə·lād′): something said or done to express praise.

while he reviewed strategies. The review led him to Dan
Blevins, the Bears' quarterback. If the signal caller would join
in, maybe Coach Williams would listen.

"Yeah, I heard," Dan said. "But, look, what about Joe
Wright at guard, Bill Slocum at right tackle, even Herbie Watson
at center. They might all want to carry the ball. What are we
110 going to do—take turns? It doesn't work that way."

So much for Dan Blevins.

The Moose found that most of the players in the backfield
agreed with Dan. They couldn't see any reason why the Moose
should carry the ball, especially in place of themselves. Even
Jerry Dixon, who owed a lot of his glory to the Moose's
blocking, gaped in disbelief at the Moose's idea. The Moose,
however, got some support from his fellow linemen. Maybe
they had dreams of their own, and saw value in a precedent.[5]

As the days went by, the word spread—not just on the
120 practice field and in the corridors of Bedford City High, but all
around town. The players by now were openly taking sides.
Some thought it a jolly good idea that the Moose carry the ball.
Others, like Dan Blevins, held to the purist[6] line—a left tackle
plays left tackle, a ball carrier carries the ball, and that's it.

Around town, the vote wasn't even close. Everyone wanted
the Moose to carry the ball.

"Look, son," Coach Williams said to the Moose on the
practice field the Thursday before the Benton Heights game,
"this has gone far enough. Fun is fun. A joke is a joke. But let's
130 drop it."

"Just once," the Moose pleaded.

Coach Williams looked at the Moose and didn't answer.

The Moose didn't know what that meant.

The Benton Heights Tigers were duck soup for the Bears, as
everyone knew they would be. The Bears scored in their first
three possessions and led 28–0 at the half. The hapless[7] Tigers
had yet to cross the fifty-yard line under their own steam.

---

5. **precedent** (pres′ə·dənt): action or statement that can serve as an example.
6. **purist** (pyoor′ist): someone who insists that rules be followed strictly.
7. **hapless**: unlucky.

IDENTIFY

The Moose tries to get
support for what he wants.
Circle the players he goes
to. Underline how they
respond.

EVALUATE

Pause at line 126. The
people in town want the
Moose to carry the ball. The
coach and the players don't.
How would you vote? Give
reasons for your answer.

INTERPRET

What do you think Coach
Williams's "look" means
(line 132)?

PREDICT

Pause at line 151. Is Coach Williams going to let the Moose carry the ball? Tell what you think will happen.

_____

_____

_____

_____

_____

_____

_____

_____

RETELL

Stop at line 160. **Retell** what's happened on the field and in the bleachers since the game started.

_____

_____

_____

.

_____

IDENTIFY

Who has won the main **conflict** in this story? Underline the sentence that gives you this information.

_____

_____

All the Bears, of course, were enjoying the way the game was going, as were the Bedford City fans jamming the
140 bleachers.

Coach Williams looked irritated when the crowd on a couple of occasions broke into a chant: "Give the Moose the ball! Give the Moose the ball!"

On the field, the Moose did not know whether to grin at hearing his name shouted by the crowd or to frown because the sound of his name was irritating the coach. Was the crowd going to talk Coach Williams into putting the Moose in the backfield? Probably not; Coach Williams didn't bow to that kind of pressure. Was the coach going to refuse to give the ball to the
150 Moose just to show the crowd—and the Moose and the rest of the players—who was boss? The Moose feared so.

In his time on the sideline, when the defensive unit was on the field, the Moose, of course, said nothing to Coach Williams. He knew better than to break the coach's concentration during a game—even a runaway victory—with a comment on any subject at all, much less his desire to carry the ball. As a matter of fact, the Moose was careful to stay out of the coach's line of vision, especially when the crowd was chanting "Give the Moose the ball!"

160 By the end of the third quarter the Bears were leading 42–0.

Coach Williams had been feeding substitutes into the game since half time, but the Bears kept marching on. And now, in the opening minutes of the fourth quarter, the Moose and his teammates were standing on the Tigers' five-yard line, about to pile on another touchdown.

The Moose saw his substitute, Larry Hidden, getting a slap on the behind and then running onto the field. The Moose turned to leave.

Then he heard Larry tell the referee, "Hinden for Holbrook."
170 Holbrook? Chad Holbrook, the fullback?

Chad gave the coach a funny look and jogged off the field.

Larry joined the huddle and said, "Coach says the Moose at fullback and give him the ball."

Dan Blevins said, "Really?"

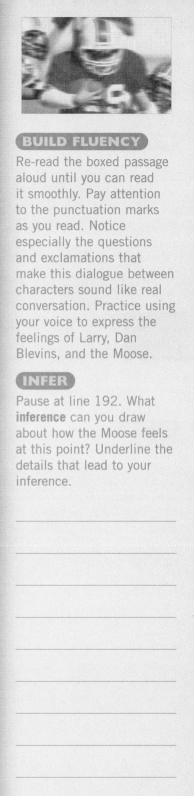

BUILD FLUENCY

Re-read the boxed passage aloud until you can read it smoothly. Pay attention to the punctuation marks as you read. Notice especially the questions and exclamations that make this dialogue between characters sound like real conversation. Practice using your voice to express the feelings of Larry, Dan Blevins, and the Moose.

INFER

Pause at line 192. What **inference** can you draw about how the Moose feels at this point? Underline the details that lead to your inference.

"Really."

The Moose was giving his grin—"sweet," some of the teachers called it; "nice," others said.

"I want to do an end run," the Moose said.

Dan looked at the sky a moment, then said, "What does it
180 matter?"

The quarterback took the snap from center, moved back and to his right while turning, and extended the ball to the Moose.

The Moose took the ball and cradled it in his right hand. So far, so good. He hadn't fumbled. Probably both Coach Williams and Dan were surprised.

He ran a couple of steps and looked out in front and said aloud, "Whoa!"

Where had all those tacklers come from?

The whole world seemed to be peopled with players in red
190 jerseys—the red of the Benton Heights Tigers. They all were looking straight at the Moose and advancing toward him. They looked very determined, and not friendly at all. And there were so many of them. The Moose had faced tough guys in the line, but usually one at a time, or maybe two. But this—five or six. And all of them heading for him.

The Moose screeched to a halt, whirled, and ran the other way.

Dan Blevins blocked somebody in a red jersey breaking through the middle of the line, and the Moose wanted to stop
200 running and thank him. But he kept going.

His reverse had caught the Tigers' defenders going the wrong way, and the field in front of the Moose looked open. But his blockers were going the wrong way, too. Maybe that was why the field looked so open. What did it matter, though, with the field clear in front of him? This was going to be a cakewalk;[8] the Moose was going to score a touchdown.

Then, again—"Whoa!"

8. **cakewalk:** easy task.

VISUALIZE

Re-read lines 215–222. Circle the details that help you picture what's happening. Which of your senses do most of these details appeal to?

_____

_____

_____

_____

INTERPRET

You've found out who wins the main **conflict**. How does the author continue to use conflict to keep you interested in the rest of the story? Who or what is on each side of this new conflict?

_____

_____

_____

_____

_____

_____

_____

_____

_____

WORDS TO OWN
ponder (pän′dər) _v._: think deeply about.

Players with red jerseys were beginning to fill the empty space—a lot of them. And they were all running toward the
210 Moose. They were kind of low, with their arms spread, as if they wanted to hit him hard and then grab him.

A picture of Jerry Dixon dancing his little jig and wriggling between tacklers flashed through the Moose's mind. How did Jerry do that? Well, no time to ponder that one right now.

The Moose lowered his shoulder and thundered ahead, into the cloud of red jerseys. Something hit his left thigh. It hurt. Then something pounded his hip, then his shoulder. They both hurt. Somebody was hanging on to him and was a terrible drag. How could he run with somebody hanging on to him? He knew
220 he was going down, but maybe he was across the goal. He hit the ground hard, with somebody coming down on top of him, right on the small of his back.

The Moose couldn't move. They had him pinned. Wasn't the referee supposed to get these guys off?

Finally the load was gone and the Moose, still holding the ball, got to his knees and one hand, then stood.

He heard the screaming of the crowd, and he saw the scoreboard blinking.

He had scored.
230 His teammates were slapping him on the shoulder pads and laughing and shouting.

The Moose grinned, but he had a strange and distant look in his eyes.

He jogged to the sideline, the roars of the crowd still ringing in his ears.

"OK, son?" Coach Williams asked.

The Moose was puffing. He took a couple of deep breaths. He relived for a moment the first sight of a half dozen players in red jerseys, all with one target—him. He saw again the
240 menacing horde of red jerseys that had risen up just when

he'd thought he had clear sailing to the goal. They all zeroed in on him, the Moose, alone.

The Moose glanced at the coach, took another deep breath, and said, "Never again."

EVALUATE

This story could have been called "Never Again." Write a sentence evaluating the story's title. Tell which title you prefer: "Just Once" or "Never Again." Give a reason for your answer.

_____

_____

_____

_____

_____

_____

_____

_____

_____

_____

_____

_____

_____

_____

_____

Conflict Scoreboard

A **conflict** is a struggle between characters or a difference of ideas. The scoreboard below lists some of the conflicts the Moose faces while trying to get what he wants: a chance to carry the ball. In the second column, fill in how each of those conflicts is **resolved,** that is, what happens to the conflict. (Are they all resolved?)

The Moose's conflict	How the conflict is resolved
With Coach in the dressing room	
With Dan Blevins	
With Coach on the practice field	
With Coach during the game	

Vocabulary and Comprehension

A. The **context** of a word—the words or sentences surrounding it—can help you figure out what the word means. In the paragraph below, each underlined word has at least one **context clue.** Circle the clues that help you guess the words' meanings.

The coach read aloud the <u>anonymous</u> note, wondering who had written it. "Please take some time to <u>ponder</u> our request carefully. You may think that it would have a <u>devastating</u> effect, but we're sure it won't ruin the sports program. It's time to be <u>tolerant</u>, accepting, and fair. After all, we've been developing and <u>nurturing</u> our dream for months. Our families have also encouraged our dream. Please let girls try out for the team."

B. Match words and definitions. Write the letter of the correct definition next to the word.

_____ **1.** anonymous   **a.** destructive

_____ **2.** ponder   **b.** nourishing

_____ **3.** devastating   **c.** nameless

_____ **4.** tolerant   **d.** accepting

_____ **5.** nurturing   **e.** think deeply

C. Write a **T** or an **F** if the following sentences about "Just Once" are true or false.

_____ **1.** Moose wants to carry the football.

_____ **2.** Everyone agrees that Moose should carry the ball.

_____ **3.** Moose makes a touchdown.

_____ **4.** Moose enjoys carrying the ball.

Ta-Na-E-Ka

Make the Connection

Choose Your Journey

Imagine that a time machine has been invented. It can take you and your family back one hundred years or two hundred years into the past. If you don't like to travel, you can choose to stay in the present. Now answer the questions below the graphic.

Past   **Present**

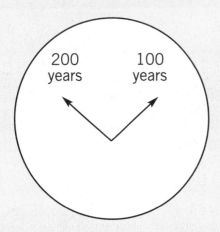

1. Will you choose to go two hundred years back, one hundred years back, or will you stay in the present? _____

2. Tell why you made that choice. _____

_____

3. If you choose the past, make a sketch inside the graphic of one thing you think you'd enjoy seeing or doing one or two hundred years ago. If you decide to stay in the present, make a sketch in the space to the right of the graphic of one thing in the present that you wouldn't want to live without.

TA-NA-E-KA

Mary Whitebird

Background

This story has to do with the traditions of the Native Americans known as the Kaw. The Kaw are also known as the Kansa. Both names are forms of a word that means "people of the south wind." The Kaw people originally lived along the Kansas River. Like most Native Americans, the Kaw lost their lands to white settlers. Eventually, the U.S. government forced the remnants of the Kaw onto a reservation in Oklahoma.

INFER

Underline the details in lines 5–15 that tell you how the grandfather looked, dressed, and acted. Based on these clues, make three **inferences**, educated guesses, about his **character**.

_____

_____

_____

_____

IDENTIFY

Circle the details that tell you what Ta-Na-E-Ka is. Underline the name and age of the **narrator**.

INTERPRET

External conflict is a struggle between a character and some outside force. The older generation is on one side of the external conflict here. Which two characters are struggling against the older generation?

_____

_____

_____

_____

_____

_____

_____

As my birthday drew closer, I had awful nightmares about it. I was reaching the age at which all Kaw Indians had to participate in Ta-Na-E-Ka. Well, not all Kaws. Many of the younger families on the reservation were beginning to give up the old customs. But my grandfather, Amos Deer Leg, was devoted to tradition. He still wore handmade beaded moccasins instead of shoes and kept his iron-gray hair in tight braids. He could speak English, but he spoke it only with white men. With his family he used a Sioux dialect.[1]

10   Grandfather was one of the last living Indians (he died in 1953, when he was eighty-one) who actually fought against the U.S. Cavalry. Not only did he fight, he was wounded in a skirmish at Rose Creek—a famous encounter in which the celebrated Kaw chief Flat Nose lost his life. At the time, my grandfather was only eleven years old.

Eleven was a magic word among the Kaws. It was the time of Ta-Na-E-Ka, the "flowering of adulthood." It was the age, my grandfather informed us hundreds of times, "when a boy could prove himself to be a warrior and a girl took the first steps to
20 womanhood."

"I don't want to be a warrior," my cousin, Roger Deer Leg, confided to me. "I'm going to become an accountant."

"None of the other tribes make girls go through the endurance ritual," I complained to my mother.

"It won't be as bad as you think, Mary," my mother said, ignoring my protests. "Once you've gone through it, you'll certainly never forget it. You'll be proud."

I even complained to my teacher, Mrs. Richardson, feeling that, as a white woman, she would side with me.

30   She didn't. "All of us have rituals of one kind or another," Mrs. Richardson said. "And look at it this way: How many girls have the opportunity to compete on equal terms with boys? Don't look down on your heritage."

---

1. Sioux (soo) **dialect:** one of the languages spoken by the Plains Indians, including the Kaw.

Heritage, indeed! I had no intention of living on a reservation for the rest of my life. I was a good student. I loved school. My fantasies were about knights in armor and fair ladies in flowing gowns being saved from dragons. It never once occurred to me that being an Indian was exciting.

But I've always thought that the Kaw were the originators
40 of the women's liberation movement. No other Indian tribe— and I've spent half a lifetime researching the subject—treated women more "equally" than the Kaw. Unlike most of the subtribes of the Sioux Nation, the Kaw allowed men and women to eat together. And hundreds of years before we were "acculturated,"[2] a Kaw woman had the right to refuse a prospective husband even if her father arranged the match.

The wisest women (generally wisdom was equated with age) often sat in tribal councils. Furthermore, most Kaw legends revolve around "Good Woman," a kind of supersquaw, a Joan
50 of Arc[3] of the high plains. Good Woman led Kaw warriors into battle after battle, from which they always seemed to emerge victorious.

And girls as well as boys were required to undergo Ta-Na-E-Ka.

The actual ceremony varied from tribe to tribe, but since the Indians' life on the plains was dedicated to survival, Ta-Na-E-Ka was a test of survival.

"Endurance is the loftiest virtue of the Indian," my grandfather explained. "To survive, we must endure. When I was a boy, Ta-Na-E-Ka was more than the mere symbol it is
60 now. We were painted white with the juice of a sacred herb and sent naked into the wilderness without so much as a knife. We couldn't return until the white had worn off. It wouldn't wash off. It took almost eighteen days, and during that time we had to stay alive, trapping food, eating insects and roots and berries, and watching out for enemies. And we did have enemies—both the white soldiers and the Omaha warriors, who were always

---

2. **acculturated** (ə·kul′chər·āt′id): adapted to a new or different culture.
3. **Joan of Arc** (1412–1431): French heroine who led her country's army to victory over the English at Orléans, France, in 1429.

INFER

At this point in the story, how does Mary feel about her Indian heritage? In lines 34–38, what else do you find out about Mary's **character** and her interests?

_____

_____

_____

INTERPRET

In lines 39–40, Mary says she's "always thought that the Kaw were the originators of the women's liberation movement." What does she mean? Circle the details that she gives to back up her opinion.

_____

_____

_____

_____

IDENTIFY

Circle the words that tell how long Ta-Na-E-Ka lasted when Grandfather was a boy.

WORDS TO OWN
loftiest (lôf′tē·əst) adj.: noblest or highest.

IDENTIFY

Re-read lines 80–85. List the *differences* between the Ta-Na-E-Ka ritual planned for Mary and Roger and the Ta-Na-E-Ka that Grandfather had.

PREDICT

Pause at line 99. What do you think Mary's idea might be?

WORDS TO OWN
shrewdest (shrōōd'əst) *adj.*
used as *n.:* cleverest;
sharpest.
grimaced (grim'ist) *v.:*
twisted the face to express
pain, anger, or disgust.

trying to capture Kaw boys and girls undergoing their endurance test. It was an exciting time."

"What happened if you couldn't make it?" Roger asked. He
70 was born only three days after I was, and we were being trained for Ta-Na-E-Ka together. I was happy to know he was frightened, too.

"Many didn't return," Grandfather said. "Only the strongest and shrewdest. Mothers were not allowed to weep over those who didn't return. If a Kaw couldn't survive, he or she wasn't worth weeping over. It was our way."

"What a lot of hooey," Roger whispered. "I'd give anything to get out of it."

"I don't see how we have any choice," I replied.
80 Roger gave my arm a little squeeze. "Well, it's only five days."

Five days! Maybe it was better than being painted white and sent out naked for eighteen days. But not much better.

We were to be sent, barefoot and in bathing suits, into the woods. Even our very traditional parents put their foot down when Grandfather suggested we go naked. For five days we'd have to live off the land, keeping warm as best we could, getting food where we could. It was May, but on the northernmost reaches of the Missouri River, the days were still chilly and the nights were fiercely cold.
90 Grandfather was in charge of the month's training for Ta-Na-E-Ka. One day he caught a grasshopper and demonstrated how to pull its legs and wings off in one flick of the fingers and how to swallow it.

I felt sick, and Roger turned green. "It's a darn good thing it's 1947," I told Roger teasingly. "You'd make a terrible warrior." Roger just grimaced.

I knew one thing. This particular Kaw Indian girl wasn't going to swallow a grasshopper no matter how hungry she got. And then I had an idea. Why hadn't I thought of it before? It
100 would have saved nights of bad dreams about squooshy grasshoppers.

I headed straight for my teacher's house. "Mrs. Richardson," I said, "would you lend me five dollars?"

"Five dollars!" she exclaimed. "What for?"

"You remember the ceremony I talked about?"

"Ta-Na-E-Ka. Of course. Your parents have written me and asked me to excuse you from school so you can participate in it."

"Well, I need some things for the ceremony," I replied, in a half-truth. "I don't want to ask my parents for the money."

110 "It's not a crime to borrow money, Mary. But how can you pay it back?"

"I'll baby-sit for you ten times."

"That's more than fair," she said, going to her purse and handing me a crisp, new five-dollar bill. I'd never had that much money at once.

"I'm happy to know the money's going to be put to a good use," Mrs. Richardson said.

A few days later the ritual began with a long speech from my grandfather about how we had reached the age of decision, 120 how we now had to fend for ourselves and prove that we could survive the most horrendous of ordeals. All the friends and relatives who had gathered at our house for dinner made jokes about their own Ta-Na-E-Ka experiences. They all advised us to fill up now, since for the next five days we'd be gorging ourselves on crickets. Neither Roger nor I was very hungry. "I'll probably laugh about this when I'm an accountant," Roger said, trembling.

"Are you trembling?" I asked.

"What do you think?"

130 "I'm happy to know boys tremble, too," I said.

At six the next morning, we kissed our parents and went off to the woods. "Which side do you want?" Roger asked. According to the rules, Roger and I would stake out "territories" in separate areas of the woods, and we weren't to communicate during the entire ordeal.

"I'll go toward the river, if it's OK with you," I said.

VISUALIZE

Re-read lines 148–162. Circle the details that help you picture the **setting**. Notice that the narrator includes details that tell you what she sees, tastes, and feels.

_____

_____

_____

_____

_____

INTERPRET

Pause at line 165. How has Mary overcome her fear?

_____

_____

_____

_____

_____

_____

PREDICT

Pause at line 171. Will the man at the counter be an enemy or a friend to Mary? Tell what you think might happen next.

_____

_____

_____

"Sure," Roger answered. "What difference does it make?"

To me, it made a lot of difference. There was a marina a few miles up the river, and there were boats moored there. At least,
140 I hoped so. I figured that a boat was a better place to sleep than under a pile of leaves.

"Why do you keep holding your head?" Roger asked.

"Oh, nothing. Just nervous," I told him. Actually, I was afraid I'd lose the five-dollar bill, which I had tucked into my hair with a bobby pin. As we came to a fork in the trail, Roger shook my hand. "Good luck, Mary."

"N'ko-n'ta," I said. It was the Kaw word for "courage."

The sun was shining and it was warm, but my bare feet began to hurt immediately. I spied one of the berry bushes
150 Grandfather had told us about. "You're lucky," he had said. "The berries are ripe in the spring, and they are delicious and nourishing." They were orange and fat, and I popped one into my mouth.

Argh! I spat it out. It was awful and bitter, and even grasshoppers were probably better tasting, although I never intended to find out.

I sat down to rest my feet. A rabbit hopped out from under the berry bush. He nuzzled the berry I'd spat out and ate it. He picked another one and ate that, too. He liked them. He
160 looked at me, twitching his nose. I watched a redheaded woodpecker bore into an elm tree, and I caught a glimpse of a civet cat[4] waddling through some twigs. All of a sudden I realized I was no longer frightened. Ta-Na-E-Ka might be more fun than I'd anticipated. I got up and headed toward the marina.

"Not one boat," I said to myself dejectedly. But the restaurant on the shore, Ernie's Riverside, was open. I walked in, feeling silly in my bathing suit. The man at the counter was big and tough-looking. He wore a sweat shirt with the words
170 "Fort Sheridan, 1944," and he had only three fingers on one of his hands. He asked me what I wanted.

---

4. **civet** (siv′it) **cat:** furry spotted skunk.

RETELL

Pause at line 198. **Retell** what has happened to Mary on her Ta-Na-E-Ka so far.

"A hamburger and a milkshake," I said, holding the five-dollar bill in my hand so he'd know I had money.

"That's a pretty heavy breakfast, honey," he murmured.

"That's what I always have for breakfast," I lied.

"Forty-five cents," he said, bringing me the food. (Back in 1947, hamburgers were twenty-five cents and milkshakes were twenty cents.)

"Delicious," I thought. "Better 'n grasshoppers—and
180 Grandfather never once mentioned that I couldn't eat hamburgers."

While I was eating, I had a grand idea. Why not sleep in the restaurant? I went to the ladies' room and made sure the window was unlocked. Then I went back outside and played along the riverbank, watching the water birds and trying to identify each one. I planned to look for a beaver dam the next day.

The restaurant closed at sunset, and I watched the three-fingered man drive away. Then I climbed in the unlocked window. There was a night light on, so I didn't turn on any
190 lights. But there was a radio on the counter. I turned it on to a music program. It was warm in the restaurant, and I was hungry. I helped myself to a glass of milk and a piece of pie, intending to keep a list of what I'd eaten so I could leave money. I also planned to get up early, sneak out through the window, and head for the woods before the three-fingered man returned. I turned off the radio, wrapped myself in the man's apron, and in spite of the hardness of the floor, fell asleep.

"What the heck are you doing here, kid?"

200 It was the man's voice.

It was morning. I'd overslept. I was scared.

"Hold it, kid. I just wanna know what you're doing here. You lost? You must be from the reservation. Your folks must be worried sick about you. Do they have a phone?"

"Yes, yes," I answered. "But don't call them."

I was shivering. The man, who told me his name was Ernie, made me a cup of hot chocolate while I explained about Ta-Na-E-Ka.

INFER

What **internal conflict** does Mary feel when Ernie says that Ta-Na-E-Ka is silly (line 212)? Underline the details that tell how she defends the ritual.

_____

_____

_____

EVALUATE

What do you like most about Mary? What do you like least about her? What's your opinion of the way Mary has endured Ta-Na-E-Ka so far?

"Darnedest thing I ever heard," he said, when I was
210 through. "Lived next to the reservation all my life and this is
the first I've heard of Ta-Na-whatever-you-call-it." He looked at
me, all goose bumps in my bathing suit. "Pretty silly thing to do
to a kid," he muttered.

That was just what I'd been thinking for months, but when
Ernie said it, I became angry. "No, it isn't silly. It's a custom
of the Kaw. We've been doing this for hundreds of years. My
mother and my grandfather and everybody in my family went
through this ceremony. It's why the Kaw are great warriors."

"OK, great warrior," Ernie chuckled, "suit yourself. And, if
220 you want to stick around, it's OK with me." Ernie went to the
broom closet and tossed me a bundle. "That's the lost-and-
found closet," he said. "Stuff people left on boats. Maybe
there's something to keep you warm."

The sweater fitted loosely, but it felt good. I felt good. And
I'd found a new friend. Most important, I was surviving Ta-Na-E-Ka.

My grandfather had said the experience would be filled with
adventure, and I was having my fill. And Grandfather had never
said we couldn't accept hospitality.

I stayed at Ernie's Riverside for the entire period. In the
230 mornings I went into the woods and watched the animals and
picked flowers for each of the tables in Ernie's. I had never felt
better. I was up early enough to watch the sun rise on the
Missouri, and I went to bed after it set. I ate everything I
wanted—insisting that Ernie take all my money for the food.
"I'll keep this in trust for you, Mary," Ernie promised, "in case
you are ever desperate for five dollars." (He did, too, but that's
another story.)

I was sorry when the five days were over. I'd enjoyed every
minute with Ernie. He taught me how to make Western omelets
240 and to make Chili Ernie Style (still one of my favorite dishes).
And I told Ernie all about the legends of the Kaw. I hadn't
realized I knew so much about my people.

But Ta-Na-E-Ka was over, and as I approached my house
at about nine-thirty in the evening, I became nervous all over

again. What if Grandfather asked me about the berries and the grasshoppers? And my feet were hardly cut. I hadn't lost a pound and my hair was combed.

"They'll be so happy to see me," I told myself hopefully, "that they won't ask too many questions."

250 I opened the door. My grandfather was in the front room. He was wearing the ceremonial beaded deerskin shirt which had belonged to *his* grandfather. "N'g'da'ma," he said. "Welcome back."

I embraced my parents warmly, letting go only when I saw my cousin Roger sprawled on the couch. His eyes were red and swollen. He'd lost weight. His feet were an unsightly mass of blood and blisters, and he was moaning: "I made it, see. I made it. I'm a warrior. A warrior."

My grandfather looked at me strangely. I was clean, 260 obviously well-fed, and radiantly healthy. My parents got the message. My uncle and aunt gazed at me with hostility.

Finally my grandfather asked, "What did you eat to keep you so well?"

I sucked in my breath and blurted out the truth: "Hamburgers and milkshakes."

"Hamburgers!" my grandfather growled.

"Milkshakes!" Roger moaned.

"You didn't say we *had* to eat grasshoppers," I said sheepishly.

270 "Tell us all about your Ta-Na-E-Ka," my grandfather commanded.

I told them everything, from borrowing the five dollars, to Ernie's kindness, to observing the beaver.

"That's not what I trained you for," my grandfather said sadly.

I stood up. "Grandfather, I learned that Ta-Na-E-Ka is important. I didn't think so during training. I was scared stiff of it. I handled it my way. And I learned I had nothing to be afraid of. There's no reason in 1947 to eat grasshoppers when you can 280 eat a hamburger."

PREDICT

How do you think Grandfather will react when he sees Mary looking healthy?

_____

_____

_____

_____

INFER

Why do you think Mary's uncle and aunt might be hostile (line 261)?

_____

_____

_____

_____

_____

BUILD FLUENCY

Re-read the boxed passage, and underline clues, like "my grandfather growled," that tell you how the characters would speak. Then, read the passage aloud. Practice reading as if you were Roger, Mary's grandfather, and the narrator.

IDENTIFY

Underline the words that tell how Mary's feelings about Ta-Na-E-Ka have changed since the beginning of the story.

INTERPRET

As a result of her experiences in this story, do you think that Mary has more or less respect for the past, especially for the traditions of her people? Tell why you think so.

_____

_____

_____

_____

_____

IDENTIFY

Circle the details that tell you that Mary's grandfather approves of the way she handled her Ta-Na-E-Ka.

EVALUATE

Rate this story with a number from 0 to 4, with 4 meaning excellent. Give a reason for your rating.

_____

_____

_____

_____

_____

_____

WORDS TO OWN
audacity (ô·das′ə·tē) *n.:* bold courage; daring.

I was inwardly shocked at my own <u>audacity</u>. But I liked it. "Grandfather, I'll bet you never ate one of those rotten berries yourself."

Grandfather laughed! He laughed aloud! My mother and father and aunt and uncle were all dumbfounded. Grandfather never laughed. Never.

"Those berries—they are terrible," Grandfather admitted. "I could never swallow them. I found a dead deer on the first day of my Ta-Na-E-Ka—shot by a soldier, probably—and he kept my belly full for the entire period of the test!"

Grandfather stopped laughing. "We should send you out again," he said.

I looked at Roger. "You're pretty smart, Mary," Roger groaned. "I'd never have thought of what you did."

"Accountants just have to be good at arithmetic," I said comfortingly. "I'm terrible at arithmetic."

Roger tried to smile but couldn't. My grandfather called me to him. "You should have done what your cousin did. But I think you are more alert to what is happening to our people today than we are. I think you would have passed the test under any circumstances, in any time. Somehow, you know how to exist in a world that wasn't made for Indians. I don't think you're going to have any trouble surviving."

Grandfather wasn't entirely right. But I'll tell about that another time.

Character-and-Conflict Chart

Fill out this character-and-conflict chart after you read "Ta-Na-E-Ka." Then analyze how the main character's personality affects the story's resolution.

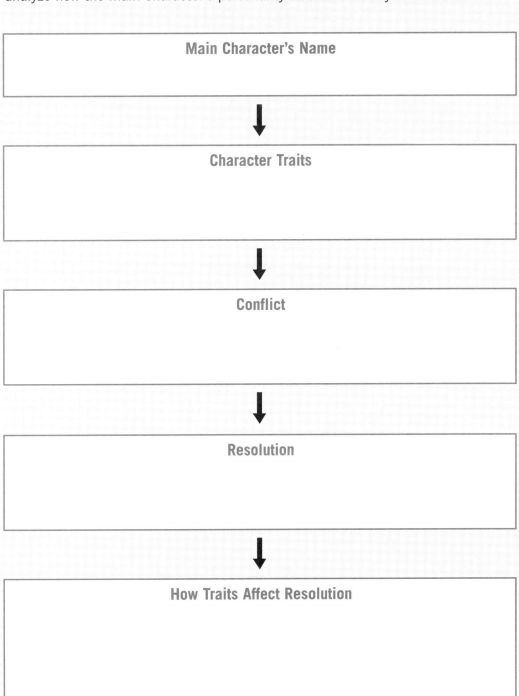

Main Character's Name

Character Traits

Conflict

Resolution

How Traits Affect Resolution

Vocabulary

A. Match words and definitions. Write the letter of the appropriate definition next to each word.

_____ **1.** gorging   **a.** noblest

_____ **2.** grimaced   **b.** cleverest

_____ **3.** loftiest   **c.** expressed disgust

_____ **4.** audacity   **d.** stuffing

_____ **5.** shrewdest   **e.** daring

> **Word Bank**
> loftiest
> shrewdest
> grimaced
> gorging
> audacity

B. Answer the following questions.

1. In your opinion, what is the loftiest quality a person can have? What is the opposite of a lofty quality?

_____

_____

2. What is the shrewdest way to deal with a class bully?

_____

_____

3. How is a grimace different from a smile?

_____

_____

4. In what situation might you be gorging yourself? Why?

_____

_____

5. What are three deeds that require audacity to carry out?

_____

_____

Comprehension

A. Write **T** or **F** next to each statement to tell whether it is true or false.

_____ **1.** Mary is eleven years old.

_____ **2.** Mary must undergo an endurance ritual.

_____ **3.** Mary is excited about the ritual.

_____ **4.** Mary adheres to the guidelines of the ritual.

_____ **5.** A restaurant owner refuses to feed Mary.

_____ **6.** Mary's grandfather admits Mary passed the test in her own way.

B. Answer the following questions about "Ta-Na-E-Ka."

1. What does Mary do in preparation for Ta-Na-E-Ka?

_____

_____

2. What does Mary do during her five days of Ta-Na-E-Ka?

_____

_____

3. What happens to Mary when she returns home after her Ta-Na-E-Ka?

_____

_____

4. What did Mary learn from her experiences?

_____

_____

The All-American Slurp

Make the Connection

Alike and Different

The main character in "The All-American Slurp" is a girl whose family has recently moved to the United States. As she becomes friends with Meg, she finds that they are different in some ways, but alike in other ways. How are you like and different from your friends? Think of your best friend or someone you know quite well but who is not related to you. Use the Venn diagram below to compare your similarities and differences. You might mention your interests, abilities, appearances, and backgrounds.

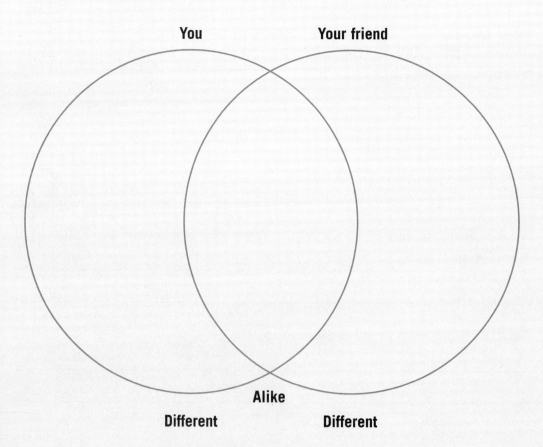

You

Your friend

Alike

Different

Different

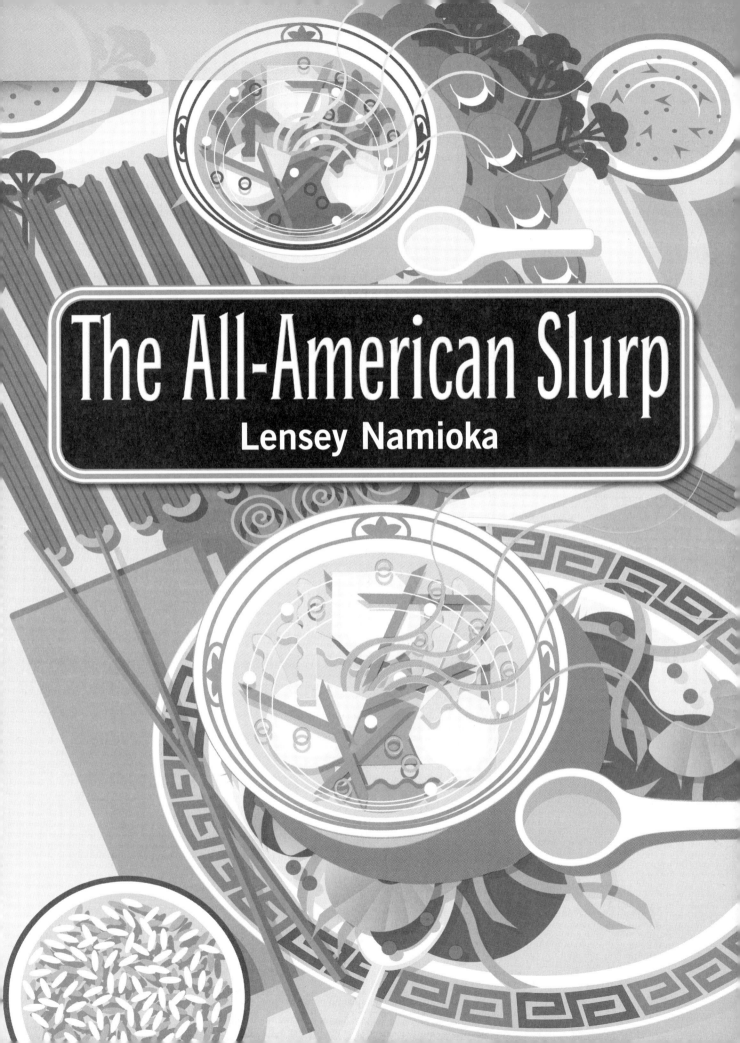

The All-American Slurp

Lensey Namioka

INFER

In this story, Chinese customs are in conflict with American customs. Underline the sentence that supports this **inference**.

IDENTIFY

In lines 5–28, underline the food items that the Lins have never eaten before.

_____

_____

_____

_____

_____

_____

_____

_____

PREDICT

Pause at line 28. The Lins are not used to American food. Do you think they will enjoy the dinner? Why or why not?

_____

_____

_____

_____

_____

_____

The first time our family was invited out to dinner in America, we disgraced ourselves while eating celery. We had immigrated to this country from China, and during our early days here we had a hard time with American table manners.

In China we never ate celery raw, or any other kind of vegetable raw. We always had to disinfect the vegetables in boiling water first. When we were presented with our first relish tray, the raw celery caught us unprepared.

We had been invited to dinner by our neighbors, the
10 Gleasons. After arriving at the house, we shook hands with our hosts and packed ourselves into a sofa. As our family of four sat stiffly in a row, my younger brother and I stole glances at our parents for a clue as to what to do next.

Mrs. Gleason offered the relish tray to Mother. The tray looked pretty, with its tiny red radishes, curly sticks of carrots, and long, slender stalks of pale-green celery. "Do try some of the celery, Mrs. Lin," she said. "It's from a local farmer, and it's sweet."

Mother picked up one of the green stalks, and Father
20 followed suit. Then I picked up a stalk, and my brother did too. So there we sat, each with a stalk of celery in our right hand.

Mrs. Gleason kept smiling. "Would you like to try some of the dip, Mrs. Lin? It's my own recipe: sour cream and onion flakes, with a dash of Tabasco sauce."

Most Chinese don't care for dairy products, and in those days I wasn't even ready to drink fresh milk. Sour cream sounded perfectly revolting. Our family shook our heads in unison.

Mrs. Gleason went off with the relish tray to the other
30 guests, and we carefully watched to see what they did. Everyone seemed to eat the raw vegetables quite happily.

Mother took a bite of her celery. _Crunch._ "It's not bad!" she whispered.

Father took a bite of his celery. _Crunch._ "Yes, it _is_ good," he said, looking surprised.

I took a bite, and then my brother. *Crunch, crunch.* It was more than good; it was delicious. Raw celery has a slight sparkle, a zingy taste that you don't get in cooked celery. When Mrs. Gleason came around with the relish tray, we each took
40 another stalk of celery, except my brother. He took two.

There was only one problem: Long strings ran through the length of the stalk, and they got caught in my teeth. When I help my mother in the kitchen, I always pull the strings out before slicing celery.

I pulled the strings out of my stalk. *Z-z-zip, z-z-zip.* My brother followed suit. *Z-z-zip, z-z-zip, z-z-zip.* To my left, my parents were taking care of their own stalks. *Z-z-zip, z-z-zip, z-z-zip.*

Suddenly I realized that there was dead silence except for
50 our zipping. Looking up, I saw that the eyes of everyone in the room were on our family. Mr. and Mrs. Gleason, their daughter Meg, who was my friend, and their neighbors the Badels—they were all staring at us as we busily pulled the strings of our celery.

That wasn't the end of it. Mrs. Gleason announced that dinner was served and invited us to the dining table. It was lavishly covered with platters of food, but we couldn't see any chairs around the table. So we helpfully carried over some dining chairs and sat down. All the other guests just stood there.

Mrs. Gleason bent down and whispered to us, "This is a
60 buffet dinner. You help yourselves to some food and eat it in the living room."

Our family beat a retreat back to the sofa as if chased by enemy soldiers. For the rest of the evening, too mortified to go back to the dining table, I nursed a bit of potato salad on my plate.

Next day, Meg and I got on the school bus together. I wasn't sure how she would feel about me after the spectacle our family made at the party. But she was just the same as usual, and the only reference she made to the party was, "Hope you and your
70 folks got enough to eat last night. You certainly didn't take very

INFER

Based on what she says to the narrator about the party (lines 69–72), what **inference** can you make about Meg's **character**?

_____

_____

_____

IDENTIFY

In lines 73–75, circle the similarity, or likeness, that the narrator sees between her family and the Gleason family.

_____

_____

_____

_____

_____

IDENTIFY

Underline the different ways the narrator, her brother, her father, and her mother try to learn English.

_____

_____

_____

_____

_____

_____

_____

much. Mom never tries to figure out how much food to prepare. She just puts everything on the table and hopes for the best."

I began to relax. The Gleasons' dinner party wasn't so different from a Chinese meal after all. My mother also puts everything on the table and hopes for the best.

Meg was the first friend I had made after we came to America. I eventually got acquainted with a few other kids in school, but Meg was still the only real friend I had.

My brother didn't have any problems making friends. He
80 spent all his time with some boys who were teaching him baseball, and in no time he could speak English much faster than I could—not better, but faster.

I worried more about making mistakes, and I spoke carefully, making sure I could say everything right before opening my mouth. At least I had a better accent than my parents, who never really got rid of their Chinese accent, even years later. My parents had both studied English in school before coming to America, but what they had studied was mostly written English, not spoken.

90 Father's approach to English was a scientific one. Since Chinese verbs have no tense, he was fascinated by the way English verbs changed form according to whether they were in the present, past, perfect, pluperfect, future, or future perfect tense. He was always making diagrams of verbs and their inflections, and he looked for opportunities to show off his mastery of the pluperfect and future perfect tenses, his two favorites. "I shall have finished my project by Monday," he would say smugly.

Mother's approach was to memorize lists of polite phrases
100 that would cover all possible social situations. She was constantly muttering things like "I'm fine, thank you. And you?" Once she accidentally stepped on someone's foot and hurriedly blurted, "Oh, that's quite all right!" Embarrassed by her slip, she resolved to do better next time. So when someone stepped on *her* foot, she cried, "You're welcome!"

In our own different ways, we made progress in learning English. But I had another worry, and that was my appearance. My brother didn't have to worry, since Mother bought him bluejeans for school, and he dressed like all the other boys. But

110 she insisted that girls had to wear skirts. By the time she saw that Meg and the other girls were wearing jeans, it was too late. My school clothes were bought already, and we didn't have money left to buy new outfits for me. We had too many other things to buy first, like furniture, pots, and pans.

The first time I visited Meg's house, she took me upstairs to her room, and I wound up trying on her clothes. We were pretty much the same size since Meg was shorter and thinner than average. Maybe that's how we became friends in the first place. Wearing Meg's jeans and T-shirt, I looked at myself in the

120 mirror. I could almost pass for an American—from the back, anyway. At least the kids in school wouldn't stop and stare at me in the hallways, which was what they did when they saw me in my white blouse and navy-blue skirt that went a couple of inches below the knees.

When Meg came to my house, I invited her to try on my Chinese dresses, the ones with a high collar and slits up the sides. Meg's eyes were bright as she looked at herself in the mirror. She struck several <u>sultry</u> poses, and we nearly fell over laughing.

130 The dinner party at the Gleasons' didn't stop my growing friendship with Meg. Things were getting better for me in other ways too. Mother finally bought me some jeans at the end of the month, when Father got his paycheck. She wasn't in any hurry about buying them at first, until I worked on her. This is what I did. Since we didn't have a car in those days, I often ran down to the neighborhood store to pick up things for her. The groceries cost less at a big supermarket, but the closest one was many blocks away. One day, when she ran out of flour, I offered to borrow a bike from our neighbor's son

140 and buy a ten-pound bag of flour at the big supermarket.

RETELL

Explain how the narrator gets her mother to buy jeans for her.

_____

_____

_____

_____

_____

_____

_____

_____

_____

_____

PREDICT

Pause at line 167. What do you think will happen to the Lin family at this fancy restaurant?

_____

_____

_____

_____

_____

_____

_____

_____

I mounted the boy's bike and waved to Mother. "I'll be back in five minutes!"

Before I started pedaling, I heard her voice behind me. "You can't go out in public like that! People can see all the way up to your thighs!"

"I'm sorry," I said innocently. "I thought you were in a hurry to get the flour." For dinner we were going to have pot stickers (fried Chinese dumplings), and we needed a lot of flour.

"Couldn't you borrow a girl's bicycle?" complained Mother.
150 "That way your skirt won't be pushed up."

"There aren't too many of those around," I said. "Almost all the girls wear jeans while riding a bike, so they don't see any point buying a girl's bike."

We didn't eat pot stickers that evening, and Mother was thoughtful. Next day we took the bus downtown and she bought me a pair of jeans. In the same week, my brother made the baseball team of his junior high school, Father started taking driving lessons, and Mother discovered rummage sales. We soon got all the furniture we needed, plus a dartboard and a
160 1,000-piece jigsaw puzzle. (Fourteen hours later, we discovered that it was a 999-piece jigsaw puzzle.) There was hope that the Lins might become a normal American family after all.

Then came our dinner at the Lakeview restaurant. The Lakeview was an expensive restaurant, one of those places where a headwaiter dressed in tails conducted you to your seat, and the only light came from candles and flaming desserts. In one corner of the room a lady harpist played tinkling melodies.

Father wanted to celebrate because he had just been promoted. He worked for an electronics company, and after his
170 English started improving, his superiors decided to appoint him to a position more suited to his training. The promotion not only brought a higher salary but was also a tremendous boost to his pride.

Up to then we had eaten only in Chinese restaurants. Although my brother and I were becoming fond of hamburgers,

my parents didn't care much for Western food, other than chow mein.

But this was a special occasion, and Father asked his co-workers to recommend a really elegant restaurant. So there we were at the Lakeview, stumbling after the headwaiter in the murky dining room.

At our table we were handed our menus, and they were so big that to read mine, I almost had to stand up again. But why bother? It was mostly in French, anyway.

Father, being an engineer, was always systematic. He took out a pocket French dictionary. "They told me that most of the items would be in French, so I came prepared." He even had a pocket flashlight the size of a marking pen. While Mother held the flashlight over the menu, he looked up the items that were in French.

"*Pâté en croûte,*" he muttered. "Let's see . . . *pâté* is paste . . . *croûte* is crust . . . hmmm . . . a paste in crust."

The waiter stood looking patient. I squirmed and died at least fifty times.

At long last Father gave up. "Why don't we just order four complete dinners at random?" he suggested.

"Isn't that risky?" asked Mother. "The French eat some rather peculiar things, I've heard."

"A Chinese can eat anything a Frenchman can eat," Father declared.

The soup arrived in a plate. How do you get soup up from a plate? I glanced at the other diners, but the ones at the nearby tables were not on their soup course, while the more distant ones were invisible in the darkness.

Fortunately my parents had studied books on Western etiquette before they came to America. "Tilt your plate," whispered my mother. "It's easier to spoon the soup up that way."

She was right. Tilting the plate did the trick. But the etiquette book didn't say anything about what you did after the soup reached your lips. As any respectable Chinese knows, the correct way to eat your soup is to slurp. This helps to cool the

INTERPRET

What does the narrator mean when she says she "squirmed and died at least fifty times" (lines 193–194)? Circle two of her father's actions that cause her to squirm.

IDENTIFY

Circle the word in line 211 that is an example of **onomatopoeia.**

VISUALIZE

Re-read lines 214–236. Circle the details that help you picture—and hear— what is happening.

INFER

Why does the narrator leave the table so abruptly (lines 228–230)?

IDENTIFY

When the narrator says that maybe an hour had passed, she is using **exaggeration** as a method of creating humor in the story. Underline an example of exaggeration in lines 243–246.

liquid and prevent you from burning your lips. It also shows your appreciation.

We showed our appreciation. *Shloop*, went my father. *Shloop*, went my mother. *Shloop, shloop*, went my brother, who was the hungriest.

The lady harpist stopped playing to take a rest. And in the silence, our family's consumption of soup suddenly seemed unnaturally loud. You know how it sounds on a rocky beach
220 when the tide goes out and the water drains from all those little pools? They go *shloop, shloop, shloop*. That was the Lin family eating soup.

At the next table a waiter was pouring wine. When a large *shloop* reached him, he froze. The bottle continued to pour, and red wine flooded the table top and into the lap of a customer. Even the customer didn't notice anything at first, being also hypnotized by the *shloop, shloop, shloop*.

It was too much. "I need to go to the toilet," I mumbled, jumping to my feet. A waiter, sensing my urgency, quickly
230 directed me to the ladies' room.

I splashed cold water on my burning face, and as I dried myself with a paper towel, I stared into the mirror. In this perfumed ladies' room, with its pink-and-silver wallpaper and marbled sinks, I looked completely out of place. What was I doing here? What was our family doing in the Lakeview restaurant? In America?

The door to the ladies' room opened. A woman came in and glanced curiously at me. I retreated into one of the toilet cubicles and latched the door.
240 Time passed—maybe half an hour, maybe an hour. Then I heard the door open again, and my mother's voice. "Are you in there? You're not sick, are you?"

There was real concern in her voice. A girl can't leave her family just because they slurp their soup. Besides, the toilet cubicle had a few drawbacks as a permanent residence. "I'm all right," I said, undoing the latch.

Mother didn't tell me how the rest of the dinner went, and I didn't want to know. In the weeks following, I managed to push the whole thing into the back of my mind, where it jumped out at me only a few times a day. Even now, I turn hot all over when I think of the Lakeview restaurant.

But by the time we had been in this country for three months, our family was definitely making progress toward becoming Americanized. I remember my parents' first PTA meeting. Father wore a neat suit and tie, and Mother put on her first pair of high heels. She stumbled only once. They met my homeroom teacher and beamed as she told them that I would make honor roll soon at the rate I was going. Of course Chinese etiquette forced Father to say that I was a very stupid girl and Mother to protest that the teacher was showing favoritism toward me. But I could tell they were both very proud.

The day came when my parents announced that they wanted to give a dinner party. We had invited Chinese friends to eat with us before, but this dinner was going to be different. In addition to a Chinese American family, we were going to invite the Gleasons.

"Gee, I can hardly wait to have dinner at your house," Meg said to me. "I just *love* Chinese food."

That was a relief. Mother was a good cook, but I wasn't sure if people who ate sour cream would also eat chicken gizzards stewed in soy sauce.

Mother decided not to take a chance with chicken gizzards. Since we had Western guests, she set the table with large dinner plates, which we never used in Chinese meals. In fact we didn't use individual plates at all, but picked up food from the platters in the middle of the table and brought it directly to our rice bowls. Following the practice of Chinese American restaurants, Mother also placed large serving spoons on the platters.

RETELL

Pause at line 251. Tell what happens at the restaurant that, years later, still makes the narrator feel embarrassed.

INTERPRET

Circle Father's and Mother's comments at the PTA meeting (lines 258–261). Why do you think they make such comments?

PREDICT

Pause at line 271. What do you think will happen at this dinner party?

BUILD FLUENCY

Re-read the boxed passage aloud. Remember to pause slightly whenever you see a colon (:) or a comma. Come to a longer stop when you see a period. When you get to the third paragraph in this passage, make your voice show the narrator's horrified surprise.

IDENTIFY

In lines 289–299, circle the mistakes that Meg and her mother make when they eat Chinese food.

INFER

Notice that Mr. Gleason is trying to eat with chopsticks (lines 300–305). Why do you think he didn't ask the Lins if he could have a fork to eat with?

INTERPRET

Pause at line 312. How is this incident like the celery-string incident on pages 30–31?

280   The dinner started well. Mrs. Gleason exclaimed at the beautifully arranged dishes of food: the colorful candied fruit in the sweet-and-sour pork dish, the noodle-thin shreds of chicken meat stir-fried with tiny peas, and the glistening pink prawns[1] in a ginger sauce.

At first I was too busy enjoying my food to notice how the guests were doing. But soon I remembered my duties. Sometimes guests were too polite to help themselves and you had to serve them with more food.

I glanced at Meg to see if she needed more food, and my
290   eyes nearly popped out at the sight of her plate. It was piled with food: The sweet-and-sour meat pushed right against the chicken shreds, and the chicken sauce ran into the prawns. She had been taking food from a second dish before she finished eating her helping from the first!

Horrified, I turned to look at Mrs. Gleason. She was dumping rice out of her bowl and putting it on her dinner plate. Then she ladled prawns and gravy on top of the rice and mixed everything together, the way you mix sand, gravel, and cement to make concrete.

300   I couldn't bear to look any longer, and I turned to Mr. Gleason. He was chasing a pea around his plate. Several times he got it to the edge, but when he tried to pick it up with his chopsticks, it rolled back toward the center of the plate again. Finally he put down his chopsticks and picked up the pea with his fingers. He really did! A grown man!

All of us, our family and the Chinese guests, stopped eating to watch the activities of the Gleasons. I wanted to giggle. Then I caught my mother's eyes on me. She frowned and shook her head slightly, and I understood the message:
310   The Gleasons were not used to Chinese ways, and they were just coping the best they could. For some reason I thought of celery strings.

When the main courses were finished, Mother brought out a platter of fruit. "I hope you weren't expecting a sweet dessert,"

---

1. **prawns:** large shrimps.

she said. "Since the Chinese don't eat dessert, I didn't think to prepare any."

"Oh, I couldn't possibly eat dessert!" cried Mrs. Gleason. "I'm simply stuffed!"

Meg had different ideas. When the table was cleared, she
320 announced that she and I were going for a walk. "I don't know about you, but I feel like dessert," she told me, when we were outside. "Come on, there's a Dairy Queen down the street. I could use a big chocolate milkshake!"

Although I didn't really want anything more to eat, I insisted on paying for the milkshakes. After all, I was still hostess.

Meg got her large chocolate milkshake and I had a small one. Even so, she was finishing hers while I was only half done. Toward the end she pulled hard on her straws and went *shloop, shloop.*

330 "Do you always slurp when you eat a milkshake?" I asked, before I could stop myself.

Meg grinned. "Sure. All Americans slurp."

EVALUATE

Which part of this story did you think was the funniest? Tell why you do or do not like the way the author uses humor in describing the difficulties of learning the customs of a different culture.

Theme Pyramid

A **theme** is an idea about life that is revealed in a work of literature. We discover a story's theme by thinking about the characters and what they learned or discovered in the story.

   After you read "The All-American Slurp," complete this pyramid. In the top section, write a word from the story you feel captures the story's essence. (Remember that no one word is right. There are many possibilities.) In the next section, describe how this word is related to the characters and their actions. Finally, in the bottom section of the pyramid, write the idea about life that is revealed in the story.

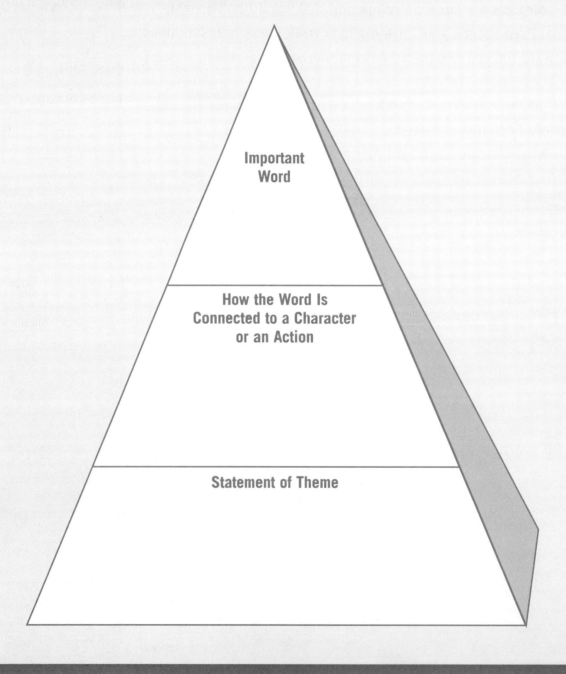

Important
Word

How the Word Is
Connected to a Character
or an Action

Statement of Theme

Vocabulary and Comprehension

A. Use the context clues in the surrounding words or sentences to decide which words from the Word Bank fit in the blanks in the paragraph below.

> **Word Bank**
> lavishly
> mortified
> spectacle
> sultry

The dance competition promised to be an impressive

_____ . The room was

_____ decorated with big bouquets of flowers and brightly

colored balloons everywhere. The dancers for the first competition looked very

_____ in their tight, sexy tango costumes. The organizers

were upset and _____ , however, when the event was

spoiled by raindrops falling through the roof onto the dance floor below.

B. Answer the following questions about "The All-American Slurp."

1. What goes wrong when the Lins have dinner at the Gleasons' house?

_____

_____

2. What goes wrong at the fancy French restaurant?

_____

_____

3. What mistakes do the Gleasons make when they have dinner at the Lins' house?

_____

_____

4. What happens at the end of the story to make the narrator feel like an American?

_____

_____

Storm

Make the Connection

Animal Talk

- Two dogs meet. One flops over on its back. It's saying, "I'm no threat. You're the boss!"
- A cat twitches the tip of its tail. It's saying, "Don't bother me!"

Animals use their behavior to communicate with each other and with us. How well do you understand what they are saying?

Below are cartoons of some of the ways animals communicate. In the thought balloons, write what you think the animal might be saying. Add your own example of animal communication. First, sketch the animal doing something, and describe the behavior on the lines below. Then, write what the animal is saying in the thought balloon.

Blue jays divebomb the cat.

The cat scratches at the door.

The dog's tail is up and wagging.

_____

_____

STORM

FROM **Woodsong**

Gary Paulsen

Background

"Storm" is taken from *Woodsong*, the true account of Gary Paulsen's adventures with his sled dogs in northern Minnesota, where this story takes place, and later in running in the Iditarod (i·dit′ə·räd), an approximately 1,160-mile dog-sled race across Alaska.

IDENTIFY

Circle the reason why the **narrator,** the person telling this story, says he is writing about "one dog."

INTERPRET

Pause at line 14. What does the narrator reveal about Storm's **character** here?

_____

_____

_____

_____

_____

_____

_____

_____

INTERPRET

How are Storm's and Fonzie's **characters** different? Underline the details that lead to your conclusion.

_____

_____

_____

_____

_____

_____

It is always possible to learn from dogs, and in fact the longer I'm with them, the more I understand how little I know. But there was one dog who taught me the most. Just one dog. Storm.

First dog. . . .

Joy, loyalty, toughness, peacefulness—all of these were part of Storm. Lessons about life and, finally, lessons about death came from him.

He had a bear's ears. He was brindle colored[1] and built like
10 a truck, and his ears were rounded when we got him, so that they looked like bear cub ears. They gave him a comical look when he was young that somehow hung on to him even when he grew old. He had a sense of humor to match his ears, and when he grew truly old, he somehow resembled George Burns.[2]

At peak, he was a mighty dog. He pulled like a machine. Until we retired him and used him only for training puppies, until we let him loose to enjoy his age, he pulled, his back over in the power curve, so that nothing could stop the sled.

In his fourth or fifth year as a puller, he started doing tricks.
20 First he would play jokes on the dog pulling next to him. On long runs he would become bored, and when we least expected it, he would reach across the gang line and snort wind into the ear of the dog next to him. I ran him with many different dogs and he did it to all of them—chuckling when the dog jumped and shook his or her head—but I never saw a single dog get mad at him for it. Oh, there was once a dog named Fonzie who nearly took his head off, but Fonzie wasn't really mad at him so much as surprised. Fonzie once nailed me through the wrist for waking him up too suddenly when he was sleeping. I'd reached
30 down and touched him before whispering his name.

Small jokes. Gentle jokes, Storm played. He took to hiding things from me. At first I couldn't understand where things were going. I would put a bootie down while working on a dog, and it would disappear. I lost a small ladle[3] I used for watering

---

1. **brindle colored:** gray or brown and streaked or spotted with a darker color.
2. **George Burns** (1896–1996): American comedian and actor with large ears.
3. **ladle:** cup-shaped spoon with a long handle for dipping out liquids.

each dog, a cloth glove liner I took off while working on a dog's feet, a roll of tape, and finally, a hat.

He was so clever.

When I lost the hat, it was a hot day and I had taken the hat off while I worked on a dog's harness. The dog was just
40 ahead of Storm, and when I knelt to work on the harness—he'd chewed almost through the side of it while running—I put the hat down on the snow near Storm.

Or thought I had. When I had changed the dog's harness, I turned and the hat was gone. I looked around, moved the dogs, looked under them, then shrugged. At first I was sure I'd put the hat down; then, when I couldn't find it, I became less sure, and at last I thought perhaps I had left it at home or dropped it somewhere on the run.

Storm sat quietly, looking ahead down the trail, not showing
50 anything at all.

I went back to the sled, reached down to <u>disengage</u> the hook, and when I did, the dogs exploded forward. I was not quite on the sled when they took off, so I was knocked slightly off balance. I leaned over to the right to <u>regain</u> myself, and when I did, I accidentally dragged the hook through the snow.

And pulled up my hat.

It had been buried off to the side of the trail in the snow, buried neatly with the snow smoothed over the top, so that it
60 was completely hidden. Had the snow hook not scraped down four or five inches, I never would have found it.

> I stopped the sled and set the hook once more. While knocking the snow out of the hat and putting it back on my head, I studied where it had happened.
>
> Right next to Storm.
>
> He had taken the hat, quickly dug a hole, buried the hat and smoothed the snow over it, then gone back to sitting, staring ahead, looking completely innocent.
>
> When I stopped the sled and picked up the hat, he looked
> 70 back, saw me put the hat on my head, and—I swear—smiled. Then he shook his head once and went back to work pulling.

RETELL

Re-read lines 19–36. **Retell** the behavior that the narrator describes as Storm's "gentle jokes."

_____

_____

_____

_____

_____

_____

_____

_____

BUILD FLUENCY

Read the boxed text aloud. Try to capture the narrator's amused tone as he describes Storm's joke. Where might his tone change to amazement? See if you can capture that change in tone when you read the text a second or third time.

WORDS TO OWN
disengage (dis′in·gāj′) v.: unfasten.
regain (ri·gān′) v.: recover.

INFER

What do you think it means that the dogs will have to "break trail" (line 83)?

_____

_____

_____

_____

_____

_____

_____

_____

PREDICT

Pause at line 96. What do you think Storm will do after the stove is loaded on the sled?

_____

_____

_____

_____

_____

_____

_____

_____

Along with the jokes, Storm had scale eyes. He watched as the sled was loaded, carefully calculated the weight of each item, and let his disapproval be known if it went too far.

One winter a friend gave us a parlor stove with nickel trim. It was not an enormous stove, but it had some weight to it and some bulk. This friend lived twelve miles away—twelve miles over two fair hills followed by about eight miles on an old, abandoned railroad grade.[4] We needed the stove badly (our old

80 barrel stove had started to burn through), so I took off with the team to pick it up. I left early in the morning because I wanted to get back that same day. It had snowed four or five inches, so the dogs would have to break trail. By the time we had done the hills and the railroad grade, pushing in new snow all the time, they were ready for a rest. I ran them the last two miles to where the stove was and unhooked their tugs so they could rest while I had coffee.

We stopped for an hour at least, the dogs sleeping quietly. When it was time to go, my friend and I carried the stove

90 outside and put it in the sled. The dogs didn't move.

Except for Storm.

He raised his head, opened one eye, did a perfect double take—both eyes opening wide—and sat up. He had been facing the front. Now he turned around to face the sled—so he was facing away from the direction we had to travel when we left— and watched us load the sled.

It took some time, as the stove barely fit on the sled and had to be jiggled and shuffled around to get it down between the side rails.

100 Through it all, Storm sat and watched us, his face a study in interest. He did not get up but sat on his back end, and when I was done and ready to go, I hooked all the dogs back in harness—which involved hooking the tugs to the rear ties on their harnesses. The dogs knew this meant we were going to head home, so they got up and started slamming against the tugs, trying to get the sled to move.

_____

4. railroad grade: rise or elevation in a railroad track.

All of them, that is, but Storm.

Storm sat backward, the tug hooked up but hanging down. The other dogs were screaming to run, but Storm sat and stared 110 at the stove.

Not at me, not at the sled, but at the stove itself. Then he raised his lips, bared his teeth, and growled at the stove.

When he was finished growling, he snorted twice, stood, turned away from the stove, and started to pull. But each time we stopped at the tops of the hills to let the dogs catch their breath after pulling the sled and stove up the steep incline, Storm turned and growled at the stove.

The enemy.

The weight on the sled.

120 I do not know how many miles Storm and I ran together. Eight, ten, perhaps twelve thousand miles. He was one of the first dogs and taught me the most, and as we worked together, he came to know me better than perhaps even my own family. He could look once at my shoulders and tell how I was feeling, tell how far we were to run, how fast we had to run—knew it all.

When I started to run long, moved from running a work team, a trap line team, to training for the Iditarod, Storm took it in stride, changed the pace down to the long trot, matched 130 what was needed, and settled in for the long haul.

He did get bored, however, and one day while we were running a long run, he started doing a thing that would stay with him—with us—until the end. We had gone forty or fifty miles on a calm, even day with no bad wind. The temperature was a perfect ten below zero. The sun was bright, everything was moving well, and the dogs had settled into the rhythm that could take them a hundred or a thousand miles.

And Storm got bored.

At a curve in the trail, a small branch came out over the 140 path we were running, and as Storm passed beneath the limb, he jumped up and grabbed it, broke a short piece off—about a foot long—and kept it in his mouth.

INTERPRET

What do you think Storm might be saying when he growls at the stove (lines 112 and 117)?

_____

_____

_____

_____

INFER

Re-read lines 111–119. What **character traits** can you **infer** from this incident?

_____

_____

_____

_____

PREDICT

Pause at line 138. Tell what you think will happen next.

_____

_____

_____

_____

VISUALIZE

Circle the details in lines 131–142 that help you picture the **setting**. Underline the details that help you see each of Storm's actions.

INFER

What do Storm's actions with the stick in lines 144–159 tell you about his **character**?

_____

_____

_____

_____

_____

_____

_____

INFER

In lines 160–173, what does the narrator reveal about his own **character**?

_____

_____

_____

_____

_____

_____

_____

_____

WORDS TO OWN
emit (ē·mit′) _v._: give out.

All day.

And into the night. He ran, carrying the stick like a toy, and when we stopped to feed or rest, he would put the stick down, eat, then pick it up again. He would put the stick down carefully in front of him, or across his paws, and sleep, and when he awakened, he would pick up the stick, and it soon became a thing between us, the stick.

150   He would show it to me, making a contact, a connection between us, each time we stopped. I would pet him on top of the head and take the stick from him—he would emit a low, gentle growl when I took the stick. I'd "examine" it closely, nod and seem to approve of it, and hand it back to him.

    Each day we ran, he would pick a different stick. And each time I would have to approve of it, and after a time, after weeks and months, I realized that he was using the sticks as a way to communicate with me, to tell me that everything was all right, that I was doing the right thing.

160   Once, when I pushed them too hard during a pre-Iditarod race—when I thought it was important to compete and win (a feeling that didn't last long)—I walked up to Storm, and as I came close to him, he pointedly dropped the stick. I picked it up and held it out, but he wouldn't take it. He turned his face away. I put the stick against his lips and tried to make him take it, but he let it fall to the ground. When I realized what he was doing, I stopped and fed and rested the team, sat on the sled, and thought about what I was doing wrong. After four hours or so of sitting—watching other teams pass me—I fed them
170 another snack, got ready to go, and was gratified to see Storm pick up the stick. From that time forward I looked for the stick always, knew when I saw it out to the sides of his head that I was doing the right thing. And it was always there.

Through storms and cold weather, on the long runs, the long, long runs where there isn't an end to it, where only the sled and the winter around the sled and the wind are there, Storm had the stick to tell me it was right, all things were right.

EVALUATE

Do you believe that Storm really did the clever actions that the narrator tells about? Or do you think the narrator made up these things, perhaps **exaggerating** (overstating) Storm's intelligence to create an interesting story? State your opinion, and give reasons for it.

Character Cluster

Animals, like people, have their own character traits that make them unique individuals. Qualities such as cleverness, laziness, stubbornness, kindness, and bravery are found in animals as in humans. Complete the graphic organizer below to show the qualities you have discovered in Storm. Write one of Storm's character traits on each line inside the dog's head. In each box attached, write a detail from the story that demonstrates that trait.

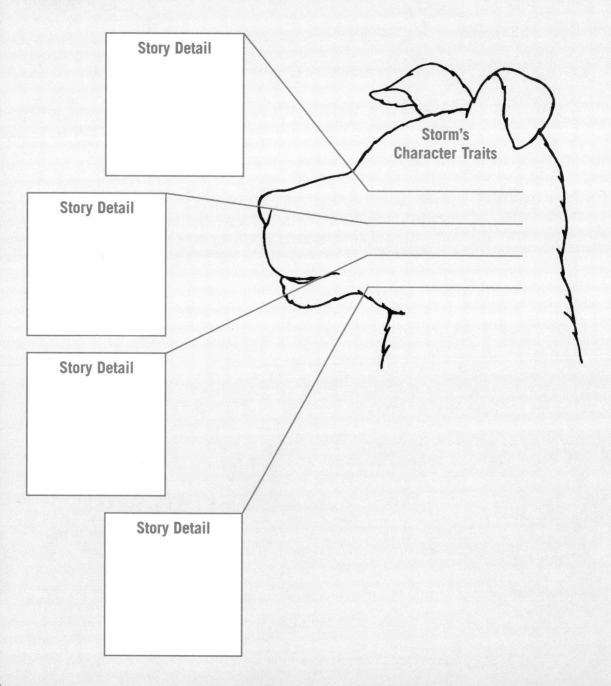

Vocabulary and Comprehension

A. Match words and definitions. Write the letter of the correct
definition next to each word.

Word Bank
disengage
regain
emit

_____ **1.** disengage   **a.** recover

_____ **2.** emit   **b.** unfasten

_____ **3.** regain   **c.** give out

B. Fill in each blank in the paragraph below with the appropriate word from the
Word Bank.

When Gary Paulsen heard Storm _____ a

deep growl, he knew he had placed too heavy a load on the sled. He

had to _____ the straps holding the load

and repack the equipment for two trips. That way he was able to

_____ the trust he had lost from his dog

team and continue on his way.

C. Use two words from the Word Bank in a sentence of your own.

1. _____

_____

2. _____

_____

D. Write **T** or **F** next to each sentence below to show whether it is true or false.

_____ **1.** Storm had bear cub ears and was half bear.

_____ **2.** Storm blew in his teammates' ears in order to upset them.

_____ **3.** Storm hid Gary Paulsen's hat in the snow.

_____ **4.** Storm measured the enormous stove on a scale.

Brother

Make the Connection

"You're the Greatest"

In her autobiography, the story of her own life, Maya Angelou says that her brother Bailey was "the greatest person in my world."

Who is the greatest person in your world? Your choice could be someone you know or a public figure you admire. It could even be someone from the past. In the middle of the star below, write the person's name. Then, inside the points of the star, write five reasons why this person is "the greatest," the most important person in your world. Write one reason inside each point.

You Are the Greatest:

_____

_____

Brother

FROM *I Know Why the Caged Bird Sings*

Boy by the Sea (1995) by Jonathan Green, Naples, Florida. Oil on canvas (18″ 3 17″). Photograph by Tim Stamm.

Maya Angelou

VISUALIZE

The author uses **description** to paint a picture in words. Underline the details in the first paragraph that help us *see* Bailey. Circle the detail that appeals to our memory of how something *feels* when we touch it.

INTERPRET

List three reasons (*not* including how Bailey looks) the author gives for believing that her brother is "the greatest." Base your answer on lines 9–35.

_____

_____

_____

_____

_____

_____

_____

_____

_____

_____

WORDS TO OWN
grating (grāt′iŋ) *adj.:* irritating or annoying.
lauded (lôd′əd) *v.:* praised.
aghast (ə·gast′) *adj.:* shocked or horrified.
precision (prē·sizh′ən) *n.:* correctness; accuracy.
apt (apt) *adj.:* quick to learn or understand.

Bailey was the greatest person in my world. And the fact that he was my brother, my only brother, and I had no sisters to share him with, was such good fortune that it made me want to live a Christian life just to show God that I was grateful. Where I was big, elbowy, and grating, he was small, graceful, and smooth. . . . He was lauded for his velvet-black skin. His hair fell down in black curls, and my head was covered with black steel wool. And yet he loved me.

10 When our elders said unkind things about my features (my family was handsome to a point of pain for me), Bailey would wink at me from across the room, and I knew that it was a matter of time before he would take revenge. He would allow the old ladies to finish wondering how on earth I came about, then he would ask, in a voice like cooling bacon grease, "Oh Mizeriz[1] Coleman, how is your son? I saw him the other day, and he looked sick enough to die."

Aghast, the ladies would ask, "Die? From what? He ain't sick."

And in a voice oilier than the one before, he'd answer with
20 a straight face, "From the Uglies."

I would hold my laugh, bite my tongue, grit my teeth, and very seriously erase even the touch of a smile from my face. Later, behind the house by the black-walnut tree, we'd laugh and laugh and howl.

Bailey could count on very few punishments for his consistently outrageous behavior, for he was the pride of the Henderson/Johnson family.

His movements, as he was later to describe those of an acquaintance, were activated with oiled precision. He was also
30 able to find more hours in the day than I thought existed. He finished chores, homework, read more books than I, and played the group games on the side of the hill with the best of them. He could even pray out loud in church and was apt at stealing pickles from the barrel that sat under the fruit counter and Uncle Willie's nose.

_____

1. Mizeriz: dialect term for "Mrs."

Once when the Store was full of lunchtime customers, he dipped the strainer, which we also used to sift weevils[2] from meal and flour, into the barrel and fished for two fat pickles. He caught them and hooked the strainer onto the side of the barrel, where they dripped until he was ready for them. When the last school bell rang, he picked the nearly dry pickles out of the strainer, jammed them into his pockets, and threw the strainer behind the oranges. We ran out of the Store. It was summer and his pants were short, so the pickle juice made clean streams down his ashy legs, and he jumped with his pockets full of loot and his eyes laughing a "How about that?" He smelled like a vinegar barrel or a sour angel.

After our early chores were done, while Uncle Willie or Momma minded the Store, we were free to play the children's games as long as we stayed within yelling distance. Playing hide-and-seek, his voice was easily identified, singing, "Last night, night before, twenty-four robbers at my door. Who all is hid? Ask me to let them in, hit 'em in the head with a rolling pin. Who all is hid?" In follow the leader, naturally he was the one who created the most daring and interesting things to do. And when he was on the tail of the pop the whip, he would twirl off the end like a top, spinning, falling, laughing, finally stopping just before my heart beat its last, and then he was back in the game, still laughing.

Of all the needs (there are none imaginary) a lonely child has, the one that must be satisfied, if there is going to be hope and a hope of wholeness, is the unshaking need for an unshakable God. My pretty black brother was my Kingdom Come.

---

2. **weevils:** small beetles that feed on grains, fruits, cotton, and so on.

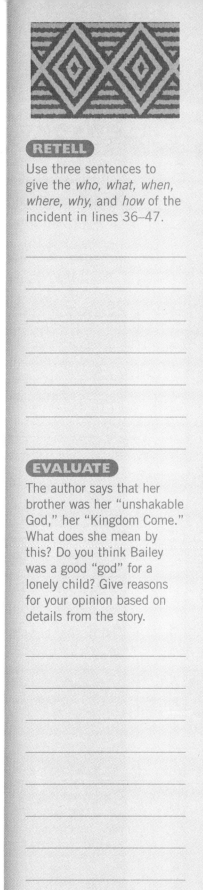

RETELL

Use three sentences to give the *who, what, when, where, why,* and *how* of the incident in lines 36–47.

EVALUATE

The author says that her brother was her "unshakable God," her "Kingdom Come." What does she mean by this? Do you think Bailey was a good "god" for a lonely child? Give reasons for your opinion based on details from the story.

Sensory Image Chart

"Brother" is full of **sensory images**—details that appeal to our five senses. Fill in the chart below with details from the story that help us see, hear, smell, feel, or taste something as if it were real. List one detail for each sense.

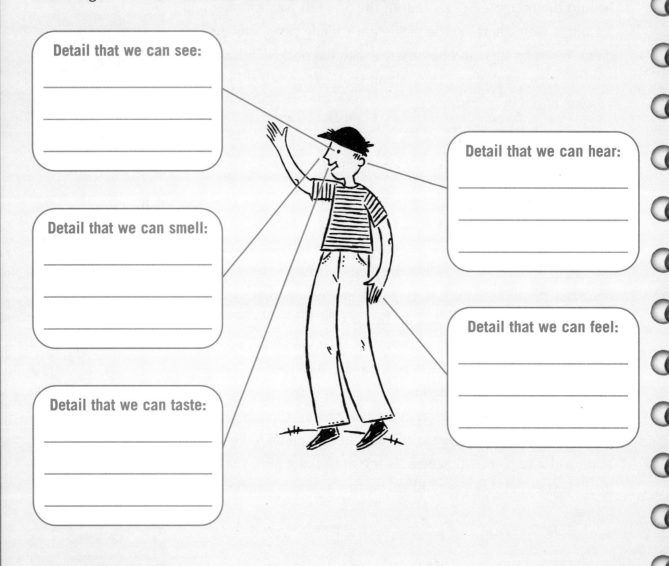

Detail that we can see:
_____
_____
_____

Detail that we can smell:
_____
_____
_____

Detail that we can taste:
_____
_____
_____

Detail that we can hear:
_____
_____
_____

Detail that we can feel:
_____
_____
_____

Vocabulary and Comprehension

A. Match words and synonyms. Write the letter of the correct synonym next to each word.

Word Bank
grating
lauded
aghast
precision
apt

_____ **1.** grating   **a.** shocked

_____ **2.** lauded   **b.** irritating

_____ **3.** aghast   **c.** praised

_____ **4.** precision   **d.** correctness

_____ **5.** apt   **e.** quick to learn

B. Complete each sentence with a word from the Word Bank.

1. Maya was big and _____, while Bailey was small and charming.

2. Everyone praised, or _____, Bailey for his good looks.

3. Bailey moved with exactness and _____.

4. His elders were often shocked and _____ at what Bailey said.

5. Bailey was smart and _____ in studies, games, and tricks.

C. Answer each question below.

1. Why does the writer like her brother so much?

_____

_____

2. In the last paragraph, the writer says she was a lonely child. Why do you think she was lonely?

_____

_____

The Mysterious Mr. Lincoln

Make the Connection

Facing History

You already know many facts about Abraham Lincoln, our sixteenth president. In your opinion, what was his greatest achievement?

Write inside the oval in the five-dollar-bill graphic below what you think was the most important thing that Abraham Lincoln did. (On a real five-dollar bill, Lincoln's picture is inside the oval.) At the left of the oval, write three things that you **already know** about Lincoln. To the right of the oval, write what you **want to know** about Lincoln.

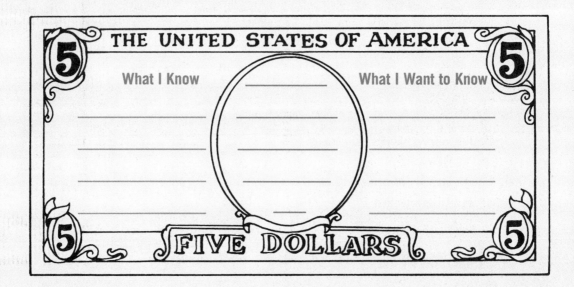

THE UNITED STATES OF AMERICA

What I Know   What I Want to Know

FIVE DOLLARS

The Mysterious Mr. Lincoln

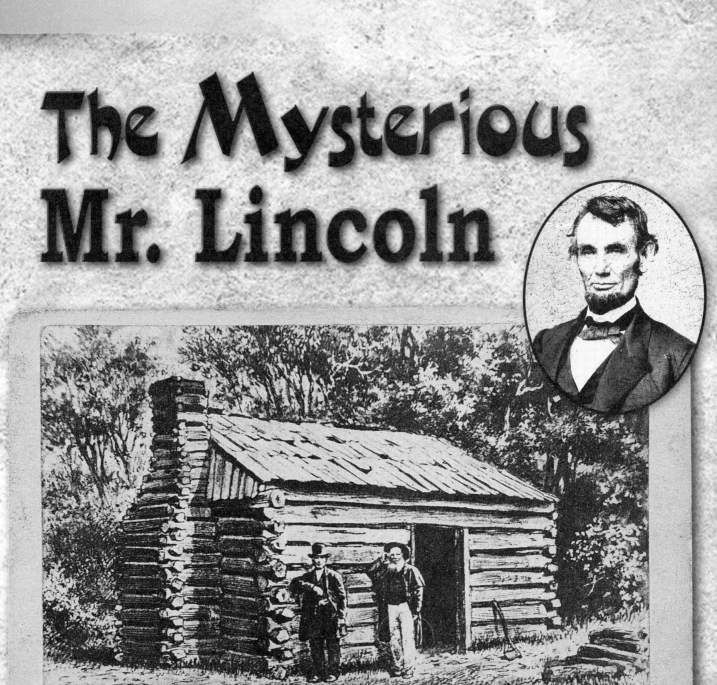

President Lincoln's first Home in Illinois.

Russell Freedman

VISUALIZE

Underline the words and
phrases in lines 1–21
that help you picture
how Lincoln looked.

_____

_____

_____

_____

_____

INFER

Pause at line 28. Why does
Lincoln look so stiff and
formal in his photographs?

_____

_____

_____

_____

WORDS TO OWN
gawky (gô′kē) *adj.:*
awkward; lacking grace or
elegance.
repose (ri·pōz′) *n.:* restful
state.
countenance (koun′tə·nəns)
n.: face or facial expression.
animation (an′i·mā′shən) *n.:*
liveliness; life.
defy (dē·fī′) *v.:* resist
completely.
reticent (ret′ə·sənt) *adj.:*
reserved; choosing not to
talk about what one thinks
and feels.

Abraham Lincoln wasn't the sort of man who could lose
himself in a crowd. After all, he stood six feet four inches tall,
and to top it off, he wore a high silk hat.

His height was mostly in his long, bony legs. When he sat
in a chair, he seemed no taller than anyone else. It was only
when he stood up that he towered above other men.

At first glance most people thought he was homely. Lincoln
thought so too, referring once to his "poor, lean, lank face." As
a young man he was sensitive about his gawky looks, but in
10 time, he learned to laugh at himself. When a rival called him
"two-faced" during a political debate, Lincoln replied: "I leave it
to my audience. If I had another face, do you think I'd wear
this one?"

According to those who knew him, Lincoln was a man
of many faces. In repose he often seemed sad and gloomy.
But when he began to speak, his expression changed. "The
dull, listless features dropped like a mask," said a Chicago
newspaperman. "The eyes began to sparkle, the mouth to
smile; the whole countenance was wreathed in animation, so
20 that a stranger would have said, "Why, this man, so angular
and solemn a moment ago, is really handsome!"

Lincoln was the most photographed man of his time, but
his friends insisted that no photo ever did him justice. It's no
wonder. Back then, cameras required long exposures. The
person being photographed had to "freeze" as the seconds
ticked by. If he blinked an eye, the picture would be blurred.
That's why Lincoln looks so stiff and formal in his photos. We
never see him laughing or joking.

Artists and writers tried to capture the "real" Lincoln that
30 the camera missed, but something about the man always
escaped them. His changeable features, his tones, gestures,
and expressions, seemed to defy description.

Today it's hard to imagine Lincoln as he really was. And he
never cared to reveal much about himself. In company he was
witty and talkative, but he rarely betrayed his inner feelings.
According to William Herndon, his law partner, he was "the
most secretive—reticent—shut-mouthed man that ever lived."

In his own time, Lincoln was never fully understood even by his closest friends. Since then, his life story has been told and
40 retold so many times he has become as much a legend as a flesh-and-blood human being. While the legend is based on truth, it is only partly true. And it hides the man behind it like a disguise.

The legendary Lincoln is known as Honest Abe, a humble man of the people who rose from a log cabin to the White House. There's no doubt that Lincoln was a poor boy who made good. And it's true that he carried his folksy manners and homespun speech to the White House with him. He said "howdy" to visitors and invited them to "stay a spell." He
50 greeted diplomats while wearing carpet slippers, called his wife "mother" at receptions, and told bawdy[1] jokes at cabinet meetings.

Lincoln may have seemed like a common man, but he wasn't. His friends agreed that he was one of the most ambitious people they had ever known. Lincoln struggled hard to rise above his log-cabin origins, and he was proud of his achievements. By the time he ran for president he was a wealthy man, earning a large income from his law practice and his many investments. As for the nickname Abe, he hated it. No one who knew him well ever called him Abe to his face.
60 They addressed him as Lincoln or Mr. Lincoln.

Lincoln is often described as a sloppy dresser, careless about his appearance. In fact, he patronized the best tailor in Springfield, Illinois, buying two suits a year. That was at a time when many men lived, died, and were buried in the same suit.

It's true that Lincoln had little formal "eddication," as he would have pronounced it. Almost everything he "larned" he taught himself. All his life he said "thar" for *there,* "git" for *get,* "kin" for *can.* Even so, he became an eloquent public speaker who could hold a vast audience spellbound and a great writer
70 whose finest phrases still ring in our ears. He was known to sit up late into the night, discussing Shakespeare's plays with White House visitors.

---

1. **bawdy:** humorous but crude.

INFER

What do you think Lincoln was like? Do you think he was an easy man to get to know? Circle details in lines 29–43 that support your opinion.

INTERPRET

Underline the details in lines 44–51 that reveal Lincoln's "folksy manners." What do you think the author means when he says Lincoln seemed like a "common man"? Circle the details in lines 52–64 that seem to show that Lincoln was *not* a common man.

WORDS TO OWN
patronized (pā′trə·nīzd′) *v.:* was a regular customer of.

IDENTIFY

In lines 73–89, each of the three paragraphs presents two sides of Lincoln's **character.** The two sides are separated by a **transitional** word, like *But* in line 74. Circle the transitional words in the next two paragraphs.

_____

_____

_____

_____

INTERPRET

Re-read lines 90–96. How did Lincoln's attitude change during the war?

_____

_____

_____

_____

_____

_____

_____

_____

WORDS TO OWN
omens (ō′mənz) *n.*: events, objects, or situations that supposedly tell what will happen in the future.
paramount (par′ə·mount′) *adj.*: most important.
crusade (krōō·sād′) *n.*: struggle for a cause or belief.

He was certainly a humorous man, famous for his rollicking stories. But he was also moody and melancholy, tormented by long and frequent bouts of depression. Humor was his therapy. He relied on his yarns,[2] a friend observed, to "whistle down sadness."

He had a cool, logical mind, trained in the courtroom, and a practical, commonsense approach to problems. Yet he was

80 deeply superstitious, a believer in dreams, omens, and visions.

We admire Lincoln today as an American folk hero. During the Civil War, however, he was the most unpopular president the nation had ever known. His critics called him a tyrant, a hick,[3] a stupid baboon who was unfit for his office. As commander in chief of the armed forces, he was denounced as a bungling amateur who meddled in military affairs he knew nothing about. But he also had his supporters. They praised him as a farsighted statesman, a military mastermind who engineered the Union victory.

90 Lincoln is best known as the Great Emancipator, the man who freed the slaves. Yet he did not enter the war with that idea in mind. "My paramount object in this struggle *is* to save the Union," he said in 1862, "and is *not* either to save or destroy slavery." As the war continued, Lincoln's attitude changed. Eventually he came to regard the conflict as a moral crusade to wipe out the sin of slavery.

No black leader was more critical of Lincoln than the fiery abolitionist[4] writer and editor Frederick Douglass. Douglass had grown up as a slave. He had won his freedom by escaping to

100 the North. Early in the war, impatient with Lincoln's cautious leadership, Douglass called him "preeminently the white man's president, entirely devoted to the welfare of white men." Later, Douglass changed his mind and came to admire Lincoln. Several years after the war, he said this about the sixteenth president:

---

2. **yarns:** entertaining stories that rely on exaggeration for their humor. Storytellers like Lincoln could be said to "spin" yarns.
3. **hick:** awkward, inexperienced person from the country.
4. **abolitionist:** anyone who wanted to end, or abolish, slavery in the United States.

"His greatest mission was to accomplish two things: first, to save his country from dismemberment[5] and ruin; and second, to free his country from the great crime of slavery. . . . Taking him for all in all, measuring the tremendous magnitude of the 110 work before him, considering the necessary means to ends, and surveying the end from the beginning, infinite wisdom has seldom sent any man into the world better fitted for his mission than Abraham Lincoln."

INTERPRET

In one sentence, summarize what Frederick Douglass concluded was most important about Lincoln.

_____

_____

_____

_____

IDENTIFY

What was the most surprising, interesting, or important new thing you learned about Lincoln in this selection?

_____

_____

_____

_____

EVALUATE

Do you think this chapter is an effective opening of a **biography** about Lincoln? Tell why it does or does not make you want to read the rest of the book.

_____

_____

_____

_____

_____

5. **dismemberment:** separating into parts; dividing up.

Metaphor Matching Map

A **metaphor** compares two things without using a comparison word such as *like* or *as*. Re-read "The Mysterious Mr. Lincoln," looking for metaphors. Write the metaphors in the boxes below, and explain what each metaphor means. The first two metaphors have been filled in for you.

Metaphor	Meaning
A rival called him "two-faced."	
He was a man of many faces.	

Vocabulary and Comprehension

A. Match words and definitions. Write the letter of the correct definition next to each word.

_____ **1.** omens   **a.** state of rest

_____ **2.** animation   **b.** liveliness

_____ **3.** crusade   **c.** most important

_____ **4.** paramount   **d.** signs of the future

_____ **5.** repose   **e.** struggle for a cause

_____ **6.** gawky   **f.** resist completely

_____ **7.** patronized   **g.** reserved

_____ **8.** defy   **h.** awkward

_____ **9.** countenance   **i.** was a customer of

_____ **10.** reticent   **j.** face

Word Bank
gawky
repose
countenance
animation
defy
reticent
patronized
omens
paramount
crusade

B. Choose two words from the Word Bank, and use each in a sentence of your own.

1. _____

_____

2. _____

_____

C. Lincoln's **character** contained many contradictions. For instance, he was humorous but also melancholy, or sad. List two other sets of opposite traits on the lines below.

1. Lincoln was _____ , but he was also _____ .

2. Lincoln was _____ , but he was also _____ .

A Glory over Everything

Make the Connection

Slavery Versus Freedom

This **biography** is the true story of Harriet Tubman, who escaped from slavery in the South to freedom in the North. Tubman then made many return trips to the South, risking her life to lead more than three hundred slaves to freedom.

What do slavery and freedom mean to you? To the left of the wall below, use words, phrases, symbols, and sketches to show what the word *slavery* means to you. To the right of the wall, do the same for the word *freedom*.

Slavery   **Freedom**

Background

In 1849, when "A Glory over Everything" takes place, a runaway from slavery who crossed into a free state was considered free. In 1850, however, a federal law decreed that runaways could be returned to their "owners." That meant that runaways were not safe until they reached Canada. In what came to be called the Underground Railroad, people opposed to slavery offered shelter, food, and transportation to those escaping to freedom in the North.

In this excerpt from her biography, we meet Harriet Tubman when she is still a slave, working as a field hand at the Brodas Plantation in Maryland. As a young girl, Harriet had received a crushing blow to her head when she refused to help tie up a runaway slave. The injury made her occasionally fall asleep quite suddenly and uncontrollably.

A Glory over Everything

FROM **Harriet Tubman: Conductor on the Underground Railroad**

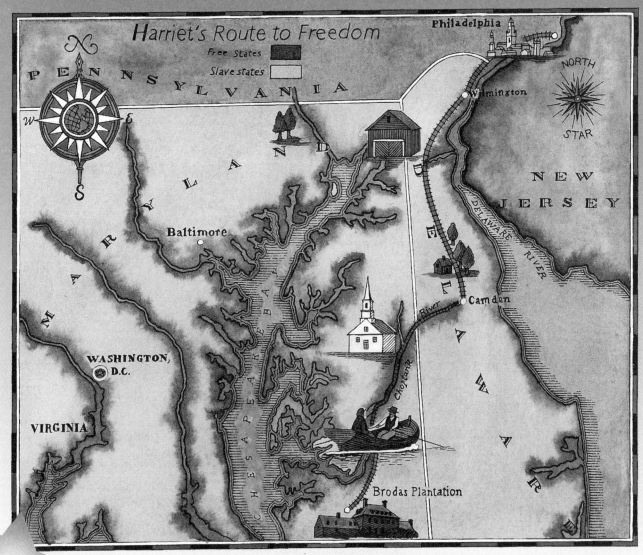

Ann Petry

IDENTIFY

Who is telling this story? Remember that it's a **biography**—a story of a person's life told by someone else.

_____

_____

_____

_____

INFER

What kind of help do you think the white woman might be referring to (lines 12–13)?

_____

_____

_____

_____

_____

IDENTIFY

Sequence is the order of events in a story. Time-order words and phrases like _soon, next,_ and _that night_ signal the order of events and the time that has passed. Circle five time-order words or phrases that you find in the first three paragraphs.

_____

_____

_____

One day in 1849, when Harriet was working in the fields near the edge of the road, a white woman wearing a faded sunbonnet went past, driving a wagon. She stopped the wagon and watched Harriet for a few minutes. Then she spoke to her, asked her what her name was, and how she had acquired the deep scar on her forehead.

Harriet told her the story of the blow she had received when she was a girl. After that, whenever the woman saw her in the fields, she stopped to talk to her. She told Harriet that she lived

10 on a farm near Bucktown. Then one day she said, not looking at Harriet but looking instead at the overseer[1] far off at the edge of the fields, "If you ever need any help, Harriet, ever need any help, why, you let me know."

That same year the young heir to the Brodas estate[2] died. Harriet mentioned the fact of his death to the white woman in the faded sunbonnet the next time she saw her. She told her of the panic-stricken talk in the quarter, told her that the slaves were afraid that the master, Dr. Thompson, would start selling them. She said that Doc Thompson no longer permitted any of

20 them to hire their time.[3] The woman nodded her head, clucked to the horse, and drove off, murmuring, "If you ever need any help—"

The slaves were right about Dr. Thompson's intention. He began selling slaves almost immediately. Among the first ones sold were two of Harriet Tubman's sisters. They went south with the chain gang[4] on a Saturday.

When Harriet heard of the sale of her sisters, she knew that the time had finally come when she must leave the plantation. She was reluctant to attempt the long trip north alone, not

---

1. **overseer:** person who supervises workers; in this case, a slave driver.
2. **Brodas estate:** Edward Brodas, the previous owner of the plantation, died in 1849 and left his property to his heir, who was not yet old enough to manage it. In the meantime the plantation was placed in the hands of the boy's guardian, Dr. Thompson.
3. **hire their time:** Some slaveholders allowed their slaves to hire themselves out for pay to other plantation owners who needed extra help. In such cases the slaves were permitted to keep their earnings.
4. **chain gang:** literally, a gang of people (slaves or prisoners) chained together.

because of John Tubman's threat to betray her[5] but because she was afraid she might fall asleep somewhere along the way and so would be caught immediately.

She persuaded three of her brothers to go with her. Having made certain that John was asleep, she left the cabin quietly and met her brothers at the edge of the plantation. They agreed that she was to lead the way, for she was more familiar with the woods than the others.

The three men followed her, crashing through the underbrush, frightening themselves, stopping constantly to say, "What was that?" or "Someone's coming."

She thought of Ben[6] and how he had said, "Any old body can go through a woods crashing and mashing things down like a cow." She said sharply, "Can't you boys go quieter? Watch where you're going!"

One of them grumbled, "Can't see in the dark. Ain't got cat's eyes like you."

"You don't need cat's eyes," she retorted. "On a night like this, with all the stars out, it's not black dark. Use your own eyes."

She supposed they were doing the best they could, but they moved very slowly. She kept getting so far ahead of them that she had to stop and wait for them to catch up with her, lest they lose their way. Their progress was slow, uncertain. Their feet got tangled in every vine. They tripped over fallen logs, and once one of them fell flat on his face. They jumped, startled, at the most ordinary sounds: the murmur of the wind in the branches of the trees, the twittering of a bird. They kept turning around, looking back.

They had not gone more than a mile when she became aware that they had stopped. She turned and went back to them. She could hear them whispering. One of them called out, "Hat!"

---

5. Harriet's husband, John Tubman, was a free man who was content with his life. He violently disapproved of his wife's plan to escape and threatened to tell the master if she carried it out.
6. **Ben:** Harriet Tubman's father. Her mother is called Old Rit.

PREDICT

Pause at line 58. Tubman's brothers seem fearful about going on. What do you think might happen next?

INTERPRET

What's the main reason why Tubman's brothers want to go back?

_____

_____

_____

_____

_____

INFER

Why do you think Tubman's brothers prevent her from continuing without them?

_____

_____

_____

_____

_____

_____

_____

_____

_____

_____

WORDS TO OWN
elude (ē·lōōd') *v.*: escape notice of.

"What's the matter? We haven't got time to keep stopping like this."

"We're going back."

"No," she said firmly. "We've got a good start. If we move fast and move quiet—"

Then all three spoke at once. They said the same thing, over and over, in frantic hurried whispers, all talking at once:

70 They told her that they had changed their minds. Running away was too dangerous. Someone would surely see them and recognize them. By morning the master would know they had "took off." Then the handbills advertising them would be posted all over Dorchester County. The patterollers[7] would search for them. Even if they were lucky enough to elude the patrol, they could not possibly hide from the bloodhounds. The hounds would be baying after them, snuffing through the swamps and the underbrush, zigzagging through the deepest woods. The bloodhounds would surely find them. And

80 everyone knew what happened to a runaway who was caught and brought back alive.

She argued with them. Didn't they know that if they went back they would be sold, if not tomorrow, then the next day, or the next? Sold south. They had seen the chain gangs. Was that what they wanted? Were they going to be slaves for the rest of their lives? Didn't freedom mean anything to them?

"You're afraid," she said, trying to shame them into action. "Go on back. I'm going north alone."

Instead of being ashamed, they became angry. They shouted

90 at her, telling her that she was a fool and they would make her go back to the plantation with them. Suddenly they surrounded her, three men, her own brothers, jostling her, pushing her along, pinioning[8] her arms behind her. She fought against them, wasting her strength, exhausting herself in a furious struggle.

She was no match for three strong men. She said, panting, "All right. We'll go back. I'll go with you."

---

7. **patterollers:** patrollers.
8. **pinioning** (pin'yən·iŋ): binding or holding someone to make the person helpless.

She led the way, moving slowly. Her thoughts were bitter.
Not one of them was willing to take a small risk in order to
be free. It had all seemed so perfect, so simple, to have her
100 brothers go with her, sharing the dangers of the trip together,
just as a family should. Now if she ever went north, she would
have to go alone.

Two days later, a slave working beside Harriet in the fields
motioned to her. She bent toward him, listening. He said the
water boy had just brought news to the field hands, and it had
been passed from one to the other until it reached him. The
news was that Harriet and her brothers had been sold to the
Georgia trader and that they were to be sent south with the
chain gang that very night.
110   Harriet went on working but she knew a moment of panic.
She would have to go north alone. She would have to start as
soon as it was dark. She could not go with the chain gang. She
might die on the way because of those inexplicable sleeping
seizures. But then she—how could she run away? She might
fall asleep in plain view along the road.

> But even if she fell asleep, she thought, the Lord would take
> care of her. She murmured a prayer, "Lord, I'm going to hold
> steady on to You, and You've got to see me through."
>   Afterward, she explained her decision to run the risk of
> 120 going north alone in these words: "I had reasoned this out in
> my mind; there was one of two things I had a *right* to, liberty
> or death; if I could not have one, I would have the other; for no
> man should take me alive; I should fight for my liberty as long
> as my strength lasted, and when the time came for me to go,
> the Lord would let them take me."

At dusk, when the work in the fields was over, she started
toward the Big House.[9] She had to let someone know that
she was going north, someone she could trust. She no longer
trusted John Tubman and it gave her a lost, lonesome feeling.
130 Her sister Mary worked in the Big House, and she planned to

---

9. **Big House:** plantation owner's house.

RETELL
Briefly **retell** what has
happened in Tubman's life
since her sisters were sold.
(See page 68, line 25.)

BUILD FLUENCY
Read the boxed passage
aloud until you can read it
smoothly. When you say
Tubman's words, try to
capture what you think her
tone of voice would be.

WORDS TO OWN
inexplicable (in′ek·splik′ə·
bəl) *adj.:* not explainable.

INFER

Why do you think Tubman wanted someone to know she was leaving?

_____

_____

_____

_____

_____

_____

INTERPRET

Why does Tubman choose to sing this particular song (lines 146–157)? Circle the details in the song that are clues for you—and for Tubman's sister.

_____

_____

_____

_____

_____

_____

_____

WORDS TO OWN
legitimate (lə·jit′ə·mət) *adj.*: reasonable; logically correct.
defiant (dē·fī′ənt) *adj.*: openly and boldly resisting.

tell Mary that she was going to run away, so someone would know.

As she went toward the house, she saw the master, Doc Thompson, riding up the drive on his horse. She turned aside and went toward the quarter. A field hand had no legitimate reason for entering the kitchen of the Big House—and yet— there must be some way she could leave word so that afterward someone would think about it and know that she had left a message.

140   As she went toward the quarter, she began to sing. Dr. Thompson reined in his horse, turned around, and looked at her. It was not the beauty of her voice that made him turn and watch her, frowning; it was the words of the song that she was singing and something defiant in her manner that disturbed and puzzled him.

> *When that old chariot comes,*
>   *I'm going to leave you,*
> *I'm bound for the promised land,*
>   *Friends, I'm going to leave you.*

150
> *I'm sorry, friends, to leave you,*
>   *Farewell! Oh, farewell!*
> *But I'll meet you in the morning,*
>   *Farewell! Oh, farewell!*

> *I'll meet you in the morning,*
>   *When I reach the promised land;*
> *On the other side of Jordan,*
>   *For I'm bound for the promised land.*

That night when John Tubman was asleep and the fire had died down in the cabin, she took the ash cake that had been
160 baked for their breakfast and a good-sized piece of salt herring and tied them together in an old bandanna. By hoarding this small stock of food, she could make it last a long time, and

with the berries and edible roots she could find in the woods, she wouldn't starve.

She decided that she would take the quilt[10] with her, too. Her hands lingered over it. It felt soft and warm to her touch. Even in the dark, she thought she could tell one color from another because she knew its pattern and design so well.

Then John stirred in his sleep, and she left the cabin
170 quickly, carrying the quilt carefully folded under her arm.

Once she was off the plantation, she took to the woods, not following the North Star, not even looking for it, going instead toward Bucktown. She needed help. She was going to ask the white woman who had stopped to talk to her so often if she would help her. Perhaps she wouldn't. But she would soon find out.

When she came to the farmhouse where the woman lived, she approached it cautiously, circling around it. It was so quiet. There was no sound at all, not even a dog barking or the sound of voices. Nothing.

180 She tapped on the door, gently. A voice said, "Who's there?" She answered, "Harriet, from Dr. Thompson's place."

When the woman opened the door, she did not seem at all surprised to see her. She glanced at the little bundle that Harriet was carrying, at the quilt, and invited her in. Then she sat down at the kitchen table and wrote two names on a slip of paper and handed the paper to Harriet.

She said that those were the next places where it was safe for Harriet to stop. The first place was a farm where there was a gate with big white posts and round knobs on top of them.
190 The people there would feed her, and when they thought it was safe for her to go on, they would tell her how to get to the next house or take her there. For these were the first two stops on the Underground Railroad—going north, from the eastern shore of Maryland.

Thus Harriet learned that the Underground Railroad that ran straight to the North was not a railroad at all. Neither did it run

INTERPRET

Why do you think Tubman decides to take the quilt (line 165)?

_____

_____

_____

_____

_____

PREDICT

Pause at line 179. Do you think the woman's at home? What do you think will happen next?

_____

_____

_____

_____

_____

_____

IDENTIFY

What is the Underground Railroad? Underline the details in lines 192–200 that tell you about it.

_____

_____

_____

_____

_____

_____

10. **the quilt:** Tubman had painstakingly stitched together a quilt before her wedding.

INFER

What does her gift to the woman tell you about Tubman's **character**?

_____

_____

_____

_____

VISUALIZE

Underline the details in lines 208–212 that help you picture what Tubman looked like.

_____

_____

_____

_____

INFER

Why does thinking of the handbills make Tubman walk faster (line 221)?

_____

_____

_____

_____

WORDS TO OWN

sinewy (sin'yoo·ē) adj.: strong; firm; tough.

underground. It was composed of a loosely organized group of people who offered food and shelter, or a place of concealment, to fugitives who had set out on the long road to the North and
200 freedom.

Harriet wanted to pay this woman who had befriended her. But she had no money. She gave her the patchwork quilt, the only beautiful object she had ever owned.

That night she made her way through the woods, crouching in the underbrush whenever she heard the sound of horses' hoofs, staying there until the riders passed. Each time, she wondered if they were already hunting for her. It would be so easy to describe her, the deep scar on her forehead like a dent, the old scars on the back of her neck, the husky speaking voice,
210 the lack of height, scarcely five feet tall. The master would say she was wearing rough clothes when she ran away, that she had a bandanna on her head, that she was muscular and strong.

She knew how accurately he would describe her. One of the slaves who could read used to tell the others what it said on those handbills that were nailed up on the trees along the edge of the roads. It was easy to recognize the handbills that advertised runaways because there was always a picture in one corner, a picture of a black man, a little running figure with a stick over his shoulder and a bundle tied on the end
220 of the stick.

Whenever she thought of the handbills, she walked faster. Sometimes she stumbled over old grapevines, gnarled and twisted, thick as a man's wrist, or became entangled in the tough sinewy vine of the honeysuckle. But she kept going.

In the morning she came to the house where her friend had said she was to stop. She showed the slip of paper that she carried to the woman who answered her knock at the back door of the farmhouse. The woman fed her and then handed her a broom and told her to sweep the yard.
230 Harriet hesitated, suddenly suspicious. Then she decided that with a broom in her hand, working in the yard, she would look as though she belonged on the place; certainly no one would suspect that she was a runaway.

That night the woman's husband, a farmer, loaded a wagon with produce. Harriet climbed in. He threw some blankets over her, and the wagon started.

It was dark under the blankets and not exactly comfortable. But Harriet decided that riding was better than walking. She was surprised at her own lack of fear, wondered how it was that she so readily trusted these strangers who might betray her. For all she knew, the man driving the wagon might be taking her straight back to the master.

She thought of those other rides in wagons, when she was a child, the same clop-clop of the horses' feet, creak of the wagon, and the feeling of being lost because she did not know where she was going. She did not know her destination this time either, but she was not alarmed. She thought of John Tubman. By this time he must have told the master that she was gone. Then she thought of the plantation and how the land rolled gently down toward the river, thought of Ben and Old Rit, and that Old Rit would be inconsolable because her favorite daughter was missing. "Lord," she prayed, "I'm going to hold steady onto You. You've got to see me through." Then she went to sleep.

The next morning, when the stars were still visible in the sky, the farmer stopped the wagon. Harriet was instantly awake.

He told her to follow the river, to keep following it to reach the next place where people would take her in and feed her. He said that she must travel only at night and she must stay off the roads because the patrol would be hunting for her. Harriet climbed out of the wagon. "Thank you," she said simply, thinking how amazing it was that there should be white people who were willing to go to such lengths to help a slave get to the North.

When she finally arrived in Pennsylvania, she had traveled roughly ninety miles from Dorchester County. She had slept on the ground outdoors at night. She had been rowed for miles up the Choptank River by a man she had never seen before. She had been concealed in a haycock[11] and had, at one point, spent

---

11. **haycock:** pile of hay in a field.

INFER
What do Tubman's thoughts and prayers while she's in the wagon reveal about her **character**?

INFER
Why do you think Tubman was amazed that white people would be willing to help her?

RETELL

Pause at line 276.
Summarize the *who, what, when, where, why,* and *how* of Tubman's escape from slavery.

_____

_____

_____

_____

_____

_____

_____

EVALUATE

Ann Petry, the author of this biography, never knew Harriet Tubman personally; yet she describes Tubman's private thoughts and feelings. Explain why you think it is or isn't right for a biographer to add such details to someone's life story.

_____

_____

_____

_____

_____

_____

_____

a week hidden in a potato hole in a cabin which belonged to a
270 family of free Negroes. She had been hidden in the attic of the
home of a Quaker. She had been befriended by stout German
farmers, whose guttural[12] speech surprised her and whose well-
kept farms astonished her. She had never before seen barns and
fences, farmhouses and outbuildings, so carefully painted. The
cattle and horses were so clean they looked as though they had
been scrubbed.

When she crossed the line into the free state of Pennsylvania,
the sun was coming up. She said, "I looked at my hands to see
if I was the same person now I was free. There was such a
280 glory over everything, the sun came like gold through the trees
and over the fields, and I felt like I was in heaven."

_____

12. **guttural:** harsh, rasping.

Biography Chart

Some biographies are written by people who know their subjects well. Others are written hundreds, even thousands, of years after the subject has died. All biographies require careful research. Most biographies contain some details that cannot be proven true—or false. These details are inferences the biographer makes, based on facts in the historical record.

List details from this biography of Harriet Tubman that can be proven true and details that are based on the biographer's educated guesswork.

The first examples are done for you.

Objective Facts Based on Research	Details Provided by Author
In 1849, Harriet Tubman meets a woman who offers to give help.	"The woman nodded her head, clucked to the horse, and drove off, murmuring. . . . "

Vocabulary and Comprehension

You may use your book to help you answer the questions below.

Word Bank
elude
inexplicable
legitimate
defiant
sinewy

A. Match words and definitions. Write the letter of the correct definition next to each word.

_____ 1. elude   **a.** not explainable

_____ 2. inexplicable   **b.** escape the notice of

_____ 3. legitimate   **c.** boldly resisting

_____ 4. defiant   **d.** reasonable

_____ 5. sinewy   **e.** tough

B. Finish each sentence with a description that fits the underlined word from the Word Bank.

1. Harriet Tubman showed that she had a defiant manner by _____

_____

2. To elude the patrol, Tubman _____

_____

3. A legitimate reason for Tubman to enter the Big House might be _____

_____

_____

4. A sinewy vine is _____

5. Harriet Tubman's sleeping spells were inexplicable because _____

_____

Vocabulary and Comprehension

C. Choose three words from the Word Bank on the previous page, and use each one in a sentence of your own.

1. _____

_____

2. _____

_____

3. _____

_____

D. Answer each question below.

1. Why wouldn't Harriet Tubman's brothers and husband try to escape with her?

_____

_____

2. What is the hidden message in the song that Tubman sings when she decides to escape north to freedom?

_____

_____

3. How did people help Tubman along the Underground Railroad?

_____

_____

_____

John Henry

Make the Connection

Anything It Can Do, I Can Do Better

What can machines do better than people? Think of some machines inside and outside your house, at school, and in factories. Remember that a machine is anything with fixed and moving parts invented by people to do some kind of work. Computers, cell phones, hair dryers, skateboards, and cars are all machines.

Machines make life easier for humans, but they can't do everything. They can't take a dog for a walk, for instance, or fly a kite or write a poem. Think of some contests that people could have with machines. In the chart below, list some that people would probably win and some that machines would probably win. Two contests have been filled in to get you started.

Contests People Would Win	Contests Machines Would Win
songwriting	washing clothes

Background

Nobody knows for sure if John Henry, the hero of this song, was a real person. People began singing about him in the early 1870s. He was said to be an African American laborer in the construction crew building the Big Bend Tunnel of the Chesapeake and Ohio Railroad. According to the legend, someone set up a contest between John Henry and a steam drill.

John Henry

Anonymous
African American

IDENTIFY

The captain (boss) of the work crew brings in a machine to do the job. Circle what the job is. Underline the name of the person who will be in **conflict** with the machine.

PREDICT

Who do you think is going to win this contest? What will happen next?

_____

_____

_____

_____

_____

_____

_____

INFER

Why will tomorrow be the shaker's "buryin' day" (line 24) if John Henry misses the piece of steel?

_____

_____

_____

_____

_____

_____

_____

John Henry was about three days old
Sittin' on his papa's knee.
He picked up a hammer and a little piece of steel
Said, "Hammer's gonna be the death of me, Lord, Lord!
Hammer's gonna be the death of me."

The captain said to John Henry,
"Gonna bring that steam drill 'round
Gonna bring that steam drill out on the job
Gonna whop that steel on down, Lord, Lord!
10   Whop that steel on down."

John Henry told his captain,
"A man ain't nothin' but a man
But before I let your steam drill beat me down
I'd die with a hammer in my hand, Lord, Lord!
I'd die with a hammer in my hand."

John Henry said to his shaker,[1]
"Shaker, why don't you sing?
I'm throwing thirty pounds from my hips on down
Just listen to that cold steel ring, Lord, Lord!
20   Listen to that cold steel ring."

John Henry said to his shaker,
"Shaker, you'd better pray
'Cause if I miss that little piece of steel
Tomorrow be your buryin' day, Lord, Lord!
Tomorrow be your buryin' day."

The shaker said to John Henry,
"I think this mountain's cavin' in!"
John Henry said to his shaker, "Man,
That ain't nothin' but my hammer suckin' wind, Lord, Lord!
30   Nothin' but my hammer suckin' wind."

---

1. **shaker:** worker who holds the drill.

The man that invented the steam drill

Thought he was mighty fine

But John Henry made fifteen feet

The steam drill only made nine, Lord, Lord!

The steam drill only made nine.

John Henry hammered in the mountain

His hammer was striking fire

But he worked so hard, he broke his poor heart

He laid down his hammer and he died, Lord, Lord!

40   He laid down his hammer and he died.

John Henry had a little woman

Her name was Polly Ann

John Henry took sick and went to his bed

Polly Ann drove steel like a man, Lord, Lord!

Polly Ann drove steel like a man.

John Henry had a little baby

You could hold him in the palm of your hand

The last words I heard that poor boy say,

"My daddy was a steel-driving man, Lord, Lord!

50   My daddy was a steel-driving man."

They took John Henry to the graveyard

And they buried him in the sand

And every locomotive comes a-roaring by

Says, "There lies a steel-driving man, Lord, Lord!

There lies a steel-driving man."

Well, every Monday morning

When the bluebirds begin to sing

You can hear John Henry a mile or more

You can hear John Henry's hammer ring, Lord, Lord!

60   You can hear John Henry's hammer ring.

INTERPRET

Circle the words in lines 31–35 that tell you that John Henry won the contest. How does the next stanza (lines 36–40) suggest that the machine might have won after all?

_____

_____

_____

IDENTIFY

A **refrain** is a repeated word, phrase, line, or group of lines in a poem, song, or speech. In this song, the last two lines of each stanza repeat, creating a refrain. Circle the refrain in any two stanzas.

BUILD FLUENCY

This song is fun to sing and to read aloud. Pick four stanzas you like, and read them aloud until you can do it smoothly. Try to give your reading the rhythm of a song.

EVALUATE

John Henry's actual story ends at line 40, but the song goes on. Why do you think the last four verses were added to the story? How do they show that the deeds of John Henry will never be forgotten?

_____

_____

_____

Refrains from the Song of Your Life

A **refrain** is a repeated word, phrase, line, or group of lines in a song, poem, or speech. A refrain appears at the end of each stanza of "John Henry."

If you were writing a song about your life, what events, thoughts, or feelings would be worthy of a refrain? Think of your favorite activities at home or school. Then, write a refrain for four of them.

News Pyramid

"John Henry" is a song that tells its story using refrains. Think about how you would rewrite the story of John Henry as a newspaper report. The format of a news report is like an inverted pyramid. The most important details of the story come first; less important details come later.

The headline is meant to grab the reader's attention. The dateline is the date and place from which the story is filed. For this story, you will have to get this information from the background text. The lead (lēd) contains the essential facts of the story: *What* happened? *When* did it happen? *Whom* did it happen to? *Why* and *how* did it happen?

To plan your news story about John Henry, fill in the details in the following graphic.

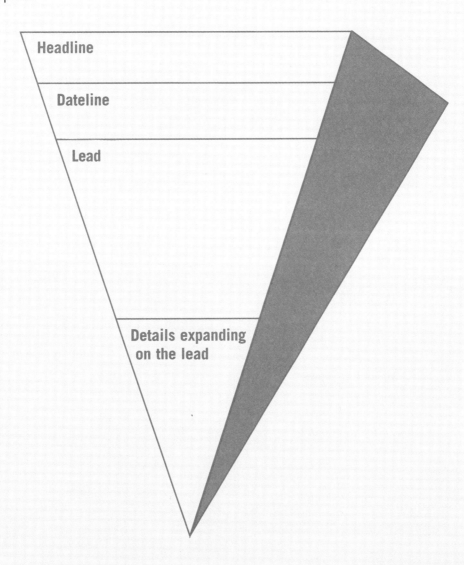

Headline

Dateline

Lead

Details expanding on the lead

Ankylosaurus

Make the Connection

Crazy about Dinosaurs

Sixty million years after dinosaurs died out, people are still crazy about them. They exist today in movies, books, computer games, and TV shows. They inhabit our imaginations and even our nightmares.

Every dinosaur had a special ability to protect itself against its natural enemies. Most of the dinosaurs we know about were huge creatures, but some of them might have been tiny. Maybe some could breathe fire (like fairy-tale dragons). Maybe another dinosaur's defense was a terrible smell or the ability to leap or even fly.

Create an imaginary dinosaur with its own way of defending itself against enemies. On the lab book below, sketch what your dinosaur looked like. Describe it in words, and tell how it defended itself.

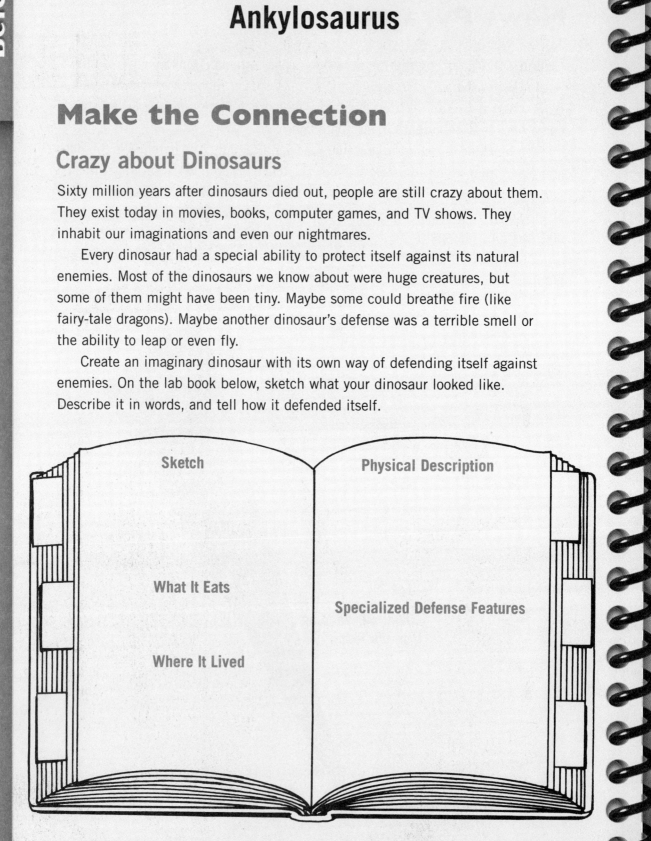

Sketch

Physical Description

What It Eats

Specialized Defense Features

Where It Lived

ANKYLOSAURUS

Jack Prelutsky

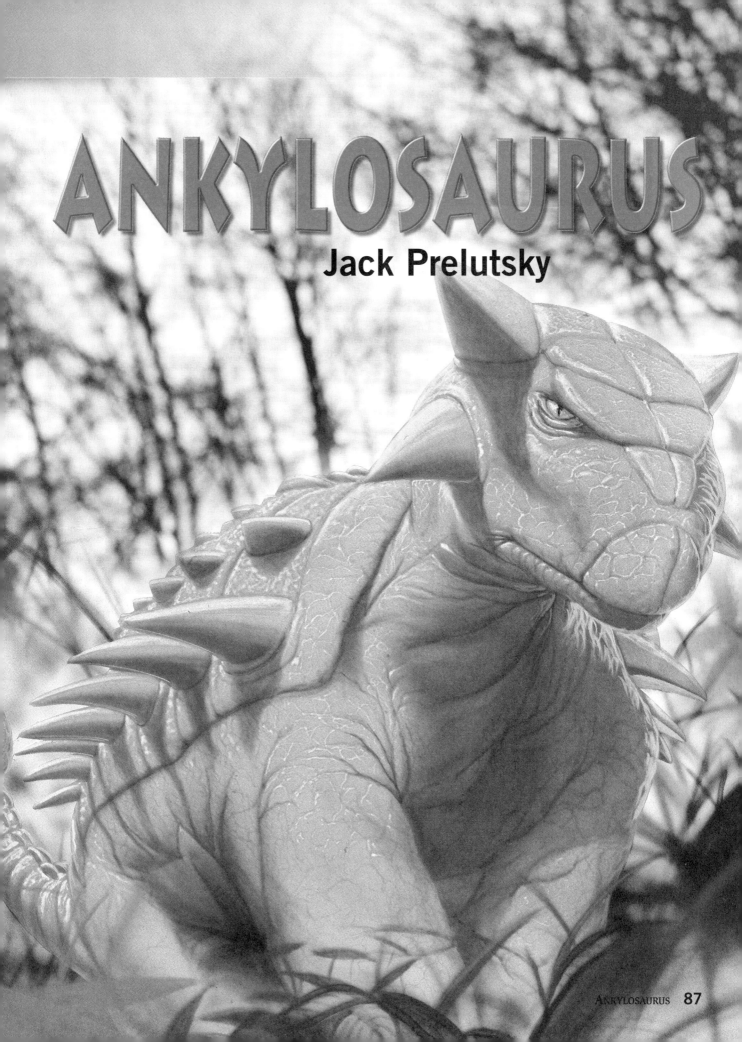

VISUALIZE

Circle the phrases that help you picture ankylosaurus.

INTERPRET

Which detail suggests that ankylosaurus was a vegetarian?

_____

_____

_____

INFER

Which part of its body did it use as a weapon?

_____

_____

_____

INTERPRET

What one word would you use to describe ankylosaurus?

_____

_____

_____

BUILD FLUENCY

Read the poem aloud listening to its sounds. Emphasize the "clankity-clank" lines and the words that rhyme. Notice how the rhythm of the poem helps you "see" the way the creature moves.

Clankity Clankity Clankity Clank!
Ankylosaurus[1] was built like a tank,
its hide was a fortress as sturdy as steel,
it tended to be an inedible meal.

It was armored in front, it was armored behind,
there wasn't a thing on its minuscule mind,
it waddled about on its four stubby legs,
nibbling on plants with a mouthful of pegs.

Ankylosaurus was best left alone,
10 its tail was a cudgel of gristle and bone,
Clankity Clankity Clankity Clank!
Ankylosaurus was built like a tank.

---

1. ankylosaurus (aŋ′kə·lō·sôr′əs): heavily armored, short-legged dinosaur; also called ankylosaur.

Onomatopoeia Chart

Onomatopoeia is the use of a word whose sound imitates or suggests its meaning. In "Ankylosaurus," Jack Prelutsky uses *clankity clank* as a sound effect that makes his monster sound like an army tank. What sounds can you create? Fill in the chart below with sounds you think the items listed might make.

Item	Sound
A washing machine	
Potato chips	
Walking in mud	
Leaves	

Zlateh the Goat

Make the Connection

What Happens Next

At first, "Zlateh the Goat" seems to be a simple story about a boy who is sent to market to sell a goat. However, the story soon turns into a suspenseful page turner that makes you eager to find out what happens next.

Suspense happens all the time in everyday life, for example, in taking a test, playing a ballgame, or trying out for a part in a play. Another example is described in the first row of the graphic organizer below. Fill in the next two rows with two suspense-filled situations. The events can be fictional or real, personal, national, or worldwide.

SUSPENSEFUL EVENTS

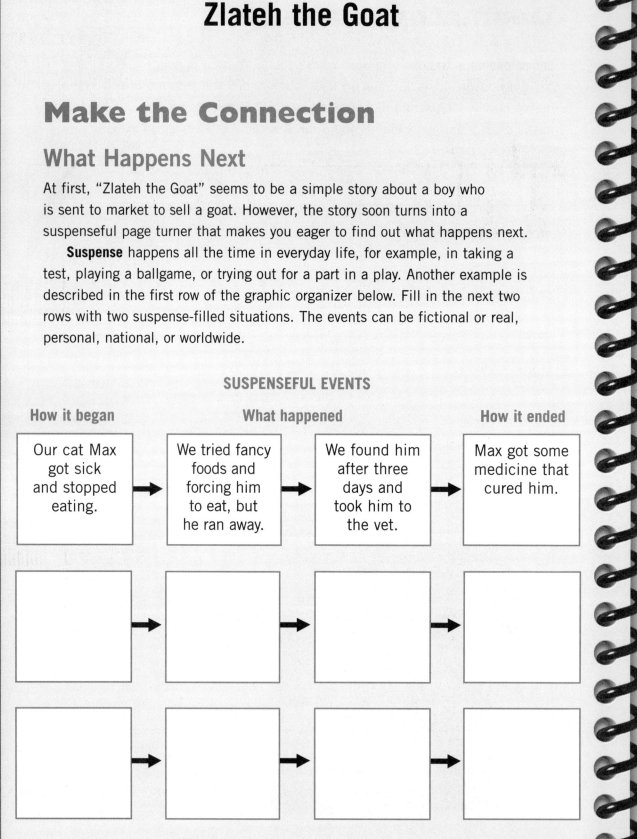

How it began	What happened		How it ended
Our cat Max got sick and stopped eating.	We tried fancy foods and forcing him to eat, but he ran away.	We found him after three days and took him to the vet.	Max got some medicine that cured him.

ZLATEH THE GOAT

Isaac Bashevis Singer

Background

"Zlateh the Goat" takes place at Hanukkah (khä′n$\overline{oo}$·kä′), an eight-day Jewish religious festival usually observed in December. Hanukkah celebrates the victory, in 165 B.C., of the Jewish fighters called Maccabees over a Syrian army. After the victory, a bit of oil for the holy lamp—barely enough for one day—lasted eight days. During the festival, one candle is lit each evening for eight nights. Gifts are exchanged, and money is given to the poor.

IDENTIFY

In lines 8–14, underline the details that describe the situation Reuven faces. Why does he decide to sell Zlateh?

_____

_____

_____

_____

_____

INFER

What does "taking the goat to Feyvel" mean? Why is the family unhappy?

_____

_____

_____

_____

INFER

Based on lines 24–28, what **inference** can you make about Zlateh's **character**?

_____

_____

_____

_____

_____

_____

At Hanukkah time the road from the village to the town is usually covered with snow, but this year the winter had been a mild one. Hanukkah had almost come, yet little snow had fallen. The sun shone most of the time. The peasants complained that because of the dry weather there would be a poor harvest of winter grain. New grass sprouted, and the peasants sent their cattle out to pasture.

For Reuven the furrier[1] it was a bad year, and after long hesitation he decided to sell Zlateh the goat. She was old and

10 gave little milk. Feyvel the town butcher had offered eight gulden[2] for her. Such a sum would buy Hanukkah candles, potatoes and oil for pancakes, gifts for the children, and other holiday necessaries for the house. Reuven told his oldest boy, Aaron, to take the goat to town.

Aaron understood what taking the goat to Feyvel meant, but he had to obey his father. Leah, his mother, wiped the tears from her eyes when she heard the news. Aaron's younger sisters, Anna and Miriam, cried loudly. Aaron put on his quilted jacket and a cap with earmuffs, bound a rope around Zlateh's

20 neck, and took along two slices of bread with cheese to eat on the road. Aaron was supposed to deliver the goat by evening, spend the night at the butcher's, and return the next day with the money.

While the family said goodbye to the goat, and Aaron placed the rope around her neck, Zlateh stood as patiently and good-naturedly as ever. She licked Reuven's hand. She shook her small white beard. Zlateh trusted human beings. She knew that they always fed her and never did her any harm.

When Aaron brought her out on the road to town, she

30 seemed somewhat astonished. She'd never been led in that direction before. She looked back at him questioningly, as if to say, "Where are you taking me?" But after a while she seemed to come to the conclusion that a goat shouldn't ask questions. Still, the road was different. They passed new fields, pastures,

---

1. **furrier:** someone who makes and repairs articles made of fur.
2. **gulden:** gold or silver coins used in several European countries.

and huts with thatched roofs. Here and there a dog barked and came running after them, but Aaron chased it away with his stick.

The sun was shining when Aaron left the village. Suddenly the weather changed. A large black cloud with a bluish center
40 appeared in the east and spread itself rapidly over the sky. A cold wind blew in with it. The crows flew low, croaking. At first it looked as if it would rain, but instead it began to hail as in summer. It was early in the day, but it became dark as dusk. After a while the hail turned to snow.

In his twelve years Aaron had seen all kinds of weather, but he had never experienced a snow like this one. It was so dense it shut out the light of the day. In a short time their path was completely covered. The wind became as cold as ice. The road to town was narrow and winding. Aaron no longer knew where
50 he was. He could not see through the snow. The cold soon penetrated his quilted jacket.

At first Zlateh didn't seem to mind the change in weather. She too was twelve years old and knew what winter meant. But when her legs sank deeper and deeper into the snow, she began to turn her head and look at Aaron in wonderment. Her mild eyes seemed to ask, "Why are we out in such a storm?" Aaron hoped that a peasant would come along with his cart, but no one passed by.

The snow grew thicker, falling to the ground in large,
60 whirling flakes. Beneath it Aaron's boots touched the softness of a plowed field. He realized that he was no longer on the road. He had gone astray. He could no longer figure out which was east or west, which way was the village, the town. The wind whistled, howled, whirled the snow about in eddies. It looked as if white imps were playing tag on the fields. A white dust rose above the ground. Zlateh stopped. She could walk no longer. Stubbornly she anchored her cleft hooves in the earth and bleated as if pleading to be taken home. Icicles hung from her white beard, and her horns were glazed with frost.
70 Aaron did not want to admit the danger, but he knew just the same that if they did not find shelter, they would freeze to

VISUALIZE

Re-read lines 38–44. Underline three details that help you picture the change in the weather.

PREDICT

Pause at line 51. What do you think will happen now that the weather has changed?

INTERPRET

How would Aaron have to answer Zlateh's question (line 56)? What do we know that Zlateh doesn't know? How does this knowledge make you feel?

WORDS TO OWN
penetrated (pen'i·trāt'id) *v.*: went through.
cleft (kleft) *adj.*: formed with a partial split.

PREDICT

Now comes a moment of great **suspense:** Will Aaron and Zlateh freeze to death? How do you think the story will end?

_____

_____

_____

_____

_____

RETELL

Retell what Aaron does to survive (lines 84–94).

_____

_____

_____

_____

_____

_____

INTERPRET

Look back at the beginning of the story. Notice in lines 9–10 one of the reasons Aaron's father decides to sell Zlateh. In lines 98–104, underline what happens that is a kind of miracle.

WORDS TO OWN

chaos (kā′äs′) *n.:* extreme confusion.

death. This was no ordinary storm. It was a mighty blizzard. The snowfall had reached his knees. His hands were numb, and he could no longer feel his toes. He choked when he breathed. His nose felt like wood, and he rubbed it with snow. Zlateh's bleating began to sound like crying. Those humans in whom she had so much confidence had dragged her into a trap. Aaron began to pray to God for himself and for the innocent animal.

Suddenly he made out the shape of a hill. He wondered
80 what it could be. Who had piled snow into such a huge heap? He moved toward it, dragging Zlateh after him. When he came near it, he realized that it was a large haystack which the snow had blanketed.

Aaron realized immediately that they were saved. With great effort he dug his way through the snow. He was a village boy and knew what to do. When he reached the hay, he hollowed out a nest for himself and the goat. No matter how cold it may be outside, in the hay it is always warm. And hay was food for Zlateh. The moment she smelled it, she became contented and
90 began to eat. Outside, the snow continued to fall. It quickly covered the passageway Aaron had dug. But a boy and an animal need to breathe, and there was hardly any air in their hide-out. Aaron bored a kind of a window through the hay and snow and carefully kept the passage clear.

Zlateh, having eaten her fill, sat down on her hind legs and seemed to have regained her confidence in man. Aaron ate his two slices of bread and cheese, but after the difficult journey he was still hungry. He looked at Zlateh and noticed her udders were full. He lay down next to her, placing himself so that when
100 he milked her, he could squirt the milk into his mouth. It was rich and sweet. Zlateh was not accustomed to being milked that way, but she did not resist. On the contrary, she seemed eager to reward Aaron for bringing her to a shelter whose very walls, floor, and ceiling were made of food.

Through the window Aaron could catch a glimpse of the chaos outside. The wind carried before it whole drifts of snow. It was completely dark, and he did not know whether night had already come or whether it was the darkness of the storm.

Thank God that in the hay it was not cold. The dried hay, grass,
110 and field flowers exuded the warmth of the summer sun. Zlateh
ate frequently; she nibbled from above, below, from the left
and right. Her body gave forth an animal warmth, and Aaron
cuddled up to her. He had always loved Zlateh, but now she
was like a sister. He was alone, cut off from his family, and
wanted to talk. He began to talk to Zlateh. "Zlateh, what do
you think about what has happened to us?" he asked.

"Maaaa," Zlateh answered.

"If we hadn't found this stack of hay, we would both be
frozen stiff by now," Aaron said.

120 "Maaaa," was the goat's reply.

"If the snow keeps on falling like this, we may have to stay
here for days," Aaron explained.

"Maaaa," Zlateh bleated.

"What does 'Maaaa' mean?" Aaron asked. "You'd better
speak up clearly."

"Maaaa. Maaaa," Zlateh tried.

"Well, let it be 'Maaaa' then," Aaron said patiently. "You
can't speak, but I know you understand. I need you and you
need me. Isn't that right?"

130 "Maaaa."

Aaron became sleepy. He made a pillow out of some hay,
leaned his head on it, and dozed off. Zlateh too fell asleep.

When Aaron opened his eyes, he didn't know whether it
was morning or night. The snow had blocked up his window.
He tried to clear it, but when he had bored through to the
length of his arm, he still hadn't reached the outside. Luckily he
had his stick with him and was able to break through to the
open air. It was still dark outside. The snow continued to fall
and the wind wailed, first with one voice and then with many.
140 Sometimes it had the sound of devilish laughter. Zlateh too
awoke, and when Aaron greeted her, she answered, "Maaaa."
Yes, Zlateh's language consisted of only one word, but it meant
many things. Now she was saying, "We must accept all that
God gives us—heat, cold, hunger, satisfaction, light, and
darkness."

INTERPRET

Re-read lines 84–115. If
Aaron or Zlateh had been
alone, neither would have
survived. List three ways
that Zlateh helps Aaron
survive. Then, list three
ways that Aaron helps
Zlateh survive.

_____

_____

_____

_____

_____

BUILD FLUENCY

Imagine that each time
Zlateh speaks, she is
responding to what Aaron
says. Write down on the
text what Zlateh might
be saying each time she
bleats, "Maaaa." Then,
read the passage aloud.
Try to say Zlateh's simple
answer in a different way
each time you read it.

EVALUATE

What do you think of this
idea about acceptance
(lines 143–145)? Do you
agree or disagree with it?
Give two reasons for your
answer.

_____

_____

WORDS TO OWN
exuded (eg·zyōōd'id) v.:
gave off.

VISUALIZE

Underline details in lines 155–170 that help you see what Aaron experiences. Circle details that help you imagine sounds (or the complete lack of sound).

INTERPRET

What does the decision in lines 175–176 reveal about Aaron's **character**? How has his experience changed him from the kind of person he was before the storm?

Aaron had awakened hungry. He had eaten up his food, but Zlateh had plenty of milk.

For three days Aaron and Zlateh stayed in the haystack. Aaron had always loved Zlateh, but in these three days he loved
150 her more and more. She fed him with her milk and helped him keep warm. She comforted him with her patience. He told her many stories, and she always cocked her ears and listened. When he patted her, she licked his hand and his face. Then she said, "Maaaa," and he knew it meant, I love you too.

The snow fell for three days, though after the first day it was not as thick and the wind quieted down. Sometimes Aaron felt that there could never have been a summer, that the snow had always fallen, ever since he could remember. He, Aaron, never had a father or mother or sisters. He was a snow child, born of
160 the snow, and so was Zlateh. It was so quiet in the hay that his ears rang in the stillness. Aaron and Zlateh slept all night and a good part of the day. As for Aaron's dreams, they were all about warm weather. He dreamed of green fields, trees covered with blossoms, clear brooks, and singing birds. By the third night the snow had stopped, but Aaron did not dare to find his way home in the darkness. The sky became clear and the moon shone, casting silvery nets on the snow. Aaron dug his way out and looked at the world. It was all white, quiet, dreaming dreams of heavenly splendor. The stars were large and close.
170 The moon swam in the sky as in a sea.

On the morning of the fourth day, Aaron heard the ringing of sleigh bells. The haystack was not far from the road. The peasant who drove the sleigh pointed out the way to him—not to the town and Feyvel the butcher, but home to the village. Aaron had decided in the haystack that he would never part with Zlateh.

Aaron's family and their neighbors had searched for the boy and the goat but had found no trace of them during the storm. They feared they were lost. Aaron's mother and sisters cried for
180 him; his father remained silent and gloomy. Suddenly one of the neighbors came running to their house with the news that Aaron and Zlateh were coming up the road.

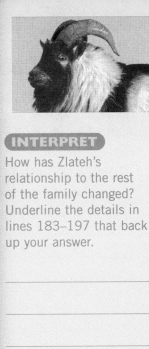

There was great joy in the family. Aaron told them how he had found the stack of hay and how Zlateh had fed him with her milk. Aaron's sisters kissed and hugged Zlateh and gave her a special treat of chopped carrots and potato peels, which Zlateh gobbled up hungrily.

Nobody ever again thought of selling Zlateh, and now that the cold weather had finally set in, the villagers needed the services of Reuven the furrier once more. When Hanukkah came, Aaron's mother was able to fry pancakes every evening, and Zlateh got her portion too. Even though Zlateh had her own pen, she often came to the kitchen, knocking on the door with her horns to indicate that she was ready to visit, and she was always admitted. In the evening, Aaron, Miriam, and Anna played dreidel.[3] Zlateh sat near the stove, watching the children and the flickering of the Hanukkah candles.

Once in a while Aaron would ask her, "Zlateh, do you remember the three days we spent together?"

And Zlateh would scratch her neck with a horn, shake her white bearded head, and come out with the single sound which expressed all her thoughts, and all her love.

INTERPRET

How has Zlateh's relationship to the rest of the family changed? Underline the details in lines 183–197 that back up your answer.

EVALUATE

Suspense in this story is caused by questions of survival. After Aaron and Zlateh survive the storm, what keeps you wondering what will happen next? How do you feel about this story's conclusion? Give reasons for your answer.

---

3. dreidel (drā′dəl): spinning top played with at Hanukkah. The top's four sides contain Hebrew letters that stand for "A great miracle happened there."

Plot Map

The plot events in "Zlateh the Goat" work together to build suspense. Re-create the plot events by filling in the plot map below. Then use a star to mark the point at which your interest in the story began to increase. Use a question mark to indicate any plot event you thought was contrived, or not believable.

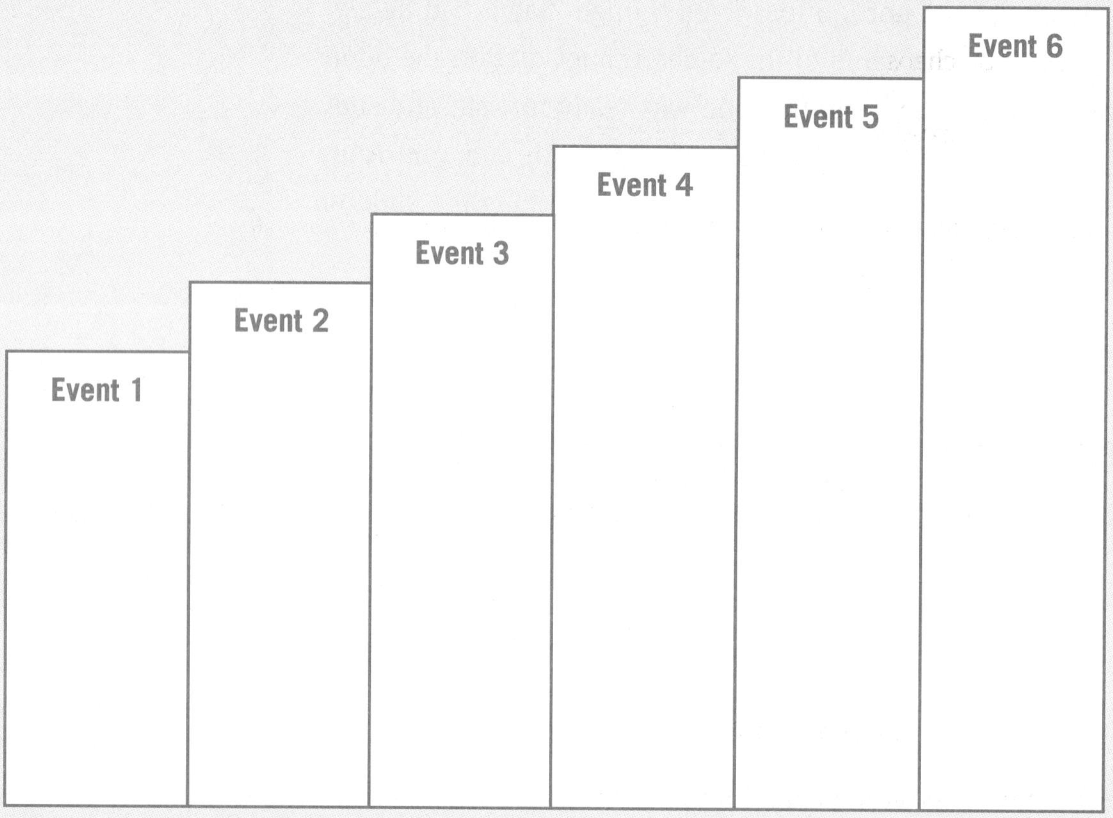

Event 1

Event 2

Event 3

Event 4

Event 5

Event 6

Was the story ❑ credible? ❑ not credible?

Why?

_____

_____

_____

_____

Vocabulary and Comprehension

A. Match words and definitions. Write the letter of the correct
definition next to each word.

_____ **1.** penetrated

_____ **2.** cleft

_____ **3.** chaos

_____ **4.** exuded

a. extreme confusion

b. gave off

c. made a way through

d. split; divided

B. Choose three words from the Word Bank. Use each word in a sentence.

1. _____

_____

2. _____

_____

3. _____

_____

C. Answer each question below.

1. Where is Aaron taking Zlateh? Why?

_____

_____

2. How do Aaron and Zlateh survive in the haystack?

_____

_____

3. How does Aaron feel about Zlateh after the blizzard has ended?

_____

_____

All Summer in a Day

Make the Connection

The Outsider

This story is set on an imaginary Venus sometime in the future. Its science fiction author, Ray Bradbury, describes a planet of unending rain where kids lead different lives from children on Earth. One thing is still the same: someone who is different from the rest of the crowd is seen as an outsider.

It's no fun to feel like an outsider. Why do you think some people won't accept someone who's different into their group?

On the arrows below, write words or phrases that describe how you think the group feels toward the outsider. Underneath the outsider's face, write how the outsider feels.

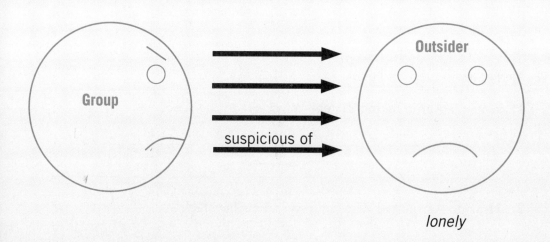

Group

Outsider

suspicious of

lonely

All Summer in a Day

Ray Bradbury

IDENTIFY

Circle how long it's been raining. Underline *where* the story takes place.

INFER

Based on lines 11–20, what **inference** can you make about *when* the story takes place?

INFER

How is Margot different from the other children? Circle details from this paragraph that back up your **inference.**

"Ready."

"Ready."

"Now?"

"Soon."

"Do the scientists really know? Will it happen today, will it?"

"Look, look; see for yourself!"

The children pressed to each other like so many roses, so many weeds, intermixed, peering out for a look at the hidden sun.

10   It rained.

It had been raining for seven years; thousands upon thousands of days compounded and filled from one end to the other with rain, with the drum and gush of water, with the sweet crystal fall of showers and the concussion[1] of storms so heavy they were tidal waves come over the islands. A thousand forests had been crushed under the rain and grown up a thousand times to be crushed again. And this was the way life was forever on the planet Venus, and this was the schoolroom of the children of the rocket men and women who had come to 20 a raining world to set up civilization and live out their lives.

"It's stopping, it's stopping!"

"Yes, yes!"

Margot stood apart from them, from these children who could never remember a time when there wasn't rain and rain and rain. They were all nine years old, and if there had been a day, seven years ago, when the sun came out for an hour and showed its face to the stunned world, they could not recall. Sometimes, at night, she heard them stir, in remembrance, and she knew they were dreaming and remembering gold or a yellow crayon or a 30 coin large enough to buy the world with. She knew they thought they remembered a warmness, like a blushing in the face, in the body, in the arms and legs and trembling hands. But then they always awoke to the tatting drum, the endless shaking down of clear bead necklaces upon the roof, the walk, the gardens, the forests, and their dreams were gone.

---

1. concussion: violent shaking or impact.

All day yesterday they had read in class about the sun. About how like a lemon it was, and how hot. And they had written small stories or essays or poems about it.

40   *I think the sun is a flower*
      That blooms for just one hour.

That was Margot's poem, read in a quiet voice in the still classroom while the rain was falling outside.

"Aw, you didn't write that!" protested one of the boys.

"I did," said Margot. *"I did."*

"William!" said the teacher.

But that was yesterday. Now the rain was slackening, the children were crushed in the great thick windows.

"Where's teacher?"

"She'll be back."

50   "She'd better hurry; we'll miss it!"

They turned on themselves like a feverish wheel, all tumbling spokes.

Margot stood alone. She was a very frail girl who looked as if she had been lost in the rain for years and the rain had washed out the blue from her eyes and the red from her mouth and the yellow from her hair. She was an old photograph dusted from an album, whitened away, and if she spoke at all her voice would be a ghost. Now she stood, separate, staring at the rain and the loud wet world beyond the huge glass.

60   "What're *you* looking at?" said William.

Margot said nothing.

"Speak when you're spoken to." He gave her a shove. But she did not move; rather she let herself be moved only by him and nothing else.

They edged away from her; they would not look at her. She felt them go away. And this was because she would play no games with them in the echoing tunnels of the underground city. If they tagged her and ran, she stood blinking after them and did not follow. When the class sang songs about happiness

70   and life and games, her lips barely moved. Only when they

INTERPRET

Why does William say that Margot didn't write the poem (line 43)?

_____

_____

_____

_____

_____

_____

_____

INTERPRET

A **simile** is a comparison between two unlike things, using a word such as *like, as, as if,* or *resembles*. Underline the simile in lines 53–56. What one adjective could be used to describe Margot's "washed-out" appearance? Why do you think Bradbury used his long simile instead of that adjective?

_____

_____

_____

_____

WORDS TO OWN
slackening (slak′ən·iŋ) *v.:* lessening.

IDENTIFY

Circle how old Margot was when she last saw the sun. Underline how old the other children were when they last saw the sun.

_____

_____

_____

_____

_____

INTERPRET

What does this incident tell you about how the **setting** has affected Margot? If Margot is in **conflict** with her setting, which side in the conflict seems to be winning?

_____

_____

_____

_____

IDENTIFY

Circle the reason, in lines 92–98, why Margot's future is different from the future the other children will face.

_____

_____

_____

_____

_____

_____

sang about the sun and the summer did her lips move as she watched the drenched windows.

And then, of course, the biggest crime of all was that she had come here only five years ago from Earth, and she remembered the sun and the way the sun was and the sky was when she was four in Ohio. And they, they had been on Venus all their lives, and they had been only two years old when last the sun came out and had long since forgotten the color and heat of it and the way it really was. But Margot
80 remembered.

"It's like a penny," she said once, eyes closed.

"No, it's not!" the children cried.

"It's like a fire," she said, "in the stove."

"You're lying; you don't remember!" cried the children.

But she remembered and stood quietly apart from all of them and watched the patterning windows. And once, a month ago, she had refused to shower in the school shower rooms, had clutched her hands to her ears and over her head, screaming the water mustn't touch her head. So after that,
90 dimly, dimly, she sensed it, she was different, and they knew her difference and kept away.

There was talk that her father and mother were taking her back to Earth next year; it seemed vital to her that they do so, though it would mean the loss of thousands of dollars to her family. And so, the children hated her for all these reasons of big and little consequence.[2] They hated her pale snow face, her waiting silence, her thinness, and her possible future.

"Get away!" The boy gave her another push. "What're you
100 waiting for?"

Then, for the first time, she turned and looked at him. And what she was waiting for was in her eyes.

"Well, don't wait around here!" cried the boy savagely. "You won't see nothing!"

Her lips moved.

---

2. **consequence:** importance; result.

"Nothing!" he cried. "It was all a joke, wasn't it?" He turned to the other children. "Nothing's happening today. Is it?"

They all blinked at him and then, understanding, laughed and shook their heads. "Nothing, nothing!"

110 "Oh, but," Margot whispered, her eyes helpless. "But this is the day, the scientists predict, they say, they *know*, the sun . . ."

"All a joke!" said the boy, and seized her roughly. "Hey everyone, let's put her in a closet before teacher comes!"

"No," said Margot, falling back.

They surged about her, caught her up and bore her, protesting, and then pleading, and then crying, back into a tunnel, a room, a closet, where they slammed and locked the door. They stood looking at the door and saw it tremble from her beating and throwing herself against it. They heard her

120 muffled cries. Then, smiling, they turned and went out and back down the tunnel, just as the teacher arrived.

"Ready, children?" She glanced at her watch.

"Yes!" said everyone.

"Are we all here?"

"Yes!"

The rain slackened still more.

They crowded to the huge door.

The rain stopped.

It was as if, in the midst of a film concerning an avalanche,

130 a tornado, a hurricane, a volcanic eruption, something had, first, gone wrong with the sound apparatus, thus muffling and finally cutting off all noise, all of the blasts and repercussions and thunders, and then, second, ripped the film from the projector and inserted in its place a peaceful tropical slide which did not move or tremor. The world ground to a standstill. The silence was so immense and unbelievable that you felt your ears had been stuffed or you had lost your hearing altogether. The children put their hands to their ears. They stood apart. The door slid back and the smell of the silent,

140 waiting world came in to them.

The sun came out.

INTERPRET

Circle the word *understanding* in line 108. What is it that the children understand?

_____

_____

PREDICT

What do you think will happen next?

_____

_____

RETELL

Pause at line 128, when the rain stops. **Retell** what has happened since the students asked where the teacher is, page 103, line 48.

_____

_____

_____

_____

_____

_____

_____

_____

WORDS TO OWN
surged (sɐrjd) *v.:* pushed hard.
tremor (trem'ɔr) *n.* used as *v.:* shake.

INTERPRET

How is the jungle of Venus different from a jungle on Earth? List two differences.

INTERPRET

How has the children's behavior changed now that they've been allowed to go outside? How is outside different for them now?

WORDS TO OWN
resilient (ri·zil′yənt) *adj.:*
springy.
savored (sā′vərd) *v.:*
delighted in; tasted or
smelled.

It was the color of flaming bronze and it was very large. And the sky around it was a blazing blue tile color. And the jungle burned with sunlight as the children, released from their spell, rushed out, yelling, into the springtime.

"Now, don't go too far," called the teacher after them. "You've only two hours, you know. You wouldn't want to get caught out!"

But they were running and turning their faces up to the sky
150 and feeling the sun on their cheeks like a warm iron; they were taking off their jackets and letting the sun burn their arms.

"Oh, it's better than the sun lamps, isn't it?"

"Much, much better!"

They stopped running and stood in the great jungle that covered Venus, that grew and never stopped growing, tumultuously,[3] even as you watched it. It was a nest of octopuses, clustering up great arms of fleshlike weed, wavering, flowering in this brief spring. It was the color of rubber and ash, this jungle, from the many years without sun. It was the
160 color of stones and white cheeses and ink, and it was the color of the moon.

The children lay out, laughing, on the jungle mattress and heard it sigh and squeak under them, resilient and alive. They ran among the trees, they slipped and fell, they pushed each other, they played hide-and-seek and tag, but most of all they squinted at the sun until tears ran down their faces; they put their hands up to that yellowness and that amazing blueness and they breathed of the fresh, fresh air and listened and listened to the silence which suspended them in a blessed sea
170 of no sound and no motion. They looked at everything and savored everything. Then, wildly, like animals escaped from their caves, they ran and ran in shouting circles. They ran for an hour and did not stop running.

And then—

In the midst of their running, one of the girls wailed.

Everyone stopped.

---

3. **tumultuously:** wildly; violently.

The girl, standing in the open, held out her hand.

"Oh, look, look," she said trembling.

They came slowly to look at her opened palm.

180 In the center of it, cupped and huge, was a single raindrop.

She began to cry, looking at it.

They glanced quietly at the sky.

"Oh. Oh."

A few cold drops fell on their noses and their cheeks and their mouths. The sun faded behind a stir of mist. A wind blew cool around them. They turned and started to walk back toward the underground house, their hands at their sides, their smiles vanishing away.

A boom of thunder startled them, and like leaves before
190 a new hurricane, they tumbled upon each other and ran. Lightning struck ten miles away, five miles away, a mile, a half-mile. The sky darkened into midnight in a flash.

They stood in the doorway of the underground for a moment until it was raining hard. Then they closed the door and heard the gigantic sound of the rain falling in tons and avalanches, everywhere and forever.

"Will it be seven more years?"

"Yes. Seven."

Then one of them gave a little cry.

200 "Margot!"

"What?"

"She's still in the closet where we locked her."

"Margot."

They stood as if someone had driven them, like so many stakes, into the floor. They looked at each other and then looked away. They glanced out at the world that was raining now and raining and raining steadily. They could not meet each other's glances. Their faces were solemn and pale. They looked at their hands and feet, their faces down.

210 "Margot."

One of the girls said, "Well . . . ?"

No one moved.

"Go on," whispered the girl.

INFER

How do the children feel when the rain starts again (line 184)? Underline the details that support your **inference**.

_____

_____

_____

BUILD FLUENCY

Re-read the boxed passage out loud. Use your voice to help put across the meaning of the words. For instance, you might want to read the first paragraph in the passage quickly to show that the children are running. Let the children's feelings determine what tone of voice you use in the **dialogue,** the words the characters speak. How will you read the last paragraph in a way that conveys the children's sadness?

_____

_____

_____

INTERPRET

Why can't the children look at each other? How do they feel now about what they've done to Margot? How are they like Margot now?

_____

_____

_____

EVALUATE

Bradbury's ending leaves some questions unaswered. Do you think he should have shown what happened when Margot got out of the closet? Or do you like the story better as it is? Give a reason for your answer.

They walked slowly down the hall in the sound of cold rain. They turned through the doorway to the room in the sound of the storm and thunder, lightning on their faces, blue and terrible. They walked over to the closet door slowly and stood by it.

Behind the closet door was only silence.

They unlocked the door, even more slowly, and let

220 Margot out.

Setting Circle

This story's setting directly affects the characters and story events. Fill in the middle circle with details about the setting. Then fill in the outside circles with plot events from the story. Finally, look over your completed setting circle to see how setting and plot interconnect.

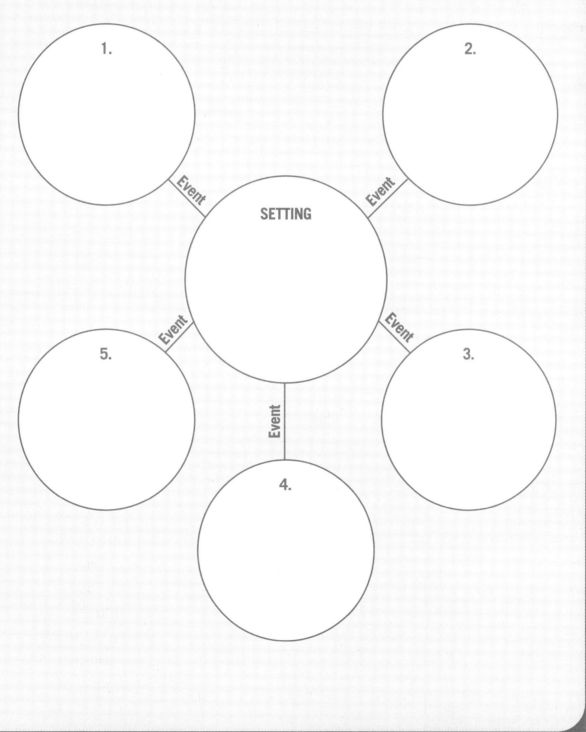

Theme Chart

To find themes in a work of literature you must look at the whole work and also at the details.

Find four (or more) details in "All Summer in a Day" that suggest a theme to you. Write these details in the Detail boxes on the chart below. State what lines they come from, and briefly describe what happens. In the Theme box, write down the idea that these details suggest to you. Be sure all the details relate to one theme.

Detail

Detail

Detail

Detail

Theme

Vocabulary and Comprehension

A. Complete each sentence with a word from the Word Bank.

Word Bank
slackening
resilient
savored
surged
tremor

1. The _____ rain made less and less noise on the windows.

2. A wave of children _____ out the door.

3. The _____ grass felt springy beneath their feet.

4. The ground seemed to _____ because the rain fell with such force.

5. The children _____ the smell of the flowers. They wanted this time to last forever.

B. Write **T** or **F** next to each statement to tell if it is true or false.

_____ **1.** The story "All Summer in a Day" takes place on Earth.

_____ **2.** All the children are nine years old.

_____ **3.** Margot was born on Earth.

_____ **4.** It has been raining on Venus for seven years.

_____ **5.** Margot doesn't remember seeing the sun.

_____ **6.** Most of the children remember seeing the sun.

_____ **7.** The children lock Margot in a closet.

_____ **8.** The sun stays out for seven years on Venus.

_____ **9.** Margot gets to see the sun on Venus.

Eleven

Make the Connection

Happy Birthday to You

This story tells about a birthday when everything went wrong. The celebration itself may have turned out OK. We don't hear about that. Rachel, the birthday girl, shares her thoughts and feelings about the bad experience she had at school on the day she became eleven.

What birthday will you always remember? Think of one birthday that made a big impression on you—good or bad. Like Rachel, you don't need to write about the party. Maybe you'll write about a year when you didn't have a party! On the birthday cake below, add candles until you get to the number you would have had on your cake that day. Then, use the questions below to recall the details of an unforgettable experience you had on one birthday.

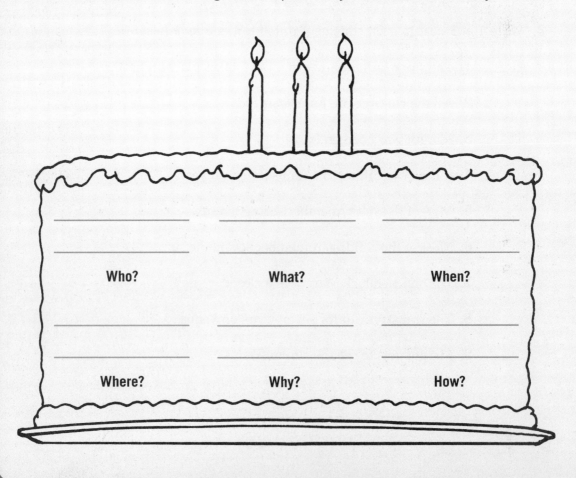

Who?   What?   When?

Where?   Why?   How?

Eleven

Sandra Cisneros

INTERPRET

In lines 16–19 Rachel compares growing old to three different things. Tell how all three are alike. Explain in your own words Rachel's idea about growing old.

_____

_____

_____

_____

_____

_____

IDENTIFY

This story is told from the **first-person point of view,** with Rachel as the narrator. She uses first-person pronouns like *I, me,* and *mine* to tell about her experience. Circle the first-person pronouns in lines 24–30. When a story is written in the first-person point of view, what can you never know about the other characters?

_____

_____

_____

_____

_____

_____

_____

_____

What they don't understand about birthdays and what they never tell you is that when you're eleven, you're also ten, and nine, and eight, and seven, and six, and five, and four, and three, and two, and one. And when you wake up on your eleventh birthday you expect to feel eleven, but you don't. You open your eyes and everything's just like yesterday, only it's today. And you don't feel eleven at all. You feel like you're still ten. And you are—underneath the year that makes you eleven.

10 Like some days you might say something stupid, and that's the part of you that's still ten. Or maybe some days you might need to sit on your mama's lap because you're scared, and that's the part of you that's five. And maybe one day when you're all grown up maybe you will need to cry like if you're three, and that's okay. That's what I tell Mama when she's sad and needs to cry. Maybe she's feeling three.

Because the way you grow old is kind of like an onion or like the rings inside a tree trunk or like my little wooden dolls that fit one inside the other, each year inside the next one. That's how being eleven years old is.

20 You don't feel eleven. Not right away. It takes a few days, weeks even, sometimes even months before you say Eleven when they ask you. And you don't feel smart eleven, not until you're almost twelve. That's the way it is.

Only today I wish I didn't have only eleven years rattling inside me like pennies in a tin Band-Aid box. Today I wish I was one hundred and two instead of eleven because if I was one hundred and two I'd have known what to say when Mrs. Price put the red sweater on my desk. I would've known how to tell her it wasn't mine instead of just sitting there with that

30 look on my face and nothing coming out of my mouth.

"Whose is this?" Mrs. Price says, and she holds the red sweater up in the air for all the class to see. "Whose? It's been sitting in the coatroom for a month."

"Not mine," says everybody. "Not me."

"It has to belong to somebody," Mrs. Price keeps saying, but nobody can remember. It's an ugly sweater with red plastic buttons and a collar and sleeves all stretched out like you could use it for a jump-rope. It's maybe a thousand years old and even if it belonged to me I wouldn't say so.

40   Maybe because I'm skinny, maybe because she doesn't like me, that stupid Sylvia Saldívar says, "I think it belongs to Rachel." An ugly sweater like that, all raggedy and old, but Mrs. Price believes her. Mrs. Price takes the sweater and puts it right on my desk, but when I open my mouth nothing comes out.

"That's not, I don't, you're not . . . Not mine," I finally say in a little voice that was maybe me when I was four.

"Of course it's yours," Mrs. Price says. "I remember you wearing it once." Because she's older and the teacher, she's right and I'm not.

50   Not mine, not mine, not mine, but Mrs. Price is already turning to page thirty-two, and math problem number four. I don't know why but all of a sudden I'm feeling sick inside, like the part of me that's three wants to come out of my eyes, only I squeeze them shut tight and bite down on my teeth real hard and try to remember today I am eleven, eleven. Mama is making a cake for me for tonight, and when Papa comes home everybody will sing Happy birthday, happy birthday to you.

But when the sick feeling goes away and I open my eyes, the red sweater's still sitting there like a big red mountain. I
60 move the red sweater to the corner of my desk with my ruler. I move my pencil and books and eraser as far from it as possible. I even move my chair a little to the right. Not mine, not mine, not mine.

In my head I'm thinking how long till lunchtime, how long till I can take the red sweater and throw it over the schoolyard fence, or leave it hanging on a parking meter, or bunch it up into a little ball and toss it in the alley. Except when math period ends Mrs. Price says loud and in front of everybody, "Now, Rachel, that's enough," because she sees I've shoved the
70 red sweater to the tippy-tip corner of my desk and it's hanging all over the edge like a waterfall, but I don't care.

"Rachel," Mrs. Price says. She says it like she's getting mad. "You put that sweater on right now and no more nonsense."

"But it's not—"

VISUALIZE
Underline the words in lines 35–39 that help you picture the sweater.

INFER
Pause at line 49. Write down three words that describe what you know about Rachel's **character** so far.

INTERPRET
Do you think that Rachel makes too big a deal out of things like the red sweater? How does knowing Rachel's feelings and thoughts make you feel about her?

RETELL
Retell what's happened to Rachel up to this point in the story.

PREDICT

Pause at line 75. What do you think will happen between Rachel and Mrs. Price?

_____

_____

_____

_____

_____

BUILD FLUENCY

Read the boxed paragraph a couple of times to yourself. Notice the words and phrases that help you experience Rachel's feelings in your imagination. Read the passage aloud pretending to be Rachel as she describes her feelings.

INFER

What do you **infer** about how Mrs. Price feels about Rachel? What do you **infer** about Mrs. Price's **character**?

_____

_____

_____

_____

_____

_____

_____

"Now!" Mrs. Price says.

This is when I wish I wasn't eleven, because all the years inside of me—ten, nine, eight, seven, six, five, four, three, two, and one—are pushing at the back of my eyes when I put one arm through one sleeve of the sweater that smells like cottage
80 cheese, and then the other arm through the other and stand there with my arms apart like if the sweater hurts me and it does, all itchy and full of germs that aren't even mine.

That's when everything I've been holding in since this morning, since when Mrs. Price put the sweater on my desk, finally lets go, and all of a sudden I'm crying in front of everybody. I wish I was invisible but I'm not. I'm eleven and it's my birthday today and I'm crying like I'm three in front of everybody. I put my head down on the desk and bury my face in my stupid clown-sweater arms. My face all hot and spit
90 coming out of my mouth because I can't stop the little animal noises from coming out of me, until there aren't any more tears left in my eyes, and it's just my body shaking like when you have the hiccups and my whole head hurts like when you drink milk too fast.

But the worst part is right before the bell rings for lunch. That stupid Phyllis Lopez, who is even dumber than Sylvia Saldívar, says she remembers the red sweater is hers! I take it off right away and give it to her, only Mrs. Price pretends like everything's okay.

100 Today I'm eleven. There's a cake Mama's making for tonight, and when Papa comes home from work we'll eat it. There'll be candles and presents and everybody will sing Happy birthday, happy birthday to you, Rachel, only it's too late.

I'm eleven today. I'm eleven, ten, nine, eight, seven, six, five, four, three, two, and one, but I wish I was one hundred and two. I wish I was anything but eleven, because I want today to be far away already, far away like a runaway balloon, like a tiny *o* in the sky, so tiny-tiny you have to close your eyes to see it.

Imagery Grid

Imagery is language that appeals to the senses. Images describe sights, smells, tastes, sounds, and the way things feel when you touch them. Writers use imagery to help us share an experience. Fill in the imagery grid below with images that Sandra Cisneros uses throughout "Eleven." Then answer the questions.

Sight	Touch

Sound	Taste	Smell

Questions

1. Which sense from the grid had the most images?

_____

2. Which had the least?

_____

3. Which image from the story do you like the most? Why?

_____

The Bracelet

Make the Connection

Bag of Memories

During World War II, the U.S. government imprisoned thousands of Japanese Americans in internment camps. In this story the author describes what it was like to be one of those imprisoned.

Suppose you and your family were forced to leave your home and relocate to a place where you would be a prisoner. Besides a bag for bedding and a suitcase big enough to hold your clothes, you can take one small suitcase for everything else. What would you choose to take with you? Inside the suitcase below, sketch or name three things you would want to take. Choose three things that would remind you of your friends, your home, and the things you used to enjoy.

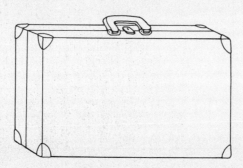

Explain why you chose each of the three things you packed.

1. _____

   _____

2. _____

   _____

3. _____

   _____

The Bracelet

Yoshiko Uchida

IDENTIFY

Who is this story's **narrator**? Circle her name.

IDENTIFY

A **figure of speech** is a comparison between two seemingly unlike things. Underline the figure of speech that the author uses to describe her empty house. Tell whether it's a **metaphor** (a comparison that says that one thing *is* another) or a **simile** (a comparison that says one thing is *like* another).

_____

_____

_____

_____

INTERPRET

Re-read lines 18–37. Based on the details in these lines, make a **generalization** about the way Japanese Americans were treated during World War II.

_____

_____

_____

_____

_____

WORDS TO OWN

evacuated (ē·vak′yo͞o·āt′id) *v.*: removed from the area.
interned (in·tʉrnd′) *v.*: confined; jailed.
aliens (āl′yənz) *n.*: people who are not U.S. citizens.

"Mama, is it time to go?"

I hadn't planned to cry, but the tears came suddenly, and I wiped them away with the back of my hand. I didn't want my older sister to see me crying.

"It's almost time, Ruri," my mother said gently. Her face was filled with a kind of sadness I had never seen before.

I looked around at my empty room. The clothes that Mama always told me to hang up in the closet, the junk piled on my dresser, the old rag doll I could never bear to part with—they 10 were all gone. There was nothing left in my room, and there was nothing left in the rest of the house. The rugs and furniture were gone, the pictures and drapes were down, and the closets and cupboards were empty. The house was like a gift box after the nice thing inside was gone; just a lot of nothingness.

It was almost time to leave our home, but we weren't moving to a nicer house or to a new town. It was April 21, 1942. The United States and Japan were at war, and every Japanese person on the West Coast was being evacuated by the 20 government to a concentration camp. Mama, my sister Keiko, and I were being sent from our home, and out of Berkeley, and eventually out of California.

The doorbell rang, and I ran to answer it before my sister could. I thought maybe by some miracle a messenger from the government might be standing there, tall and proper and buttoned into a uniform, come to tell us it was all a terrible mistake, that we wouldn't have to leave after all. Or maybe the messenger would have a telegram from Papa, who was interned in a prisoner-of-war camp in Montana because he had worked 30 for a Japanese business firm.

The FBI had come to pick up Papa and hundreds of other Japanese community leaders on the very day that Japanese planes had bombed Pearl Harbor. The government thought they were dangerous enemy aliens. If it weren't so sad, it would have been funny. Papa could no more be dangerous than the mayor of our city, and he was every bit as loyal to the United States. He had lived here since 1917.

When I opened the door, it wasn't a messenger from anywhere. It was my best friend, Laurie Madison, from next
40 door. She was holding a package wrapped up like a birthday present, but she wasn't wearing her party dress, and her face drooped like a wilted tulip.

"Hi," she said. "I came to say goodbye."

She thrust the present at me and told me it was something to take to camp. "It's a bracelet," she said before I could open the package. "Put it on so you won't have to pack it." She knew I didn't have one inch of space left in my suitcase. We had been instructed to take only what we could carry into camp, and Mama had told us that we could each take only two suitcases.

50 "Then how are we ever going to pack the dishes and blankets and sheets they've told us to bring with us?" Keiko worried.

"I don't really know," Mama said, and she simply began packing those big impossible things into an enormous duffel bag—along with umbrellas, boots, a kettle, hot plate, and flashlight.

"Who's going to carry that huge sack?" I asked.

But Mama didn't worry about things like that. "Someone will help us," she said. "Don't worry." So I didn't.

Laurie wanted me to open her package and put on the
60 bracelet before she left. It was a thin gold chain with a heart dangling on it. She helped me put it on, and I told her I'd never take it off, ever.

"Well, goodbye then," Laurie said awkwardly. "Come home soon."

"I will," I said, although I didn't know if I would ever get back to Berkeley again.

I watched Laurie go down the block, her long blond pigtails bouncing as she walked. I wondered who would be sitting in my desk at Lincoln Junior High now that I was gone. Laurie
70 kept turning and waving, even walking backward for a while, until she got to the corner. I didn't want to watch anymore, and I slammed the door shut.

The next time the doorbell rang, it was Mrs. Simpson, our other neighbor. She was going to drive us to the Congregational

IDENTIFY

Pause at line 49. Underline the words that tell you what Laurie gives Ruri.

INFER

Why does Laurie's gift mean a lot to Ruri? What does a heart usually **symbolize**, or stand for? Why does Ruri say she will never take it off?

RETELL

Pause at line 83. **Retell** what has happened to Ruri and her family up to this point in the story.

_____

_____

_____

_____

_____

_____

_____

INFER

Based on lines 84–93, what **inference** can you make about Ruri's parents?

_____

_____

_____

_____

_____

_____

_____

_____

_____

_____

WORDS TO OWN
forsaken (fər·sā′kən) _adj._: abandoned; deserted.

Church, which was the Civil Control Station where all the Japanese of Berkeley were supposed to report.

It was time to go. "Come on, Ruri. Get your things," my sister called to me.

It was a warm day, but I put on a sweater and my coat so I
80 wouldn't have to carry them, and I picked up my two suitcases. Each one had a tag with my name and our family number on it. Every Japanese family had to register and get a number. We were Family Number 13453.

Mama was taking one last look around our house. She was going from room to room, as though she were trying to take a mental picture of the house she had lived in for fifteen years, so she would never forget it.

I saw her take a long last look at the garden that Papa loved. The irises beside the fish pond were just beginning to bloom. If
90 Papa had been home, he would have cut the first iris blossom and brought it inside to Mama. "This one is for you," he would have said. And Mama would have smiled and said, "Thank you, Papa San"[1] and put it in her favorite cut-glass vase.

But the garden looked shabby and forsaken now that Papa was gone and Mama was too busy to take care of it. It looked the way I felt, sort of empty and lonely and abandoned.

When Mrs. Simpson took us to the Civil Control Station, I felt even worse. I was scared, and for a minute I thought I was going to lose my breakfast right in front of everybody. There
100 must have been over a thousand Japanese people gathered at the church. Some were old and some were young. Some were talking and laughing, and some were crying. I guess everybody else was scared too. No one knew exactly what was going to happen to us. We just knew we were being taken to the Tanforan Racetracks, which the army had turned into a camp for the Japanese. There were fourteen other camps like ours along the West Coast.

What scared me most were the soldiers standing at the doorway of the church hall. They were carrying guns with

_____

1. San: Japanese term added to names to indicate respect.

110 mounted bayonets. I wondered if they thought we would try to run away and whether they'd shoot us or come after us with their bayonets if we did.

A long line of buses waited to take us to camp. There were trucks, too, for our baggage. And Mama was right; some men were there to help us load our duffel bag. When it was time to board the buses, I sat with Keiko, and Mama sat behind us. The bus went down Grove Street and passed the small Japanese food store where Mama used to order her bean-curd cakes and pickled radish. The windows were all boarded up, but there was a sign
120 still hanging on the door that read, "We are loyal Americans."

The crazy thing about the whole evacuation was that we were all loyal Americans. Most of us were citizens because we had been born here. But our parents, who had come from Japan, couldn't become citizens because there was a law that prevented any Asian from becoming a citizen. Now everybody with a Japanese face was being shipped off to concentration camps.

"It's stupid," Keiko muttered as we saw the racetrack looming up beside the highway. "If there were any Japanese spies around, they'd have gone back to Japan long ago."
130 "I'll say," I agreed. My sister was in high school and she ought to know, I thought.

When the bus turned into Tanforan, there were more armed guards at the gate, and I saw barbed wire strung around the entire grounds. I felt as though I were going into a prison, but I hadn't done anything wrong.

We streamed off the buses and poured into a huge room, where doctors looked down our throats and peeled back our eyelids to see if we had any diseases. Then we were given our housing assignments. The man in charge gave Mama a slip of
140 paper. We were in Barrack 16, Apartment 40.

"Mama!" I said. "We're going to live in an apartment!" The only apartment I had ever seen was the one my piano teacher lived in. It was in an enormous building in San Francisco, with an elevator and thick-carpeted hallways. I thought how

BUILD FLUENCY

Read the boxed passage out loud. Try to use a voice that shows how scared Ruri feels. When you read the passage carefully, you'll notice other feelings too. For instance, Ruri's amazed to see how many Japanese people have gathered. See if your voice can capture all of Ruri's different feelings.

INTERPRET

Pause at line 126. Were the Japanese Americans evacuated because they were disloyal or because they were Japanese? Give reasons for your answer.

PREDICT

Pause at line 146. What do you think Ruri's apartment will be like? Tell why you think so.

_____

_____

_____

VISUALIZE

Circle the details that help you picture Apartment 40. Notice the phrases like "on each side of the door" that help you know where things are located. Draw a diagram of the apartment below.

INFER

Pause at line 177. Why do you think it takes so long for Ruri to realize that her bracelet is missing?

_____

_____

wonderful it would be to have our own elevator. A house was all right, but an apartment seemed elegant and special.

We walked down the racetrack, looking for Barrack 16. Mr. Noma, a friend of Papa's, helped us carry our bags. I was so busy looking around I slipped and almost fell on the muddy
150 track. Army barracks had been built everywhere, all around the racetrack and even in the center oval.

Mr. Noma pointed beyond the track toward the horse stables. "I think your barrack is out there."

He was right. We came to a long stable that had once housed the horses of Tanforan, and we climbed up the wide ramp. Each stall had a number painted on it, and when we got to 40, Mr. Noma pushed open the door.

"Well, here it is," he said, "Apartment 40."

The stall was narrow and empty and dark. There were two
160 small windows on each side of the door. Three folded army cots were on the dust-covered floor, and one light bulb dangled from the ceiling. That was all. This was our apartment, and it still smelled of horses.

Mama looked at my sister and then at me. "It won't be so bad when we fix it up," she began. "I'll ask Mrs. Simpson to send me some material for curtains. I could make some cushions too, and . . . well . . ." She stopped. She couldn't think of anything more to say.

Mr. Noma said he'd go get some mattresses for us. "I'd
170 better hurry before they're all gone." He rushed off. I think he wanted to leave so that he wouldn't have to see Mama cry. But he needn't have run off, because Mama didn't cry. She just went out to borrow a broom and began sweeping out the dust and dirt. "Will you girls set up the cots?" she asked.

It was only after we'd put up the last cot that I noticed my bracelet was gone. "I've lost Laurie's bracelet!" I screamed. "My bracelet's gone!"

We looked all over the stall and even down the ramp. I wanted to run back down the track and go over every inch of
180 ground we'd walked on, but it was getting dark and Mama wouldn't let me.

I thought of what I'd promised Laurie. I wasn't ever going to take the bracelet off, not even when I went to take a shower. And now I had lost it on my very first day in camp. I wanted to cry.

I kept looking for it all the time we were in Tanforan. I didn't stop looking until the day we were sent to another camp, called Topaz, in the middle of a desert in Utah. And then I gave up.

But Mama told me never mind. She said I didn't need a
190 bracelet to remember Laurie, just as I didn't need anything to remember Papa or our home in Berkeley or all the people and things we loved and had left behind.

"Those are things we can carry in our hearts and take with us no matter where we are sent," she said.

And I guess she was right. I've never forgotten Laurie, even now.

INTERPRET

Circle what Mama says in lines 193–194. She suggests the story's **theme,** the main idea or special message that the author is saying about life. State the theme in your own words.

_____

_____

_____

_____

_____

EVALUATE

Yoshiko Uchida said that she wrote about the internment of Japanese Americans so that nothing like that would ever happen in the United States again. In a war situation, where people fear a group whose members look like the enemy, would recalling this story—and other stories and movies like it—do any good? What seems most unjust to you about what happens to Ruri? Give reasons for your answer.

_____

_____

_____

_____

_____

Theme Chart

The revelation a story makes about life is its **theme.** One way to find a story's theme is to examine what we and the characters discover in the course of the story. That discovery is usually the same as the story's theme.

Complete this graphic organizer after you read "The Bracelet."

Main character(s)

_____

↓

Key experiences

_____

_____

_____

↓

What we discover from these experiences

_____

_____

_____

↓

Statement of theme

_____

_____

_____

Vocabulary and Comprehension

A. Match words and definitions. Write the letter of the correct definition next to each word.

Word Bank
evacuated
interned
aliens
forsaken

_____ **1.** aliens   **a.** removed from an area

_____ **2.** evacuated   **b.** imprisoned or confined

_____ **3.** forsaken   **c.** foreigners

_____ **4.** interned   **d.** abandoned; deserted

B. Choose three words from above. Use each word in a sentence.

1. _____

_____

2. _____

_____

3. _____

_____

C. Answer each question below.

1. How does Ruri describe her garden?

_____

_____

2. Why weren't Ruri's parents American citizens?

_____

_____

3. What did Apartment 40 look like?

_____

_____

The Dog of Pompeii

Make the Connection

Run or Hide?

It's a hot day near the end of summer. As you walk home, you hear rumblings in the distance. It sounds as if a big storm might be coming. Suddenly the sky turns dark as night. You hear people shouting, "What's going on?" One person screams an answer, "The volcano's erupting!"

Will you start running to get as far away as you can? Will you look for a place to hide? On the volcanoes below write down some advantages and disadvantages of each choice. Put a big star beside the course of action you would choose.

Run   **Hide**

Background

This story takes place in Pompeii, a real Roman city in southern Italy that was buried by a volcanic eruption in A.D. 79. When archaeologists uncovered Pompeii, they found the bones of humans and animals who had not been able to escape. They even found rock-hard loaves of bread baked almost two thousand years ago. The author of this story weaves some of these facts with fiction to bring a piece of history to life.

THE DOG OF POMPEII

Louis Untermeyer

IDENTIFY

Underline details of **setting** that tell you *where* the story takes place. Circle details that tell you that the story is set in a *time* long ago.

INFER

Pause at line 19. Why do you think Tito and Bimbo are so close to one another? How is the bond between them different from the usual relationship between a human and a dog?

Tito and his dog Bimbo lived (if you could call it living) under the wall where it joined the inner gate. They really didn't live there; they just slept there. They lived anywhere. Pompeii was one of the gayest of the old Latin towns, but although Tito was never an unhappy boy, he was not exactly a merry one. The streets were always lively with shining chariots and bright red trappings; the open-air theaters rocked with laughing crowds; sham[1] battles and athletic sports were free for the asking in the great stadium. Once a year the Caesar[2] visited the pleasure city
10 and the fireworks lasted for days; the sacrifices[3] in the forum were better than a show.

But Tito saw none of these things. He was blind—had been blind from birth. He was known to everyone in the poorer quarters. But no one could say how old he was, no one remembered his parents, no one could tell where he came from. Bimbo was another mystery. As long as people could remember seeing Tito—about twelve or thirteen years—they had seen Bimbo. Bimbo had never left his side. He was not only dog but nurse, pillow, playmate, mother, and father to Tito.

20 Did I say Bimbo never left his master? (Perhaps I had better say comrade, for if anyone was the master, it was Bimbo.) I was wrong. Bimbo did trust Tito alone exactly three times a day. It was a fixed routine, a custom understood between boy and dog since the beginning of their friendship, and the way it worked was this: Early in the morning, shortly after dawn, while Tito was still dreaming, Bimbo would disappear. When Tito awoke, Bimbo would be sitting quietly at his side, his ears cocked, his stump of a tail tapping the ground, and a fresh-baked bread— more like a large round roll—at his feet. Tito would stretch
30 himself; Bimbo would yawn; then they would breakfast. At noon, no matter where they happened to be, Bimbo would put his paw on Tito's knee and the two of them would return to the inner gate. Tito would curl up in the corner (almost like a dog)

---

1. **sham:** make-believe.
2. **Caesar** (sē′zər): Roman emperor. The word *Caesar* comes from the family name of Julius Caesar, a great general who ruled Rome as dictator from 49 to 44 B.C.
3. **sacrifices:** offerings (especially of slaughtered animals) to a god or gods.

and go to sleep, while Bimbo, looking quite important (almost like a boy), would disappear again. In half an hour he'd be back with their lunch. Sometimes it would be a piece of fruit or a scrap of meat, often it was nothing but a dry crust. But sometimes there would be one of those flat rich cakes, sprinkled with raisins and sugar, that Tito liked so much. At

40 suppertime the same thing happened, although there was a little less of everything, for things were hard to snatch in the evening, with the streets full of people. Besides, Bimbo didn't approve of too much food before going to sleep. A heavy supper made boys too restless and dogs too stodgy[4]—and it was the business of a dog to sleep lightly with one ear open and muscles ready for action.

But, whether there was much or little, hot or cold, fresh or dry, food was always there. Tito never asked where it came from and Bimbo never told him. There was plenty of rainwater

50 in the hollows of soft stones; the old egg woman at the corner sometimes gave him a cupful of strong goat's milk; in the grape season the fat winemaker let him have drippings of the mild juice. So there was no danger of going hungry or thirsty. There was plenty of everything in Pompeii—if you knew where to find it—and if you had a dog like Bimbo.

As I said before, Tito was not the merriest boy in Pompeii. He could not romp with the other youngsters and play "hare and hounds" and "I spy" and "follow your master" and "ball against the building" and "jackstones" and "kings and robbers"

60 with them. But that did not make him sorry for himself. If he could not see the sights that delighted the lads of Pompeii, he could hear and smell things they never noticed. He could really see more with his ears and nose than they could with their eyes. When he and Bimbo went out walking, he knew just where they were going and exactly what was happening.

"Ah," he'd sniff and say, as they passed a handsome villa,[5] "Glaucus Pansa is giving a grand dinner tonight. They're going to have three kinds of bread, and roast pigling, and stuffed

---

4. stodgy (stä´jē): heavy and slow in movement.
5. villa: large house.

IDENTIFY

Events in the **plot** of a story are usually organized in **chronological,** or time, order—the order in which they happen. Circle the words and phrases in lines 20–46 that tell you when events happen.

_____

_____

RETELL

Pause at line 46. Describe the routine that Tito and Bimbo follow every day, from dawn until evening.

_____

_____

_____

_____

_____

_____

INFER

Re-read lines 56–65. Write down three words that describe what you know about Tito's **character** so far.

_____

_____

_____

INFER

What does the author mean when he says in lines 62–64 that Tito could "see more with his ears and nose" than the other boys of Pompeii could see with their eyes? Circle three things in lines 66–91 that Tito "sees" with his nose.

_____

_____

_____

_____

_____

_____

_____

_____

_____

_____

_____

_____

_____

_____

WORDS TO OWN
ambitious (am·bish′əs) *adj.:* eager to succeed or to achieve.

goose, and a great stew—I think bear stew—and a fig pie."

70 And Bimbo would note that this would be a good place to visit tomorrow.

Or, "H'm," Tito would murmur, half through his lips, half through his nostrils. "The wife of Marcus Lucretius is expecting her mother. She's shaking out every piece of goods in the house; she's going to use the best clothes—the ones she's been keeping in pine needles and camphor[6]—and there's an extra girl in the kitchen. Come, Bimbo, let's get out of the dust!"

Or, as they passed a small but elegant dwelling opposite the public baths, "Too bad! The tragic poet is ill again. It must be a

80 bad fever this time, for they're trying smoke fumes instead of medicine. Whew! I'm glad I'm not a tragic poet!"

Or, as they neared the forum, "Mm-m! What good things they have in the macellum[7] today!" (It really was a sort of butcher-grocer-marketplace, but Tito didn't know any better. He called it the macellum.) "Dates from Africa, and salt oysters from sea caves, and cuttlefish, and new honey, and sweet onions, and—ugh!—water-buffalo steaks. Come, let's see what's what in the forum." And Bimbo, just as curious as his comrade, hurried on. Being a dog, he trusted his ears and nose (like Tito)

90 more than his eyes. And so the two of them entered the center of Pompeii.

The forum was the part of the town to which everybody came at least once during the day. It was the central square, and everything happened here. There were no private houses; all was public—the chief temples, the gold and red bazaars, the silk shops, the town hall, the booths belonging to the weavers and jewel merchants, the wealthy woolen market, the shrine of the household gods. Everything glittered here. The buildings looked as if they were new—which, in a sense, they

100 were. The earthquake of twelve years ago had brought down all the old structures and, since the citizens of Pompeii were ambitious to rival Naples and even Rome, they had seized the

---

6. **camphor** (kam′fər): strong-smelling substance used to keep moths away from clothing. Camphor is still used for this purpose.
7. **macellum** (mə·sel′əm): market, especially a meat market.

VISUALIZE

Re-read lines 92–105. List three details that help you picture the forum.

_____

_____

_____

_____

opportunity to rebuild the whole town. And they had done it all within a dozen years. There was scarcely a building that was older than Tito.

Tito had heard a great deal about the earthquake, though being about a year old at the time, he could scarcely remember it. This particular quake had been a light one—as earthquakes go. The weaker houses had been shaken down, parts of the
110 outworn wall had been wrecked; but there was little loss of life, and the brilliant new Pompeii had taken the place of the old. No one knew what caused these earthquakes. Records showed they had happened in the neighborhood since the beginning of time. Sailors said that it was to teach the lazy city folk a lesson and make them appreciate those who risked the dangers of the sea to bring them luxuries and protect their town from invaders. The priests said that the gods took this way of showing their anger to those who refused to worship properly and who failed to bring enough sacrifices to the altars and (though they didn't
120 say it in so many words) presents to the priests. The tradesmen said that the foreign merchants had corrupted the ground and it was no longer safe to traffic in imported goods that came from strange places and carried a curse with them. Everyone had a different explanation and everyone's explanation was louder and sillier than his neighbor's.

They were talking about it this afternoon as Tito and Bimbo came out of the side street into the public square. The forum was the favorite promenade[8] for rich and poor. What with the priests arguing with the politicians, servants doing the day's
130 shopping, tradesmen crying their wares, women displaying the latest fashions from Greece and Egypt, children playing hide-and-seek among the marble columns, knots of soldiers, sailors, peasants from the provinces[9]—to say nothing of those who merely came to lounge and look on—the square was crowded to its last inch. His ears even more than his nose guided Tito to the place where the talk was loudest. It was in front of the

IDENTIFY

What natural disaster had caused most of Pompeii to be rebuilt? How old was Tito when this disaster happened? Circle the detail that tells you how old Tito is when this story takes place.

_____

_____

_____

INTERPRET

Besides being different, loud, and silly, how are all these explanations of earthquakes alike—from a twenty-first century point of view?

_____

_____

_____

8. **promenade** (präm′ə·nād′): public place where people stroll.
9. **provinces**: places far from the capital, under Roman control.

IDENTIFY

Underline the superstition that Rufus gives as a reason why he doesn't fear earthquakes. Circle the stranger's argument *against* the superstition.

_____

_____

_____

IDENTIFY

Underline the name of the volcano that can be seen from Pompeii.

_____

_____

_____

_____

IDENTIFY

Circle the details that tell you about changes in the column of smoke rising from the volcano.

_____

_____

_____

_____

_____

WORDS TO OWN

proverb (präv′ʉrb′) *n.:* traditional saying that expresses a truth.

shrine of the household gods that, naturally enough, the householders were arguing.

"I tell you," rumbled a voice which Tito recognized as bath
140 master Rufus's, "there won't be another earthquake in my lifetime or yours. There may be a tremble or two, but earthquakes, like lightnings, never strike twice in the same place."

"Do they not?" asked a thin voice Tito had never heard. It had a high, sharp ring to it and Tito knew it as the accent of a stranger. "How about the two towns of Sicily that have been ruined three times within fifteen years by the eruptions of Mount Etna? And were they not warned? And does that column of smoke above Vesuvius mean nothing?"

"That?" Tito could hear the grunt with which one question
150 answered another. "That's always there. We use it for our weather guide. When the smoke stands up straight, we know we'll have fair weather; when it flattens out, it's sure to be foggy; when it drifts to the east—"

"Yes, yes," cut in the edged voice. "I've heard about your mountain barometer.[10] But the column of smoke seems hundreds of feet higher than usual and it's thickening and spreading like a shadowy tree. They say in Naples—"

"Oh, Naples!" Tito knew this voice by the little squeak that went with it. It was Attilio the cameo cutter.[11] "They talk while
160 we suffer. Little help we got from them last time. Naples commits the crimes and Pompeii pays the price. It's become a proverb with us. Let them mind their own business."

"Yes," grumbled Rufus, "and others', too."

"Very well, my confident friends," responded the thin voice, which now sounded curiously flat. "We also have a proverb— and it is this: *Those who will not listen to men must be taught by the gods.* I say no more. But I leave a last warning. Remember the holy ones. Look to your temples. And when the smoke tree above Vesuvius grows to the shape of an umbrella
170 pine, look to your lives."

---

10. **barometer** (bə·räm′ət·ər): instrument for measuring atmospheric pressure. Barometers are used in forecasting changes in the weather.
11. **cameo cutter:** artist who carves delicate pictures on gems or shells.

Tito could hear the air whistle as the speaker drew his toga about him, and the quick shuffle of feet told him the stranger had gone.

"Now what," said the cameo cutter, "did he mean by that?"

"I wonder," grunted Rufus. "I wonder."

Tito wondered, too. And Bimbo, his head at a thoughtful angle, looked as if he had been doing a heavy piece of pondering. By nightfall the argument had been forgotten. If the smoke had increased, no one saw it in the dark. Besides, it was
180 Caesar's birthday and the town was in a holiday mood. Tito and Bimbo were among the merrymakers, dodging the charioteers who shouted at them. A dozen times they almost upset baskets of sweets and jars of Vesuvian wine, said to be as fiery as the streams inside the volcano, and a dozen times they were cursed and cuffed. But Tito never missed his footing. He was thankful for his keen ears and quick instinct—most thankful of all for Bimbo.

They visited the uncovered theater, and though Tito could not see the faces of the actors, he could follow the play better
190 than most of the audience, for their attention wandered—they were distracted by the scenery, the costumes, the byplay,[12] even by themselves—while Tito's whole attention was centered in what he heard. Then to the city walls, where the people of Pompeii watched a mock naval battle in which the city was attacked by the sea and saved after thousands of flaming arrows had been exchanged and countless colored torches had been burned. Though the thrill of flaring ships and lighted skies was lost to Tito, the shouts and cheers excited him as much as any, and he cried out with the loudest of them.

200 The next morning there were two of the beloved raisin-and-sugar cakes for his breakfast. Bimbo was unusually active and thumped his bit of a tail until Tito was afraid he would wear it out. The boy could not imagine whether Bimbo was urging him to some sort of game or was trying to tell him something. After a

---

12. **byplay:** action taking place outside the main action of a play.

PREDICT

Pause at line 173. Do you think another earthquake will strike Pompeii? Tell what you think will happen next in the story.

_____

_____

_____

_____

_____

_____

_____

_____

_____

_____

_____

RETELL

Pause at line 199. **Retell** where Tito and Bimbo went, what they heard, and what happened on the afternoon and evening of Caesar's birthday.

_____

_____

_____

_____

IDENTIFY

Pause at line 223. What changes in the weather does Tito notice the next morning?

_____

_____

_____

_____

_____

_____

_____

_____

_____

PREDICT

Pause at line 232. What do you think is happening? What's your **prediction** about what will happen next in the story?

_____

_____

_____

WORDS TO OWN
coaxed (kōkst) v.: gently persuaded.
revived (ri·vīvd´) v.: brought back to life.

while, he ceased to notice Bimbo. He felt drowsy. Last night's late hours had tired him. Besides, there was a heavy mist in the air— no, a thick fog rather than a mist—a fog that got into his throat and scraped it and made him cough. He walked as far as the marine gate[13] to get a breath of the sea. But the blanket of haze
210 had spread all over the bay and even the salt air seemed smoky.

He went to bed before dusk and slept. But he did not sleep well. He had too many dreams—dreams of ships lurching in the forum, of losing his way in a screaming crowd, of armies marching across his chest, of being pulled over every rough pavement of Pompeii.

He woke early. Or, rather, he was pulled awake. Bimbo was doing the pulling. The dog had dragged Tito to his feet and was urging the boy along. Somewhere. Where, Tito did not know. His feet stumbled uncertainly; he was still half asleep. For a
220 while he noticed nothing except the fact that it was hard to breathe. The air was hot. And heavy. So heavy that he could taste it. The air, it seemed, had turned to powder—a warm powder that stung his nostrils and burned his sightless eyes.

Then he began to hear sounds. Peculiar sounds. Like animals under the earth. Hissings and groanings and muffled cries that a dying creature might make dislodging the stones of his underground cave. There was no doubt of it now. The noises came from underneath. He not only heard them—he could feel them. The earth twitched; the twitching changed to
230 an uneven shrugging of the soil. Then, as Bimbo half pulled, half coaxed him across, the ground jerked away from his feet and he was thrown against a stone fountain.

The water—hot water—splashing in his face revived him. He got to his feet, Bimbo steadying him, helping him on again. The noises grew louder; they came closer. The cries were even more animal-like than before, but now they came from human throats. A few people, quicker of foot and more hurried by fear, began to rush by. A family or two—then a section—then, it seemed, an army broken out of bounds. Tito, bewildered

---

13. **marine gate:** gate in a city wall leading to the sea.

240 though he was, could recognize Rufus as he bellowed past him, like a water buffalo gone mad. Time was lost in a nightmare.

It was then the crashing began. First a sharp crackling, like a monstrous snapping of twigs; then a roar like the fall of a whole forest of trees; then an explosion that tore earth and sky. The heavens, though Tito could not see them, were shot through with continual flickerings of fire. Lightnings above were answered by thunders beneath. A house fell. Then another. By a miracle the two companions had escaped the dangerous side streets and were in a more open space. It was the forum. They
250 rested here awhile—how long, he did not know.

Tito had no idea of the time of day. He could feel it was black—an unnatural blackness. Something inside—perhaps the lack of breakfast and lunch—told him it was past noon. But it didn't matter. Nothing seemed to matter. He was getting drowsy, too drowsy to walk. But walk he must. He knew it. And Bimbo knew it; the sharp tugs told him so. Nor was it a moment too soon. The sacred ground of the forum was safe no longer. It was beginning to rock, then to pitch, then to split. As they stumbled out of the square, the earth wriggled like a
260 caught snake and all the columns of the temple of Jupiter[14] came down. It was the end of the world—or so it seemed. To walk was not enough now. They must run. Tito was too frightened to know what to do or where to go. He had lost all sense of direction. He started to go back to the inner gate; but Bimbo, straining his back to the last inch, almost pulled his clothes from him. What did the creature want? Had the dog gone mad?

Then suddenly he understood. Bimbo was telling him the way out—urging him there. The sea gate, of course. The sea
270 gate—and then the sea. Far from falling buildings, heaving ground. He turned, Bimbo guiding him across open pits and dangerous pools of bubbling mud, away from buildings that had caught fire and were dropping their burning beams. Tito could no longer tell whether the noises were made by the

---

14. **Jupiter:** the supreme god in the religion of the Romans.

VISUALIZE

Underline details in lines 224–250 that help you *hear* what Tito hears. Circle details that help you *picture* the terrifying **setting**.

IDENTIFY

Circle the **simile,** the imaginative comparison using a comparing word such as *like* or *as,* that helps you imagine the scary way the earth is moving.

INFER

Underline the details that lead you to **infer** that what is happening here is more than an earthquake. What's your best guess as to what might be happening to Pompeii?

_____

_____

_____

INTERPRET

Pause at line 303. In what ways does Bimbo help Tito get to the marine gate?

_____

_____

_____

BUILD FLUENCY

Re-read this suspenseful passage out loud. This is where you find the story's **climax**, its most exciting moment, when the outcome of the conflict, boy vs. the forces of nature, is decided. Try to read the short sentences quickly. Use your voice to show increased excitement until the climax, when Tito falls—and Bimbo saves the day.

_____

_____

_____

shrieking sky or the agonized people. He and Bimbo ran on— the only silent beings in a howling world.

New dangers threatened. All Pompeii seemed to be thronging toward the marine gate and, squeezing among the crowds, there was the chance of being trampled to death. But 280 the chance had to be taken. It was growing harder and harder to breathe. What air there was choked him. It was all dust now— dust and pebbles, pebbles as large as beans. They fell on his head, his hands—pumice stones from the black heart of Vesuvius. The mountain was turning itself inside out. Tito remembered a phrase that the stranger had said in the forum two days ago: "Those who will not listen to men must be taught by the gods." The people of Pompeii had refused to heed the warnings; they were being taught now—if it was not too late.

Suddenly it seemed too late for Tito. The red-hot ashes 290 blistered his skin, the stinging vapors tore his throat. He could not go on. He staggered toward a small tree at the side of the road and fell. In a moment Bimbo was beside him. He coaxed. But there was no answer. He licked Tito's hands, his feet, his face. The boy did not stir. Then Bimbo did the last thing he could—the last thing he wanted to do. He bit his comrade, bit him deep in the arm. With a cry of pain, Tito jumped to his feet, Bimbo after him. Tito was in despair, but Bimbo was determined. He drove the boy on, snapping at his heels, worrying his way through the crowd, barking, baring his teeth, 300 heedless of kicks or falling stones. Sick with hunger, half dead with fear and sulfur fumes, Tito pounded on, pursued by Bimbo. How long, he never knew. At last he staggered through the marine gate and felt soft sand under him. Then Tito fainted. . . .

Someone was dashing seawater over him. Someone was carrying him toward a boat.

"Bimbo," he called. And then louder, "Bimbo!" But Bimbo had disappeared.

Voices jarred against each other. "Hurry—hurry!" "To the boats!" "Can't you see the child's frightened and starving!" "He 310 keeps calling for someone!" "Poor boy, he's out of his mind." "Here, child—take this!"

They tucked him in among them. The oarlocks creaked; the oars splashed; the boat rode over toppling waves. Tito was safe. But he wept continually.

"Bimbo!" he wailed. "Bimbo! Bimbo!"

He could not be comforted.

Eighteen hundred years passed. Scientists were restoring the ancient city; excavators[15] were working their way through the stones and trash that had buried the entire town. Much had
320 already been brought to light—statues, bronze instruments, bright mosaics,[16] household articles; even delicate paintings had been preserved by the fall of ashes that had taken over two thousand lives. Columns were dug up, and the forum was beginning to emerge.

It was at a place where the ruins lay deepest that the director paused.

"Come here," he called to his assistant. "I think we've discovered the remains of a building in good shape. Here are four huge millstones that were most likely turned by slaves or
330 mules—and here is a whole wall standing with shelves inside it. Why! It must have been a bakery. And here's a curious thing. What do you think I found under this heap where the ashes were thickest? The skeleton of a dog!"

"Amazing!" gasped his assistant. "You'd think a dog would have had sense enough to run away at the time. And what is that flat thing he's holding between his teeth? It can't be a stone."

"No. It must have come from this bakery. You know it looks to me like some sort of cake hardened with the years. And,
340 bless me, if those little black pebbles aren't raisins. A raisin cake almost two thousand years old! I wonder what made him want it at such a moment."

"I wonder," murmured the assistant.

---

15. **excavators** (ĕks′kə·vāt′ərz): diggers; here, archaeologists.
16. **mosaics** (mō·zā′iks): pictures or designs made by inlaying small bits of stone, glass, tile, or other materials in mortar.

RETELL

Pause at line 314. **Retell** what has happened to Tito since Bimbo woke him up that morning (page 136, line 216).

_____

_____

_____

_____

_____

INTERPRET

Why did Bimbo return to Pompeii after taking Tito to a safe place? Underline the details that back up your answer.

_____

_____

EVALUATE

Do you like the way this story ends, or is the ending too sad? Would a happy ending (with Bimbo beside Tito in the boat) weaken the story and make it less interesting? Give reasons for your answer.

_____

_____

_____

_____

_____

Chain of Events Chart

Trace the plot events in "The Dog of Pompeii" by filling in the chain of events chart below. You can summarize plot events or choose actual lines from the story for your chart entries. Did you find the plot credible? Contrived? Put a question mark beside events you did NOT find credible. Then fill in the notes at the bottom of the chart with your reasons.

Event	Event	Event	Event

Event	Event	Event	Event

Was the story ❑ credible? ❑ not credible?

Why?

_____

_____

Vocabulary and Comprehension

A. Match words and definitions. Write the letter of the correct definition next to each word.

_____ **1.** proverb   **a.** eager to succeed

_____ **2.** ambitious   **b.** persuaded

_____ **3.** revived   **c.** short traditional saying that ex-presses a truth

_____ **4.** coaxed   **d.** awakened; brought back to life

B. Answer each question below.

1. What routine do Tito and Bimbo follow each day?

_____

_____

_____

_____

2. Describe how Bimbo leads Tito to safety.

_____

_____

_____

_____

3. What do the archaeologists find in Bimbo's mouth? Why do you think Bimbo was carrying this when he died?

_____

_____

_____

Medusa's Head

Make the Connection

Foretelling the Future

The idea of fate is important in this Greek myth. *Fate* refers to a power that is believed to decide the future no matter what we do. We learn right away in this story that a king has received bad news from an oracle (ôr′ə·kəl)—a priest or priestess who can foretell the future. He has learned that one day he will be killed by his own grandson.

Today, we know that no oracle or fortuneteller can tell what lies ahead. But suppose you lived back in the days when people believed such things. Suppose you hear about an oracle with a terrific reputation for knowing the future. (This one supposedly sees the future by looking into a crystal ball.) On the rays at the left of the crystal ball below, write three questions about the future that you wouldn't mind having the oracle answer. On the rays at the right, put three questions about the future you'd *not* want to have answered.

I Want to Know   **I Don't Want to Know**

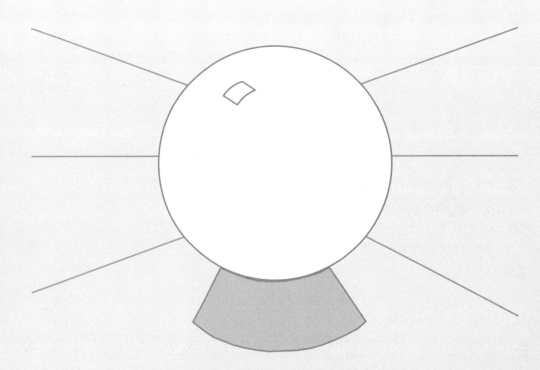

Characters and Places

King Acrisios (ə·crē′sē·ōs′) **of Argos** (är′gäs′): Argos was an ancient city and kingdom in southern Greece.

Proitos (prō·ē′tōs): brother of King Acrisios.

Danae (dan′ā·ē′): daughter of King Acrisios. She bears Zeus's son Perseus.

Apollo: Greek god of light, medicine, poetry, and prophecy. The oracle of Apollo was a priest or priestess through whom the god was believed to speak.

Zeus (zyōos): king of the Greek gods.

Dictys (dic′tis): fisherman, brother of Polydectes. They lived on the island of Seriphos.

Polydectes (päl′ē·dek′tēz): king of Seriphos.

Perseus (pur′sē·əs): son of Danae and Zeus.

Gorgons: three fearful sisters who had brass hands, gold wings, and serpentlike scales.

Medusa, the youngest Gorgon, had snakes for hair and could turn people to stone merely by looking at them.

Athene (ə·thē′nē): Greek goddess of crafts, war, and wisdom. Also spelled *Athena*.

Phorcides (fôr′sə·dēz): three sisters who live in a cave and have only one eye and one tooth between them.

Hermes (hur′mēz′): messenger of the gods.

Cepheus (sē′fē·əs): king of Ethiopia.

Cassiopeia (kas′ē·ō·pē′ə): queen of Ethiopia.

Andromeda (an·dräm′ə·də): daughter of King Cepheus and Queen Cassiopeia. She was chained to a rock to calm the anger of the sea god Poseidon.

Nereus (nir′ē·əs): a minor sea god.

Poseidon (pō·sī′dən): god of the sea.

MEDUSA'S HEAD

a Greek myth, retold by
Olivia Coolidge

King Acrisios of Argos was a hard, selfish man. He hated his brother, Proitos, who later drove him from his kingdom, and he cared nothing for his daughter, Danae. His whole heart was set on having a son who should succeed him, but since many years went by and still he had only the one daughter, he sent a message to the oracle of Apollo to ask whether he should have more children of his own. The answer of the oracle was terrible. Acrisios should have no son, but his daughter, Danae, would bear him a grandchild who should grow up to kill him. At these
10 words Acrisios was beside himself with fear and rage. Swearing that Danae should never have a child to murder him, he had a room built underground and lined all through with brass. Thither he conducted Danae and shut her up, bidding her spend the rest of her life alone.

It is possible to thwart the plans of mortal men, but never those of the gods. Zeus himself looked with pity on the unfortunate girl, and it is said he <u>descended</u> to her through the tiny hole that gave light and air to her chamber, pouring himself down into her lap in the form of a shower of gold.

20 When word came to the king from those who brought food and drink to his daughter that the girl was with child, Acrisios was angry and afraid. He would have liked best to murder both Danae and her infant son, Perseus, but he did not dare for fear of the gods' anger at so hideous a crime. He made, therefore, a great chest of wood with bands of brass about it. Shutting up the girl and her baby inside, he cast them into the sea, thinking that they would either drown or starve.

Again the gods came to the help of Danae, for they caused the planks of the chest to swell until they fitted tightly and let
30 no water in.

The chest floated for some days and was cast up at last on an island. There Dictys, a fisherman, found it and took Danae to his brother, Polydectes, who was king of the island. Danae was made a servant in the palace, yet before many years had passed, both Dictys and Polydectes had fallen in love with the silent, golden-haired girl. She in her heart preferred Dictys, yet

IDENTIFY

Circle two words in the first paragraph that describe Acrisios. Then, come up with another adjective, not in this paragraph but based on its details, to describe him.

_____

IDENTIFY

What does the oracle tell Acrisios? List and number the three parts of the oracle's answer below.

_____

_____

INFER

Although Acrisios tries to avoid his fate, how does Zeus make the *second* part of the oracle's prediction come true (lines 15–19)?

_____

_____

_____

IDENTIFY

Underline the details that tell how the gods help Danae a second time (lines 28–30).

WORDS TO OWN
descended (dē·send′id) *v.*: moved from a high place to a lower one; came down.

RETELL

Pause at line 41. Since the action in this plot is moving so quickly, take a minute to **retell** below the major events that have happened so far.

_____

_____

_____

_____

_____

_____

_____

INFER

Perseus is a **mythic hero,** a person of unusual gifts. Why do you think he might be better looking and stronger than the other youths? What gave him a head start?

_____

_____

_____

_____

_____

_____

_____

since his brother was king, she did not dare to make her choice. Therefore she hung always over Perseus, pretending that mother love left her no room for any other, and year after year

40 a silent frown would cross Polydectes' face as he saw her caress the child.

At last, Perseus became a young man, handsome and strong beyond the common and a leader among the youths of the island, though he was but the son of a poor servant. Then it seemed to Polydectes that if he could once get rid of Perseus, he could force Danae to become his wife, whether she would or not. Meanwhile, in order to lull the young man's suspicions, he pretended that he intended to marry a certain noble maiden and would collect a wedding gift for her. Now the custom was

50 that this gift of the bridegroom to the bride was in part his own and in part put together from the marriage presents of his friends and relatives. All the young men, therefore, brought Polydectes a present, excepting Perseus, who was his servant's son and possessed nothing to bring. Then Polydectes said to the others, "This young man owes me more than any of you, since I took him in and brought him up in my own house, and yet he gives me nothing."

Perseus answered in anger at the injustice of the charge, "I have nothing of my own, Polydectes, yet ask me what you will,

60 and I will fetch it, for I owe you my life."

At this Polydectes smiled, for it was what he had intended, and he answered, "Fetch me, if this is your boast, the Gorgon's head."

Now the Gorgons, who lived far off on the shores of the ocean, were three fearful sisters with hands of brass, wings of gold, and scales like a serpent. Two of them had scaly heads and tusks like the wild boar, but the third, Medusa, had the face of a beautiful woman with hair of writhing serpents, and so terrible was her expression that all who looked on it were

70 immediately turned to stone. This much Perseus knew of the Gorgons, but of how to find or kill them, he had no idea. Nevertheless, he had given his promise, and though he saw now the satisfaction of King Polydectes, he was bound to keep

his word. In his perplexity, he prayed to the wise goddess Athene, who came to him in a vision and promised him her aid.

"First, you must go," she said, "to the sisters Phorcides, who will tell you the way to the nymphs who guard the hat of darkness, the winged sandals, and the knapsack which can hold the Gorgon's head. Then I will give you a shield, and my brother 80 Hermes will give you a sword, which shall be made of adamant, the hardest rock. For nothing else can kill the Gorgon, since so venomous is her blood that a mortal sword, when plunged in it, is eaten away. But when you come to the Gorgons, invisible in your hat of darkness, turn your eyes away from them and look only on their reflection in your gleaming shield. Thus you may kill the monster without yourself being turned to stone. Pass her sisters by, for they are immortal, but smite off the head of Medusa with the hair of writhing snakes. Then put it in your knapsack and return, and I will be with you."

90 The vision ended, and with the aid of Athene, Perseus set out on the long journey to seek the Phorcides. These live in a dim cavern in the far north, where nights and days are one and where the whole earth is overspread with perpetual twilight. There sat the three old women mumbling to one another, crouched in a dim heap together, for they had but one eye and one tooth between them, which they passed from hand to hand. Perseus came quietly behind them, and as they fumbled for the eye, he put his strong, brown hand next to one of the long, yellow ones, so that the old crone thought 100 that it was her sister's and put the eye into it. There was a high scream of anger when they discovered the theft, and much clawing and groping in the dim recesses of the cavern. But they were helpless in their blindness and Perseus could laugh at them. At length, for the price of their eye, they told him how to reach the nymphs, and Perseus, laying the eye quickly in the hand of the nearest sister, fled as fast as he could before she could use it.

Again it was a far journey to the garden of the nymphs, where it is always sunshine and the trees bear golden apples. 110 But the nymphs are friends of the wise gods and hate the

INTERPRET
Mythic heroes often go on a quest (a dangerous journey) where they take on superhuman tasks. What is Perseus's quest? What is his superhuman task?

IDENTIFY
Re-read lines 76–79. Underline and number in the text three ways the gods help (or will help) Perseus in his conflict with the Gorgons.

PREDICT
Pause at line 89. Will Perseus follow Athene's detailed directions and succeed? What do you think might happen next?

WORDS TO OWN
perplexity (pər·pleks'ə·tē) n.: bewilderment; confusion.
perpetual (pər·pech'oo·əl) adj.: continual; constant.
recesses (rē'ses·əz) n.: hollow places.

VISUALIZE

Circle the details in this paragraph that help you picture what Perseus sees on his journey.

_____

_____

_____

_____

_____

_____

_____

PREDICT

Even though Athene has told Perseus how to kill Medusa, why do you think he still might be terrified? What could go wrong?

_____

_____

_____

_____

_____

_____

_____

WORDS TO OWN
hovered (huv′ərd) _v._: stayed suspended in the air.

monsters of darkness and the spirits of anger and despair. Therefore, they received Perseus with rejoicing and put the hat of darkness on his head, while on his feet they bound the golden, winged sandals, which are those Hermes wears when he runs down the slanting sunbeams or races along the pathways of the wind. Next, Perseus put on his back the silver sack with the gleaming tassels of gold, and flung across his shoulder the black-sheathed sword that was the gift of Hermes. On his left arm he fitted the shield that Athene gave, a gleaming
120 silver shield like a mirror, plain without any marking. Then he sprang into the air and ran, invisible like the rushing wind, far out over the white-capped sea, across the yellow sands of the eastern desert, over strange streams and towering mountains, until at last he came to the shores of the distant ocean which flowed round all the world.

There was a gray gorge of stone by the ocean's edge, where lay Medusa and her sisters sleeping in the dim depths of the rock. All up and down the cleft, the stones took fantastic shapes of trees, beasts, birds, or serpents. Here and there, a
130 man who had looked on the terrible Medusa stood forever with horror on his face. Far over the twilit gorge Perseus hovered invisible, while he loosened the pale, strange sword from its black sheath. Then, with his face turned away and eyes on the silver shield, he dropped, slow and silent as a falling leaf, down through the rocky cleft, twisting and turning past countless strange gray shapes, down from the bright sunlight into a chill, dim shadow echoing and reechoing with the dashing of waves on the tumbled rocks beneath. There on the heaped stones lay the Gorgons sleeping together in the dimness, and even as he
140 looked on them in the shield, Perseus felt stiff with horror at the sight.

Two of the Gorgons lay sprawled together, shaped like women, yet scaled from head to foot as serpents are. Instead of hands they had gleaming claws like eagles, and their feet were dragons' feet. Skinny metallic wings like bats' wings hung from their shoulders. Their faces were neither snake nor woman, but part both, like faces in a nightmare. These two lay arm in arm

and never stirred. Only the blue snakes still hissed and writhed round the pale, set face of Medusa, as though even in sleep
150 she were troubled by an evil dream. She lay by herself, arms outstretched, face upwards, more beautiful and terrible than living man may bear. All the crimes and madnesses of the world rushed into Perseus' mind as he gazed at her image in the shield. Horror stiffened his arm as he hovered over her with his sword uplifted. Then he shut his eyes to the vision and in the darkness struck.

There was a great cry and a hissing. Perseus groped for the head and seized it by the limp and snaky hair. Somehow he put it in his knapsack and was up and off, for at the dreadful
160 scream the sister Gorgons had awakened. Now they were after him, their sharp claws grating against his silver shield. Perseus strained forward on the pathway of the wind like a runner, and behind him the two sisters came, smelling out the prey they could not see. Snakes darted from their girdles,[1] foam flew from their tusks, and the great wings beat the air. Yet the winged sandals were even swifter than they, and Perseus fled like the hunted deer with the speed of desperation. Presently the horrible noise grew faint behind him, the hissing of snakes and the sound of the bat wings died away. At last the Gorgons could
170 smell him no longer and returned home unavenged.

By now, Perseus was over the Libyan desert, and as the blood from the horrible head touched the sand, it changed to serpents, from which the snakes of Africa are descended.

The storms of the Libyan desert blew against Perseus in clouds of eddying sand, until not even the divine sandals could hold him on his course. Far out to sea he was blown, and then north. Finally, whirled around the heavens like a cloud of mist, he alighted in the distant west, where the giant Atlas held up on his shoulders the heavens from the earth. There the weary
180 giant, crushed under the load of centuries, begged Perseus to show him Medusa's head. Perseus uncovered for him the dreadful thing, and Atlas was changed to the mighty mountain

---

1. **girdles:** belts or sashes.

VISUALIZE
Lines 142–156 are filled with **imagery,** language that appeals to the senses. Most images are visual. Circle the images in this paragraph that help you see the Gorgons.

INFER
Why do you think Atlas wants to look at Medusa's head (lines 179–181)?

INTERPRET

Myths often explain where things came from or how they came to be. Re-read lines 171–186. What two things are explained here?

_____

_____

_____

PREDICT

What do you think Perseus will do now that he sees this maiden in distress?

_____

_____

_____

_____

_____

_____

_____

_____

_____

_____

_____

_____

_____

_____

_____

whose rocks rear up to reach the sky near the gateway to the Atlantic. Perseus himself, returning eastwards and still battling with the wind, was driven south to the land of Ethiopia, where King Cepheus reigned with his wife, Cassiopeia.

As Perseus came wheeling in like a gull from the ocean, he saw a strange sight. Far out to sea the water was troubled, seething and boiling as though stirred by a great force moving 190 in its depths. Huge, sullen waves were starting far out and washing inland over sunken trees and flooded houses. Many miles of land were under water, and as he sped over them, he saw the muddy sea lapping around the foot of a black, upstanding rock. Here on a ledge above the water's edge stood a young girl chained by the arms, lips parted, eyes open and staring, face white as her linen garment. She might have been a statue, so still she stood, while the light breeze fluttered her dress and stirred her loosened hair. As Perseus looked at her and looked at the sea, the water began to boil again, and miles 200 out a long gray scaly back of vast length lifted itself above the flood. At that, there was a shriek from a distant knoll where he could dimly see the forms of people, but the girl shrank a little and said nothing. Then Perseus, taking off the hat of darkness, alighted near the maiden to talk to her, and she, though nearly mad with terror, found words at last to tell him her tale.

Her name was Andromeda, and she was the only child of the king and of his wife, Cassiopeia. Queen Cassiopeia was exceedingly beautiful, so that all people marveled at her. She herself was proud of her dark eyes, her white, slender fingers, 210 and her long black hair, so proud that she had been heard to boast that she was fairer even than the sea nymphs, who are daughters of Nereus. At this, Nereus in wrath stirred up Poseidon, who came flooding in over the land, covering it far and wide. Not content with this, he sent a vast monster from the dark depths of the bottomless sea to ravage the whole coast of Ethiopia. When the unfortunate king and queen had sought the advice of the oracle on how to appease the god, they had been ordered to sacrifice their only daughter to the sea monster Poseidon had sent. Not daring for their people's sake to

220 disobey, they had chained her to this rock, where she now awaited the beast who should devour her.

Perseus comforted Andromeda as he stood by her on the rock, and she shrank closer against him while the great gray back writhed its half-mile length slowly towards the land. Then, bidding Andromeda hide her face, Perseus sprang once more into the air, unveiling the dreadful head of dead Medusa to the monster, which reared its dripping jaws yards high into the air. The mighty tail stiffened all of a sudden, the boiling of the water ceased, and only the gentle waves of the receding ocean
230 lapped around a long, gray ridge of stone. Then Perseus freed Andromeda and restored her to her father and beautiful mother. Thereafter, with their consent, he married her amid scenes of tremendous rejoicing, and with his bride set sail at last for the kingdom of Polydectes.

Polydectes had lost no time on the departure of Perseus. First he had begged Danae to become his wife, and then he had threatened her. Undoubtedly, he would have got his way by force if Danae had not fled in terror to Dictys. The two took refuge at the altar of a temple whence Polydectes did not dare
240 drag them away. So matters stood when Perseus returned. Polydectes was enraged to see him, for he had hoped at least that Danae's most powerful protector would never return. But now, seeing him famous and with a king's daughter to wife, he could not contain himself. Openly he laughed at the tale of Perseus, saying that the hero had never killed the Gorgon, only pretended to, and that now he was claiming an honor he did not deserve. At this, Perseus, enraged by the insult and by reports of his mother's persecution, said to him, "You asked me for the Gorgon's head. Behold it!" And with that he lifted it
250 high, and Polydectes became stone.

Then Perseus left Dictys to be king of that island, but he himself went back to the Grecian mainland to seek out his grandfather, Acrisios, who was once again king of Argos. First, however, he gave back to the gods the gifts they had given him. Hermes took back the golden sandals and the hat of darkness, for both are his. But Athene took Medusa's head, and she hung it on

EVALUATE

Does the sacrifice of Andromeda seem unfair to you? Tell why or why not. Who, if anyone, should the gods have punished?

_____

_____

RETELL

Go back to line 157, and **retell** what's happened to Perseus since he cut off Medusa's head.

_____

_____

_____

_____

_____

_____

_____

BUILD FLUENCY

Read this boxed passage carefully to make sure you understand the details. Then, decide how you will read it out loud to make its meaning clear to a young listener. Review how the names are pronounced so you won't stumble over them. Read slowly, emphasizing the names so your listener will be able to recall them. Which part of the passage will you say angrily and triumphantly?

Myths often reveal the characteristics that the people who created them admired. List three of Perseus's **character** traits that the Greeks valued highly. Tell briefly how Perseus showed each of the three character traits.

_____

_____

_____

_____

_____

_____

_____

_____

EVALUATE

One reason why the Greeks created this myth was to show that no one can escape fate. How good a job does it do? What do you think of the ancient Greek idea that everything is determined in advance by fate? Give reasons for your answer.

_____

_____

_____

_____

_____

_____

a fleece around her neck as part of her battle equipment, where it may be seen in statues and portraits of the warlike goddess.

Perseus took ship for Greece, but his fame had gone before 260 him, and King Acrisios fled secretly from Argos in terror, since he remembered the prophecy and feared that Perseus had come to avenge the wrongs of Danae. The trembling old Acrisios took refuge in Larissa, where it happened the king was holding a great athletic contest in honor of his dead father.

Heroes from all over Greece, among whom was Perseus, came to the games. As Perseus was competing at the discus throwing, he threw high into the air and far beyond the rest. A strong wind caught the discus as it spun, so that it left the course marked out for it and was carried into the stands. People 270 scrambled away to right and left. Only Acrisios was not nimble enough. The heavy weight fell full on his foot and crushed his toes, and at that, the feeble old man, already weakened by his terrors, died from the shock. Thus the prophecy of Apollo was fulfilled at last; Acrisios was killed by his grandson. Then Perseus came into his kingdom, where he reigned with Andromeda long and happily.

Myth Chart

Myths, an early form of fiction, have their own unique characteristics. Show that "Medusa's Head" is a myth by filling in this chart with details from the story.

Characteristics of Myths	Examples from "Medusa's Head"
Heroes often have supernatural power.	
Gods and goddesses aid the hero.	
Monsters threaten the hero.	
Explanations are provided for natural occurrences.	
The hero saves a society from ruin.	
Cultural values are expressed.	

Vocabulary

A. Replace the word or words in parentheses with a word from the Word Bank.

1. He lit a candle and entered the dark (*hollow places*)

_____ of the cave.

2. In his (*confusion*) _____ he went down the wrong tunnel.

3. As he followed the path, he (*came down*) _____ deeper into the cave.

4. The cave walls were always wet from the (*constant*) _____ dripping of water from the stream above.

5. It seemed as if a thousand bats (*remained suspended in the air*)

_____ above his head.

B. Choose four words from the Word Bank. Use each word in a sentence.

1. _____

_____

2. _____

_____

3. _____

_____

4. _____

_____

Comprehension

A. Put the events in order. Number the events on the blanks.

_____ Perseus cuts off Medusa's head.

_____ Perseus turns Polydectes to stone.

_____ The oracle tells Acrisios he will be killed by his grandson.

_____ Perseus returns home to Greece.

_____ Perseus rescues Andromeda by turning the sea monster to stone.

_____ With Athene's guidance, Perseus sets out to find the Gorgons.

_____ Danae and Perseus are cast out to sea and are discovered by Dictys.

_____ Acrisios is killed by Perseus' discus.

_____ Polydectes orders Perseus to fetch the Gorgon's head.

_____ Perseus finds Andromeda chained to a rock.

B. Answer each question below.

1. Why does Perseus set off on his dangerous journey?

_____

_____

2. Describe how Perseus cuts off the Gorgon's head.

_____

_____

3. What happens to Polydectes at the end of the story?

_____

_____

4. Describe how King Acrisios tries twice to escape his fate.

_____

_____

The Emperor's New Clothes

Make the Connection

Sending a Message

The emperor in this story has an interest that many of us share. He loves new clothes. Some people don't care about clothes. They love to play computer games or surf the Internet. Some people love to skateboard or to dance. Others love to play with a pet animal, listen to CDs, watch TV, or play basketball. Most of us love different activities and things as we grow older. What we like best sends a message about who we are at different times in our lives.

Think about some interests or objects—such as toys or games—that seemed terrifically important to you when you were younger. In each box below, write down words or draw pictures that tell about those interests and objects. Try to think of at least two different items for each box. (It's OK to repeat something that you loved for longer than three years.)

What interests or objects did you love most?

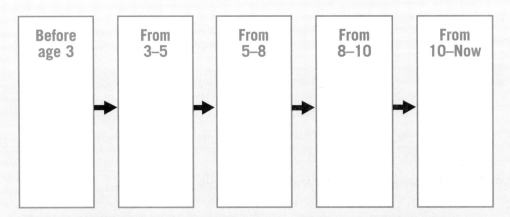

Before age 3	From 3–5	From 5–8	From 8–10	From 10–Now

Choose one or several of your boxes above. Based on what you loved at that time, what message were you sending about the kind of person you were?

_____

_____

_____

THE EMPEROR'S NEW CLOTHES

Hans Christian Andersen

IDENTIFY

Underline the emperor's biggest interest in life. Considering that an emperor is the leader of a country, what message is he sending about himself by having *that* major interest?

_____

_____

_____

_____

_____

INFER

Based on the details in lines 16–26, write down a definition for the word *swindler*.

_____

_____

_____

_____

_____

INFER

Pause at line 32. Write down three words that describe what you know about the emperor's **character** so far.

_____

_____

_____

Many years ago there lived an Emperor who was so fond of new clothes that he spent all his money on them. He did not care for his soldiers, or for the theater, or for driving in the woods, except to show off his new clothes. He had an outfit for every hour of the day, and just as they say of a king, "He is in the council chamber," so they always said of him, "The Emperor is in his dressing room."

The great city where he lived was very lively, and every day many strangers came there. One day two swindlers came. They claimed that they were weavers and said they could weave the finest cloth imaginable. Their colors and patterns, they said, were not only exceptionally beautiful, but the clothes made of this material possessed the wonderful quality of being invisible to any man who was unfit for his office, or who was hopelessly stupid.

"Those must be wonderful clothes," thought the Emperor. "If I wore them, I should be able to find out which men in my empire were unfit for their posts, and I could tell the clever from the stupid. Yes, I must have this cloth woven for me without delay." So he gave a lot of money to the two swindlers in advance, so that they could set to work at once.

They set up two looms[1] and pretended to be very hard at work, but they had nothing on the looms. They asked for the finest silk and the most precious gold, all of which they put into their own bags, and worked at the empty looms till late into the night.

"I should very much like to know how they are getting on with the cloth," thought the Emperor. But he felt rather uneasy when he remembered that whoever was not fit for his office could not see it. He believed, of course, that he had nothing to fear for himself, yet he thought he would send somebody else first to see how things were progressing.

Everybody in the town knew what a wonderful property the cloth possessed, and all were anxious to see how bad or stupid their neighbors were.

---

1. **looms:** machines used for weaving thread into cloth.

"I will send my honest old minister to the weavers," thought the Emperor. "He can judge best how the cloth looks, for he is intelligent, and nobody is better fitted for his office than he."

So the good old minister went into the room where the two
40 swindlers sat working at the empty looms. "Heaven help us!" he thought, and opened his eyes wide. "Why, I cannot see anything at all," but he was careful not to say so.

Both swindlers bade him be so good as to step closer and asked him if he did not admire the exquisite pattern and the beautiful colors. They pointed to the empty looms, and the poor old minister opened his eyes even wider, but he could see nothing, for there was nothing to be seen. "Good Lord!" he thought, "can I be so stupid? I should never have thought so, and nobody must know it! Is it possible that I am not fit for
50 my office? No, no, I must not tell anyone that I couldn't see the cloth."

"Well, have you got nothing to say?" said one, as he wove.

"Oh, it is very pretty—quite enchanting!" said the old minister, peering through his glasses. "What a pattern, and what colors! I shall tell the Emperor that I am very much pleased with it."

"Well, we are glad of that," said both the weavers, and they described the colors to him and explained the curious pattern. The old minister listened carefully, so that he might tell the
60 Emperor what they said.

Now the swindlers asked for more money, more silk, and more gold, which they required for weaving. They kept it all for themselves, and not a thread came near the loom, but they continued, as before, working at the empty looms.

Soon afterward the Emperor sent another honest official to the weavers to see how they were getting on and if the cloth was nearly finished. Like the old minister, he looked and looked but could see nothing, as there was nothing to be seen.

70 "Is it not a beautiful piece of cloth?" said the two swindlers, showing and explaining the magnificent pattern, which, however, was not there at all.

PREDICT
Will the minister be able to see the clothes? What will he tell the emperor about them?

_____

_____

IDENTIFY
Circle and number the two questions that the minister asks himself before he decides he must lie.

_____

_____

_____

INTERPRET
Pause at line 56. Why do you think the old minister never questions the weavers' honesty?

_____

_____

_____

_____

_____

_____

_____

_____

_____

RETELL

Summarize the important events that have happened in the story since the strangers came to town.

_____

_____

_____

_____

_____

BUILD FLUENCY

As you re-read the boxed passage aloud, imagine that you're the emperor reacting to the "invisible cloth." Change the rate, volume, pitch, and tone of your voice to show how you feel and how you hide your true feelings. Use your voice to reveal the emperor's **character**.

PREDICT

Pause at line 104. What will the emperor do when it's time to wear his new clothes? Will anyone dare to tell him the truth? If not, what will happen?

_____

_____

_____

_____

_____

"I am not stupid," thought the man, "so it must be that I am unfit for my high post. It is ludicrous,[2] but I must not let anyone know it." So he praised the cloth, which he did not see, and expressed his pleasure at the beautiful colors and the fine pattern. "Yes, it is quite enchanting," he said to the Emperor.

Everybody in the whole town was talking about the beautiful cloth. At last the Emperor wished to see it himself 80 while it was still on the loom. With a whole company of chosen courtiers, including the two honest councilors who had already been there, he went to the two clever swindlers, who were now weaving away as hard as they could but without using any thread.

"Is it not magnificent?" said both the honest statesmen. "Look, Your Majesty, what a pattern! What colors!" And they pointed to the empty looms, for they imagined the others could see the cloth.

"What is this?" thought the Emperor. "I do not see anything at all. This is terrible! Am I stupid? Am I unfit to be Emperor? 90 That would indeed be the most dreadful thing that could happen to me!"

"Yes, it is very beautiful," said the Emperor. "It has our highest approval," and nodding contentedly, he gazed at the empty loom, for he did not want to say that he could see nothing. All the attendants who were with him looked and looked, and, although they could not see anything more than the others, they said, just like the Emperor, "Yes, it is very fine." They all advised him to wear the new magnificent clothes at a 100 great procession that was soon to take place. "It is magnificent! beautiful, excellent!" went from mouth to mouth, and everybody seemed delighted. The Emperor awarded each of the swindlers the cross of the order of knighthood to be worn in their buttonholes, and the title of Imperial Court Weavers.

Throughout the night preceding the procession, the swindlers were up working, and they had more than sixteen candles burning. People could see how busy they were, getting

---

2. ludicrous (loo'di·krəs): ridiculous; laughable.

VISUALIZE

Re-read lines 105–117. Circle the words and phrases that help you "see" the swindlers as they trick everyone into believing they are working. Underline the comment that is the swindlers' answer to a question that no one dares to ask. What is that question?

the Emperor's new clothes ready. They pretended to take the cloth from the loom, they snipped the air with big scissors, they

110 sewed with needles without any thread, and at last said: "Now the Emperor's new clothes are ready!"

The Emperor, followed by all his noblest courtiers, then came in. Both the swindlers held up one arm as if they held something, and said: "See, here are the trousers! Here is the coat! Here is the cloak!" and so on. "They are all as light as a cobweb! They make one feel as if one had nothing on at all, but that is just the beauty of it."

"Yes!" said all the courtiers, but they could not see anything, for there was nothing to see.

120 "Will it please Your Majesty graciously to take off your clothes?" said the swindlers. "Then we may help Your Majesty into the new clothes before the large mirror!"

The Emperor took off all his clothes, and the swindlers pretended to put on the new clothes, one piece after another. Then the Emperor looked at himself in the glass from every angle.

"Oh, how well they look! How well they fit!" said all. "What a pattern! What colors! Magnificent indeed!"

"They are waiting outside with the canopy which is to be

130 borne over Your Majesty in the procession," announced the master of ceremonies.

"Well, I am quite ready," said the Emperor. "Doesn't my suit fit me beautifully?" And he turned once more to the mirror so that people would think he was admiring his garments.

The chamberlains, who were to carry the train, fumbled with their hands on the ground as if they were lifting up a train. Then they pretended to hold something up in their hands. They didn't dare let people know that they could not see anything.

140 And so the Emperor marched in the procession under the beautiful canopy, and all who saw him in the street and out of the windows exclaimed: "How marvelous the Emperor's new suit is! What a long train he has! How well it fits him!" Nobody would let the others know that he saw nothing, for then he

INTERPRET

Why is the child able to tell the truth that the adults cannot tell (line 147)?

_____

_____

_____

INTERPRET

The emperor continues to march even though he and everyone else know he's got nothing on. What message does he send by this action?

_____

_____

_____

INFER

You **infer** a message or **theme** from what happens in a story. The theme goes beyond the story to state a truth about real life. What message about life can you take from this story? Provide details that support your **inference.**

_____

_____

_____

_____

_____

_____

_____

would have been shown to be unfit for his office or too stupid. None of the Emperor's clothes had ever been such a success.

"But he has nothing on at all," said a little child.

"Good heavens! Hear what the innocent child says!" said the father, and then each whispered to the other what the child

150 said: "He has nothing on—a little child says he has nothing on at all!" "He has nothing on at all," cried all the people at last. And the Emperor too was feeling very worried, for it seemed to him that they were right, but he thought to himself, "All the same, I must go through with the procession." And he held himself stiffer than ever, and the chamberlains walked on, holding up the train which was not there at all.

Theme Chart

Theme is the meaning of a story. Often the author will not directly state the theme. Instead you must figure it out by analyzing the story. To find a story's theme, think about the main characters' actions and what they learn in the story. Look at how the actions and the details of the story relate to real life. Fill in the actions of the main characters in the chart below. Then, think about what you learned as you shared their experience and fill in the theme box below.

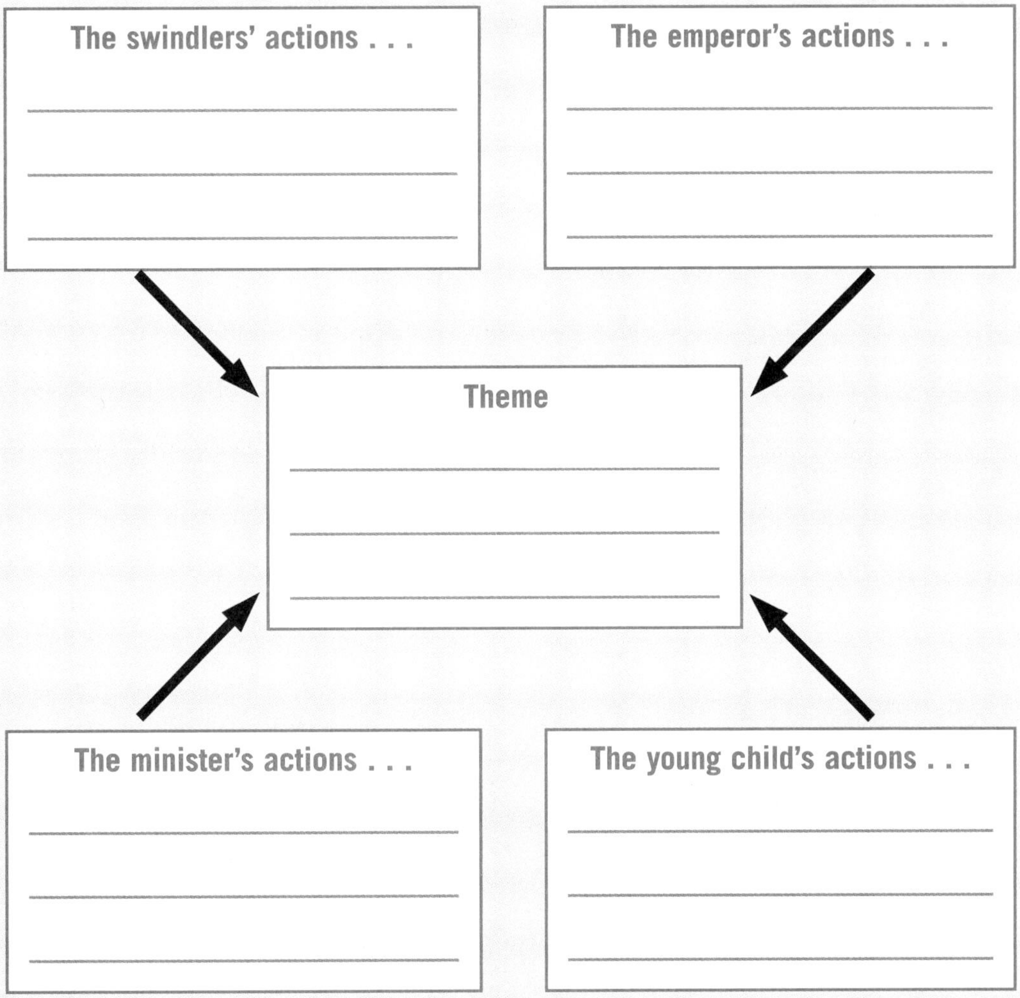

The swindlers' actions . . .	The emperor's actions . . .
_____	_____
_____	_____
_____	_____

Theme

_____

_____

_____

The minister's actions . . .	The young child's actions . . .
_____	_____
_____	_____
_____	_____

PART 2   READING INFORMATIONAL MATERIALS

The Wind People

Creating an Outline

Outlining is a good way to organize and record information in factual writing. **Outlining** usually involves three steps:

1. getting the main ideas
2. taking notes
3. putting the notes into outline form

   Use the informational reading on the Kaw to practice outlining.

1. **Getting the main ideas.** You'll probably have to read the article more than once to identify the main ideas. Note that the article has four **subheads.** You should look for a main idea and supporting details for each of these four sections of the article:

   - the Kaw creation myth
   - encounters with European explorers
   - winds of change
   - the end of the Kaw

2. **Taking notes.** Your responses to the questions alongside the selection will be your notes.

3. **Putting the notes into outline form.** Once you have your notes, it is time to organize them in an outline. An outline is set up this way:

   I. Main idea
      A. Detail supporting point I
         1. Detail supporting point A
            a. Detail supporting point 1

   Make sure that there are at least two headings at each level.

The Wind People

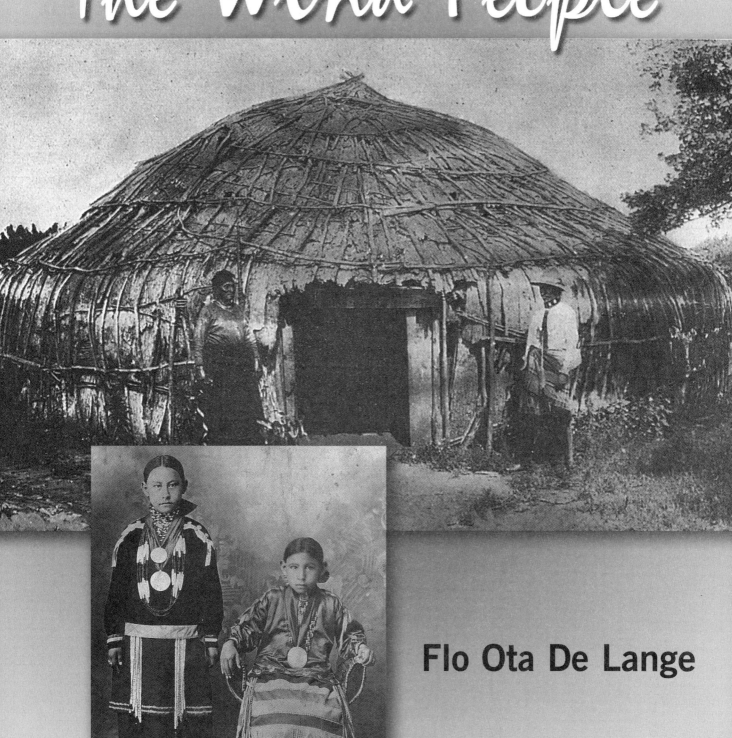

Flo Ota De Lange

IDENTIFY

According to the creation story (lines 6–15), how did the Great Spirit cause the Kaw's island to enlarge?

_____

_____

_____

_____

_____

_____

CLARIFY

For the section "Encounters with European Explorers," answer these **clarifying questions:**
Who first met the Kaw?

_____

_____

When? _____

_____

Where? _____

_____

What happened? _____

_____

Why? _____

_____

On April 23, 2000, a sad story appeared in many American newspapers. William Mehojah, eighty-two years old, had died. Mr. Mehojah was the last member of the Sovereign Nation[1] of the Kaw. With his death, the Kaw people were gone forever.

The Kaw Creation Myth

According to a Kaw creation story, the Kaw originally lived on an island that was too small for their numbers. Because there were so many Kaw people in those days, the Kaw mothers offered prayers to the Great Spirit begging for more living space.
10 The Great Spirit responded to their pleas. He sent beavers, muskrats, and turtles to enlarge the Kaw's island, using materials from the bottom of the great waters. In time the earth took shape. Plants and animals thrived. The world became spacious and vibrant. The Kaw population problem was resolved.

Encounters with European Explorers

By the early 1800s, the Kaw nation was prospering. Their land stretched over twenty million acres, from what is now Kansas east into Missouri and Iowa and north into Nebraska. The first
20 Europeans who came in contact with the Kaw were French explorers. The French were interested in commerce, and that required a working knowledge of the geography of the Great Southern Plains and Mississippi Valley, as well as knowledge of the people who lived there and of the languages they spoke. To obtain this knowledge, the French (just like the English and Spanish explorers in other parts of the country) would ask for the names of the new animals, trees, rivers, and mountains they saw and of the new people they met. "What do you call this?" the French would ask. "And this? And this?" Then the French
30 would eagerly record the answers in their ledgers and on their maps. But though the names they wrote down might have sounded roughly like the original names, they were spelled the way the French would spell them. Furthermore, many of the

---

1. **Sovereign Nation:** Native American nations govern themselves and are not subject to the laws of the U.S. government except through treaty or agreement.

sounds the European explorers heard had no equivalents in their own languages, so the new words usually bore little resemblance to the native words. This is how *U-Moln-Holn* became *Omaha* and *Wi-Tsi-Ta* became *Wichita.* The Kaw (or Kansa) called themselves Koln-Za or Kanza; the names we know them by are the French and English versions of those
40 names.

Winds of Change

The Kaw are also known as the Wind People or the People of the South Wind. They believed that since they could not control the wind, they should try to form a relationship with it. But when the winds of change hit the Kaw, with the westward push of European immigrants, the Kaw were helpless. They saw their lands and their population shrink. The European settlers brought deadly diseases with them—diseases such as influenza and smallpox, to which the Kaw had no immunity. Battles with
50 other Native American peoples further reduced the Kaw's numbers.

The End of the Kaw

The most devastating blow to the Kaw was struck by the U.S. government. Beginning in 1825, other peoples were permitted to occupy Kaw land; the Kaw themselves were confined to two million acres in what is now the Kansas, or Kaw, River valley. In 1872, the federal government moved the nation from the valley to a 100,000-acre reservation in Oklahoma. After the Kaw were removed from their native land, struggles over leadership broke out, dividing and fatally weakening the nation.
60   By 1995, only four Kaw were left: Mr. Mehojah, his brother, and two nephews. Mr. Mehojah's last surviving nephew died in 1998. By the year 2000, the Kaw were gone.

IDENTIFY

State the **main idea** of the "Encounters" section in your own words. Then, underline two **details** that support the main idea.

_____

_____

_____

_____

IDENTIFY

Underline **details** in the section "The End of the Kaw" that support the **main idea** that the U.S. government did the most damage to the Kaw.

INTERPRET

Complete the outline of the "Winds of Change" section.

I. Winds of change hit the Kaw.

  A. _____

    _____

    _____

  B. The Kaw people are infected with disease.

  C. _____

    _____

Outline Organizer

Good readers often outline informational texts to be sure they understand the facts. Complete the outline below, giving subtopics and supporting details in "The Wind People." The topics represented by Roman numerals are filled in for you. Add subtopics using capital letters (A, B, C, and so on) and supporting details using Arabic numerals (1, 2, 3, and so on) as you read them. The first section has been done for you below, so begin with section II.

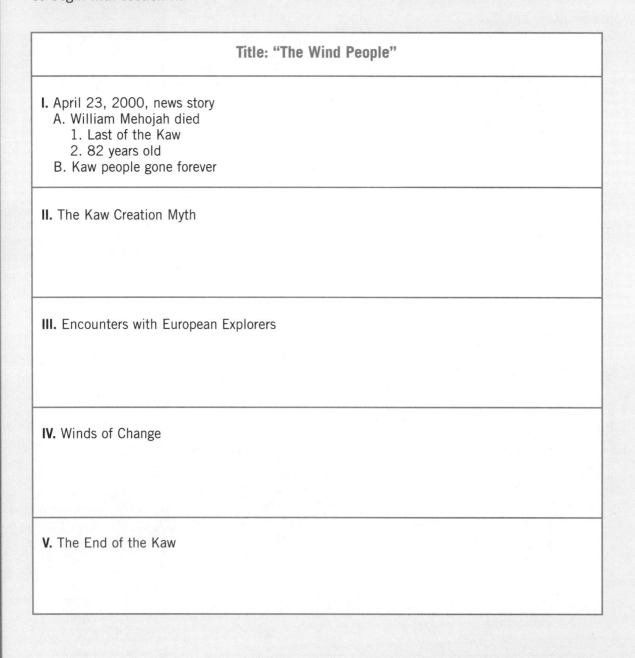

Title: "The Wind People"

I. April 23, 2000, news story
  A. William Mehojah died
    1. Last of the Kaw
    2. 82 years old
  B. Kaw people gone forever

II. The Kaw Creation Myth

III. Encounters with European Explorers

IV. Winds of Change

V. The End of the Kaw

Reading Check

1. Restate the Kaw creation story in your own words (be sure to focus on only the **main ideas** of the myth).

_____

_____

2. List three Kaw names that were modified by the French and English.

_____

Test Practice

Circle the correct answer.

1. The writer probably tells the Kaw creation myth because —

  A it contrasts with what eventually happened to the Kaw

  B it explains why the Kaw died out

  C it predicts what happened to the Kaw

  D it explains how they got the name Kaw

2. Suppose an **outline** of this article lists these main ideas:

  I. The Kaw creation myth

  II.

  III. Winds of change

  IV. The end of the Kaw

Which **main idea** should be Roman numeral II?

  F Last Kaw dies on April 23, 2000

  G Encounters with European explorers

  H Europeans bring disease

  J Other people allowed to occupy Kaw land

3. French explorers learned Kaw names for local peoples and places by —

  A studying a textbook

  B talking to the Kaw

  C taking part in Kaw rituals

  D looking at maps of the Mississippi Valley

4. Suppose an **outline** of this article has a main heading that reads "Winds of Change." Which of these details does _not_ support that main idea?

  F With European immigration, Kaw lands and population shrink.

  G Deadly diseases spread among Kaw.

  H Kaw fight with other Native Americans and reduce population further.

  J French explorers change Kaw names.

Everybody Is Different, but the Same Too

Summarizing the Evidence

In some informational texts, the writer presents **evidence** and then draws a **conclusion** based on that evidence. As a reader, your job is to evaluate the conclusion. Writers aren't perfect. Just because a text looks nice and neat on a printed page doesn't mean it's well thought out. One way to evaluate a writer's conclusion is to **summarize** the evidence in your own words. Then, review your summary to make sure that the evidence supports the writer's conclusion.

Background. In the selection that follows, a young girl from Iran talks about fitting into American life. As a Jewish girl, Nilou had felt out of place in Iran after a new government suppressed religious freedom in 1979. She had to go to school on Saturday, the Jewish day of rest and worship. Her family had few freedoms and feared for their future, so they decided to leave the country. In 1985, they finally flew to New York and then settled in Maryland.

Use the background information above to practice writing a **summary**. State only the most important points in your own words.

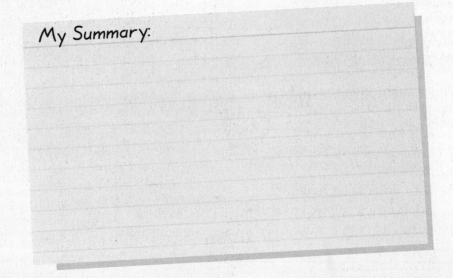

My Summary:

Everybody Is Different, but the Same Too

FROM Newcomers to America

Nilou

IDENTIFY

Circle the writer's nationality. Underline the ways the author keeps her culture alive.

INFER

Define "politically correct" (line 10). Underline the context clues that help you understand the meaning of this term.

_____

_____

_____

_____

_____

EVALUATE

What is the writer's definition of *American?* Do you agree or disagree with her definition?

_____

_____

_____

_____

_____

_____

_____

INTERPRET

The title of this article is *Everybody Is Different, but the Same Too.* Underline the ways that the writer says people are different, and circle the ways that she says people are the same.

Keeping a culture alive is hard. I think I am partly Iranian, partly American—I don't know. We keep our culture alive by traditions and by the five holidays that we celebrate.

I have changed definitely. In Iran, as a woman, I'd go to school, but universities are very hard to get into. In Iran I would have to get a job after high school and get married when I'm twenty or something. Most women don't work in very high positions, especially because the culture is very sexist. I'm happy to be here. Everybody is trying to be more
10 politically correct here.

In schools there is a Spanish club, a Chinese club, but I don't know if there is an Iranian club. We are trying to make an Iranian club but I don't know if it will work—there are [only] about eleven or twelve kids.

I think a club is a way of trying to keep the culture alive. In the Hispanic club, every Thursday, they get together and they dance, and on Tuesdays, they have meetings. We also have an international concert that we can go to. [You can] sing if you like, dance, bring food, you know, just whatever you want to
20 do, whatever you want to present of your culture.

About fitting into American life: When I came to public school, I saw that America is really a melting pot; it borrows things from other cultures—schools, building, furniture, everything from different cultures—and so there is no American way. You can't look at people and say they look like Americans, because America is really borrowing from everything else and everybody is American. And that was when I realized I am American—because all Americans are different.

We should teach that people are people and everybody is
30 the same. They just have different ways of handling their problems and different lifestyles. But we probably have the same goals.

My friends are from all different parts of the world. My American friends are different, my Iranian friends are different, everybody is different, but the same too.

EVALUATE

The **conclusion** of this article appears in both its title and its last line. Explain why you agree or disagree with this conclusion.

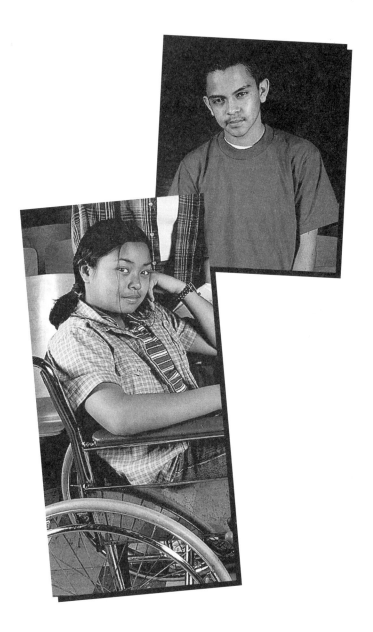

Evidence Flow Chart

In the interview called "Everybody Is Different, but the Same Too," Nilou comes to a conclusion about life in America. Read the evidence listed below that leads up to her conclusion. Then, look for her conclusion at the end of the interview. Restate Nilou's conclusion in our own words. Evaluate the evidence, and tell whether or not you think it adds up to the conclusion.

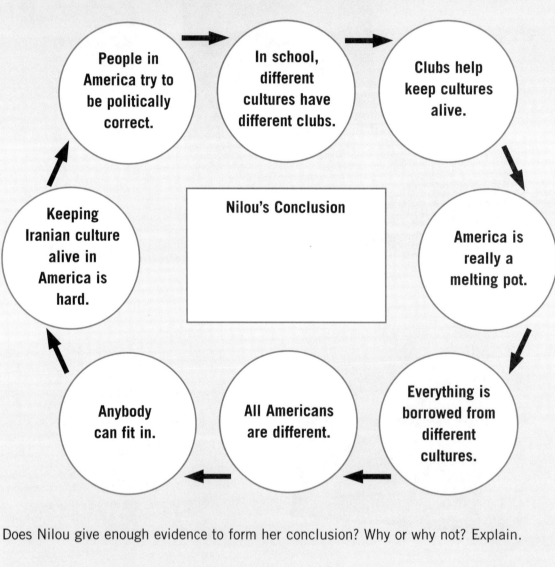

People in America try to be politically correct.

In school, different cultures have different clubs.

Clubs help keep cultures alive.

Keeping Iranian culture alive in America is hard.

Nilou's Conclusion

America is really a melting pot.

Anybody can fit in.

All Americans are different.

Everything is borrowed from different cultures.

Does Nilou give enough evidence to form her conclusion? Why or why not? Explain.

_____

_____

_____

_____

Reading Check

1. What does Nilou think would have happened to her after high school if she had stayed

   in Iran? _____

   _____

2. What did Nilou learn about fitting in to American life when she started public school?

   _____

   _____

3. What ideas about people would Nilou like to see taught? _____

   _____

Test Practice

Circle the correct answer.

1. According to Nilou, a major difference between the United States and Iran is that in the United States —

   A women have more opportunities

   B there is more prejudice

   C most people do not appreciate what it means to be free

   D anyone who wants to can go to college

2. Nilou suggests all of these ways of keeping a culture alive *except* —

   F celebrating the holidays of that culture

   G having a club for students of that cultural background

   H following the traditions of that culture

   J refusing to mix with people of different cultures

3. When Nilou says, "America is really a melting pot," she is using a **metaphor** that compares America to —

   A a pot of rice

   B a pot in which all kinds of ingredients are melted together

   C a bucket of melted steel, which will harden and become strong

   D different kinds of foods

4. Which statement best expresses Nilou's **conclusion**?

   F The differences between people will always cause trouble.

   G People change a great deal when they move to a new country.

   H We have small differences, but people are all just about the same.

   J You have to work very hard if you want to keep your culture alive.

Before You Read THE ARTICLES

Bringing Tang Home *and* Where the Heart Is

Linking Across Selections

The subject of a piece of writing can usually be stated in just a word or two: *love, dogs, growing up.* The **main idea** is the most important thing a writer has to say *about* the subject. The main idea answers the question "What about it?"—what about love or dogs or growing up?

Finding a main idea takes some practice. Sometimes it's clearly stated, but sometimes you have to read carefully to figure it out. Sometimes there's more than one main idea.

The two selections that follow have animals as their subject. The chart below shows two possible main ideas for an animal story. Write four ideas of your own about animals in the empty boxes. When you have finished reading the selections, come back to this chart. Put a star next to any ideas that were the main ideas of the articles.

Possible Main Ideas	
Humans and animals have a special bond.	Humans can learn from animals.

BRINGING TANG HOME

Gina Spadafori

IDENTIFY

In the first two paragraphs, underline what the writer says she is doing.

IDENTIFY

Circle what the opossum, raccoon, and skunk do when people approach. How is the cats' behavior different?

_____

_____

_____

_____

_____

_____

_____

_____

_____

_____

IDENTIFY

In lines 25–32, the writer finally says why they are waiting for cats. Underline the reason.

WORDS TO OWN
furtive (fur′tiv) *adj.:* done in a sneaky or secretive way.
formidable (fôr′mə·də·bəl) *adj.:* fearsome.
feral (fir′əl) *adj.:* untamed, wild.
lure (loor) *v.:* tempt; attract.

In the warm half-light at the end of a summer day, the woods near my home fall quiet as if holding their breath waiting for the wild creatures of the night. Twilight is nature's shift change: In an hour's time the day will be gone and night will be filled with the furtive rustlings of animals who'd rather their comings and goings be unnoticed by the residents of the nearby houses.

I let my own breath out slowly, quietly, for I am also waiting, as is the woman beside me. The night creatures we wait for, though, aren't meant to be wild: We are waiting for cats.

10 **Among the Wild Things**
The opossum, the raccoon, and the skunk steal food from their human neighbors on the other side of the river levee but want nothing in the way of affection. They flee from the sound of footsteps and bare formidable teeth if cornered. "Approach at your peril!" they snarl before melting into the shadows.

But the cats aren't quite so anxious to run. Perhaps this is because their kind and ours have been linked for countless generations, or perhaps it is because, among all the animals, cats alone chose the path of their own domestication and
20 remember it still. Whatever the reason, in the heart of these cats—of every cat gone feral—remains a memory of how pleasant is the company of a human, or how sweet is the feel of a hand swept warmly from just behind the ears and along the supple spine to the end of the tail.

My companion tonight is one of those people who work to return the wild ones to a life of such pleasures. The cats in these woods belong to her, as much as they belong to anyone. She traps the older ones and has them fixed and vaccinated before releasing them to these woods again, for they are too
30 wild to be good pets. The kittens—for despite all the spaying and neutering, there are always new cats, and so, new kittens— she traps, and tames, and finds homes for.

We are after the last of the spring kittens this night, a pale orange tabby male she has named Tang (as in orange Tang). The older cats know what the trap is about, and only the most desperate starvation would lure them inside again. The kittens

aren't so worldly-wise. The appeal of canned food is enough for them, and all but Tang have already been enticed inside for the first step on their journey back to domestication.

40 The Task of Taming

In the dimming light we can barely see the half-grown kitten move inside. The trap slams shut with a crack that scatters the cats—all but the young tabby, who now cannot flee. He hurls himself against the sides of his cage, yowls in fear, and hisses in anger.

The sound beside me is no less explosive. "Yes!" cries my companion. "We got him!"

Tang doesn't yet know it, but he is on his way home. After a few weeks of gentle and gradual socialization, he'll be placed
50 with someone who'll love him. A better fate, surely, than the one he faced as one of the ferals, whose short lives are full of desperation—and often end brutally.

Despite the dangers that claim so many, wild cats are everywhere on the edges of our lives, from the alleys of our cities and the parks of our suburbs to the wild areas and farmland that fill in the gaps between. And in many of those places are people like Tang's captor, quietly pursuing a labor of love that can be as thankless as it often is controversial. Some people would rather see the ferals killed, but these volunteers
60 see another way.

One kitten, one summer evening at a time, they are making a difference. Few thoughts are as pleasant to contemplate as the summer night hugs me in a warm embrace.

IDENTIFY
What causes Tang to enter the trap?

INFER
What is the **main idea** of this article? (There may be more than one.)

EVALUATE
Some people think these wild cats should be killed, while others believe them worth saving. What do you think, and why?

WORDS TO OWN
controversial
(kän′trə·vʉr′shəl) adj.: debatable, tending to stir up argument.

Where the Heart Is

Sheri Henderson

IDENTIFY

Track Bobby's route by underlining the places he visited on his journey.

INFER

Pause at line 17. Why do you think Bobby made such a journey?

On a cold February evening in 1924, a gaunt dog limped up to a farmhouse in Silverton, Oregon, where he had once lived with his family as a pup. But the house was silent, the family long departed. Since August, the dog's lonely journey had taken him across Illinois and Iowa. He had swum rivers, including the dangerous and icy Missouri; he had crossed the great Rocky Mountains in the middle of winter. He had caught squirrels and rabbits for food. At times he had been helped by strangers: He had eaten stew with hobos and Thanksgiving dinner with a

10   family who sheltered him for several weeks. But once he had regained his strength, the dog traveled on, always heading west. The dog lay down to rest for the night at the empty farmhouse. In the morning, on paws with pads worn almost to bone, he made his way slowly into town, into the restaurant where his family now lived, and climbed upstairs to a bedroom, to lick the face of the man he had walked some three thousand miles to find. Bobby had come home.

Two-year-old Bobby, partly English sheepdog but mostly collie, had become separated from Frank Brazier while on

20   vacation in Indiana. When word got out about Bobby's remarkable journey, the president of the Oregon Humane Society decided to document the facts and find the people who had seen or helped Bobby along the way. Bobby eventually became one of the most honored heroes in dog history, recognized with numerous medals and awards for his courage, devotion, and perseverance.

How did Bobby find his way home? Nobody knows for sure. We do know that Bobby's story is unusual but not unique. For centuries there have been reports of animals performing

30   mystifying and wonderful feats like Bobby's. There are stories of other animals who tracked their families, sometimes over thousands of miles, to places where the animals themselves had never been, over routes the owners had never traveled. The story of Sugar may be the longest recorded trip of this kind.

Stacy Woods, a high school principal, planned to move from Anderson, California, to a farm in Gage, Oklahoma, 1,500 miles

IDENTIFY

What do Bobby, Sugar, and Hugh's homing pigeon have in common?

_____

_____

_____

_____

_____

_____

_____

_____

_____

PREDICT

Pause at line 57. What special abilities do you think the researchers have found in animals?

_____

_____

_____

_____

_____

_____

_____

IDENTIFY

The article cites two examples of senses animals possess that humans lack. Underline them (lines 58–69).

away. She couldn't take her cat Sugar, because he was terrified of riding in the car. So a neighbor agreed to adopt him. Fourteen months later, as Stacy Woods was milking a cow in her
40 Oklahoma barn, Sugar jumped through an open window onto her shoulder. The astonished Woods family later learned that Sugar had disappeared three weeks after they had left him with the neighbor. Proving that the cat was really Sugar was easy because Sugar had an unusual hip deformity. But the main question remains unanswered today: How did Sugar find his owner? Similar questions have been raised about many other animals. How did Hugh Brady Perkins's homing pigeon find his way to Hugh's hospital window, 120 miles from his home, after the boy was rushed to the hospital in the middle of the night?
50 How do some pets know when their favorite family members are coming home unexpectedly? How do some pets know from great distances when their family members are hurt or ill or in trouble?

In recent decades, researchers have studied questions like these. They have pondered the possibility that animals draw on information picked up in some way other than through the five well-known senses (sight, hearing, smell, taste, and touch).

Researchers have found that some animals have senses humans lack, like bats' ability to detect objects from echoes
60 and certain snakes' ability to sense tiny temperature differences through special organs. Some people theorize that animals have a form of ESP (extrasensory perception). At Duke University, Joseph Banks Rhine collected more than five hundred stories of unexplainable animal feats that seem to support this theory. Rhine devoted his life to researching these events. Studies conducted at the Research Institute at Rockland State Hospital in New York also support the notion of an extrasensory connection between animals and humans, particularly humans the animals know well and trust.
70 Of course, whatever our theories say, we don't really know what goes on in the heart and mind of an animal. Perhaps the question of *how* they find us is not the most important one. A

better question to ponder may be *why* they find us, even when faced with overwhelming difficulties. It has been said that home is where the heart is. It's clear that for Bobby and Sugar and countless others, home is where one particular heart is.

IDENTIFY

What do you think is the **main idea** of this article?

Main-Idea Web

Sometimes you are asked to connect the main ideas in one reading selection to those in another. Here is a Main-Idea Web that will help you connect "Bringing Tang Home" with "Where the Heart Is"

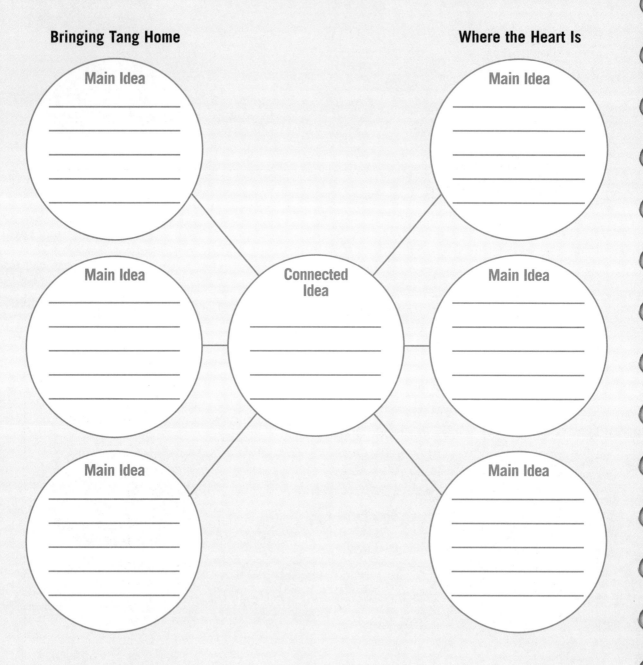

Bringing Tang Home

Main Idea

Main Idea

Main Idea

Connected Idea

Where the Heart Is

Main Idea

Main Idea

Main Idea

Reading Check

1. Go back to the chart of possible main ideas that you made before you read "Bringing Tang Home" and "Where the Heart Is" (page 178). Write the titles of these two selections under the main ideas that they best illustrate or support.

2. Which of the main ideas applies to both "Bringing Tang Home," and "Where the Heart Is"? Support your answer with examples from each selection.

_____

_____

Test Practice

Circle the correct answer.

1. The writers of both selections would probably agree that —

   A dogs and cats are not intelligent

   B relationships between animals and people benefit both

   C abandoned and lost animals should be left to survive on their own

   D dogs and cats stay with humans only because humans feed them

2. According to the writer of "Bringing Tang Home," how are feral cats different from racoons, skunks, and other wild animals?

   F Feral cats do not want affection from humans.

   G Feral cats are more willing to steal food from humans.

   H Feral cats are not as anxious to run from humans.

   J Feral cats are primarily found on farmland.

3. Which statement from "Where the Heart Is" supports the **main idea** that pets have a special bond with their owners?

   A ". . . we don't really know what goes on in the heart and mind of an animal."

   B "Proving that the cat was really Sugar was easy because Sugar had an unusual hip deformity."

   C "Bobby eventually became one of the most honored heroes in dog history. . . ."

   D "There are stories of other animals who tracked their families, sometimes over thousands of miles. . . ."

4. Which statement about the **point of view** of these selections is accurate?

   F Both selections are written from the first-person point of view.

   G Only the story of Tang is told from the first-person point of view.

   H Only "Where the Heart Is" is told from the first-person point of view.

   J Both selections are told from the third-person point of view.

Vocabulary and Comprehension

Bringing Tang Home

A. Read each of the quotations below, using **context clues** in the surrounding words to help you choose the correct meaning of the underlined word. Circle the letter of your choice.

> **Word Bank**
> furtive
> formidable
> feral
> lure
> controversial

1. "In an hour's time the day will be gone and night will be filled with the <u>furtive</u> rustlings of animals who'd rather their comings and goings be unnoticed by the residents of the nearby houses."

   a. playful   **b.** secretive   **c.** noisy   **d.** foolish

2. "They flee from the sound of footsteps and bare <u>formidable</u> teeth if cornered. 'Approach at your peril!' they snarl before melting into the shadows."

   a. surprising   **b.** playful   **c.** fearsome   **d.** weak

3. "The night creatures we wait for . . . aren't meant to be wild: We are waiting for cats. . . . in the heart of these cats—of every cat gone <u>feral</u>—remains a memory of how pleasant is the company of a human. . . ."

   a. tame   **b.** fierce   **c.** insane   **d.** wild

4. "The older cats know what the trap is about, and only the most desperate starvation would <u>lure</u> them inside again."

   a. yank   **b.** want   **c.** tempt   **d.** shove

5. "And in many of those places are people like Tang's captor, quietly pursuing a labor of love that can be as thankless as it often is <u>controversial</u>. Some people would rather see the ferals killed, but these volunteers see another way."

   a. debatable   **b.** fair   **c.** humorous   **d.** persuasive

Vocabulary and Comprehension

B. Answer each question below.

1. Describe Tang. What will happen to him after he has been trapped?

_____

_____

2. Why are the volunteers trapping feral cats?

_____

_____

Where the Heart Is

A. Answer each question below.

1. Describe Bobby's journey from Indiana to Oregon.

_____

_____

2. What do you think helped Bobby survive?

_____

_____

3. What did Sugar do after he had been adopted by a neighbor?

_____

_____

4. In your own words, tell what you think "home is where the heart is" means.

_____

_____

Lincoln's Humor

Supporting Assertions

An **assertion** is a statement or claim. In "Lincoln's Humor," Louis W. Koenig makes several assertions about Lincoln, which he supports with lots of **evidence,** such as examples, facts, and quotations.

Here is an assertion you may agree with: **Humor makes the world a better place.** What evidence can you think of to support this claim? Fill in the globe below with examples, facts, statistics, or quotations from experts.

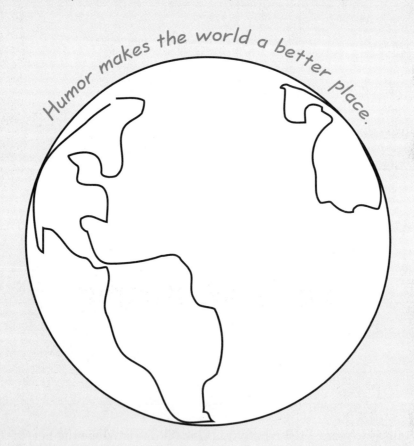

Humor makes the world a better place.

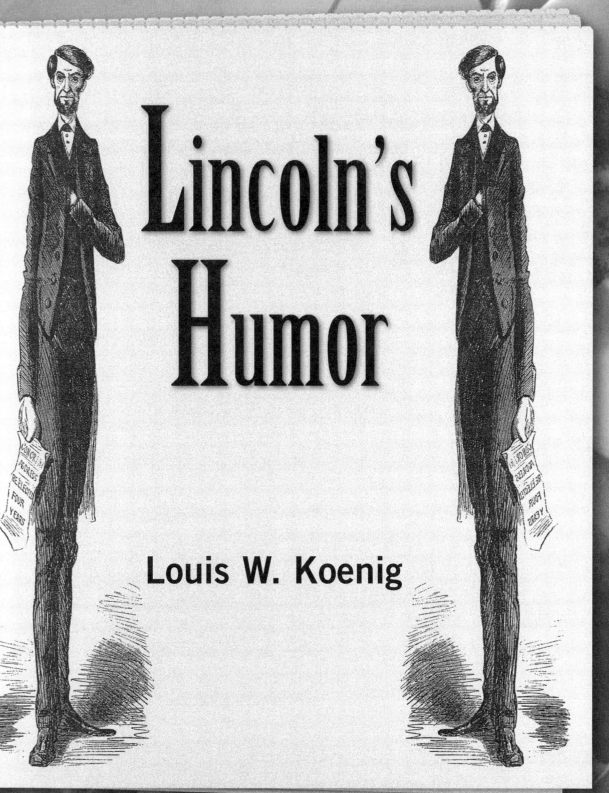

Lincoln's Humor

Louis W. Koenig

INTERPRET

Explain the statement "He could make a cat laugh" (line 4). What does that say about Lincoln's humor?

_____

_____

_____

_____

_____

_____

RETELL

Pause at line 21. List the different ways that Lincoln used humor.

_____

_____

_____

_____

_____

_____

_____

_____

_____

IDENTIFY

Underline the joke in this example of Lincoln's humor (lines 31–33).

It is puzzling how Lincoln could laugh, joke, and tell stories, despite his terrible burdens as president during the Civil War. Lincoln was the first and the best humorist ever to occupy the White House. A friend said, "He could make a cat laugh."

Lincoln called laughter "the joyous, beautiful, universal evergreen of life." For Lincoln laughter relieved life's pressures and soothed its disappointments. Both as a lawyer and as a politician, he used amusing stories to make important points clear to his listeners. Storytelling put people at ease or nudged
10 them from an unwanted topic or point of view. It also pleasantly brought an interview to a close and a visitor's welcome departure from the president's office.

Political opponents feared Lincoln's humorous jabs, which often destroyed their best arguments. Stephen A. Douglas, Lincoln's opponent in a Senate race, said, "Every one of his stories seems like a whack upon my back. . . . When he begins to tell a story, I feel that I am to be overmatched."

Lincoln's words got extra force from his facial expressions and gestures—a shrug of his shoulders, raised eyebrows, a
20 turned-down mouth, a comically twisted face—which made his audiences roar with laughter.

Here is a sampling of Lincoln's humor and the uses he made of it:

- As a young lawyer, Lincoln once defended a farmer who had been attacked by his neighbor's dog. To fend off the dog, the farmer had poked it with a pitchfork, wounding it. The dog's owner then took the case to court to recover damages. His lawyer argued that the farmer should have struck the dog with the handle end
30 of the pitchfork to avoid causing it serious harm. In the farmer's defense, Lincoln exclaimed that the dog should have avoided frightening the farmer by approaching him with its other end.

- As president, Lincoln was besieged with visitors seeking jobs and favors. One day while a visitor was pressing his demands, Lincoln's doctor entered the room. Lincoln, holding out his hands, asked him, "Doctor, what are those blotches?" "They're a mild smallpox," the doctor replied. "They're all over me," said Lincoln. "It's 40 contagious, I believe." "Very contagious," said the doctor as the visitor hastily departed. "There is one good thing about this," said Lincoln to his doctor after the caller had left. "I now have something I can give to everybody."

- Impatient with his Civil War generals, who were slow to engage their forces in battle, Lincoln began requiring frequent reports of their progress. An irritated general sent this telegram to the White House: "We have just captured six cows. What shall we do with them?" Lincoln replied, "Milk them."

EVALUATE

The writer of this article gives three examples of Lincoln's humor to support his **assertion** that Lincoln was a great humorist. Choose one example, and explain why you think it is, or isn't, funny.

Assertion Chart

An **assertion** is a statement or claim. Assertions can be supported by evidence, such as examples, facts, statistics, or quotations from experts. Complete the assertion chart below, after you read "Lincoln's Humor." Record each assertion in the left column. Then, list the evidence for each assertion in the right column. The first one has been done for you.

Assertion	Evidence
"Lincoln was the first and the best humorist ever to occupy the White House."	*". . . Lincoln could laugh, joke, and tell stories, despite his terrible burdens. . . ."* *"A friend said, 'He could make a cat laugh.'"*

Reading Check

1. What **assertion** about Lincoln does the writer make in the first paragraph?

   _____

   _____

2. How does the writer **support** his assertion that Lincoln's sense of humor helped him?

   _____

   _____

Test Practice

Circle the correct answer.

1. The information in this article supports the **assertion** that —

   A   Lincoln used humor to cope with the difficulties of being president
   B   Lincoln should have appeared more serious to the public
   C   Lincoln was the most popular president ever
   D   Lincoln worried about his health

2. What **evidence** from the article suggests that Lincoln would do well in a debate if he were a candidate today?

   F   Lincoln was handsome, so he would look good on television.
   G   Lincoln always seemed more intelligent than his opponents.
   H   The quotation by Stephen A. Douglas shows that Lincoln used humor effectively to defeat debating opponents.
   J   Lincoln's plain speaking appealed to people all over the country.

3. We can reasonably **assert** that this essay was written mainly to —

   A   persuade people to like Lincoln
   B   persuade people to laugh more
   C   describe Lincoln's sense of humor
   D   criticize Lincoln's character

4. The information in this essay supports the **assertion** that —

   F   Lincoln disliked the military
   G   Lincoln used humor and amusing stories throughout his career
   H   Lincoln did not get impatient during the Civil War
   J   Lincoln told funny stories only when he was a lawyer

5. The three samples of Lincoln's humor at the end of this article support the **assertion** that —

   A   Lincoln told jokes for no reason at all
   B   Lincoln used humor to cope with problems
   C   Lincoln used humor to hurt people
   D   Lincoln's humor went over the heads of most people

All Aboard with Thomas Garrett

Using Prior Knowledge

You may not yet know who Thomas Garrett is, but you probably know something about another person mentioned in the article you are about to read: Harriet Tubman. You also probably know something about the Underground Railroad, which they both helped keep running.

    In the chart below, fill in your **prior knowledge**—what you already know—about the Underground Railroad, Harriet Tubman, and Thomas Garrett. On the lines below the chart, make a prediction, based on your prior knowledge of the subjects, of what the **main idea** of this article will be. Don't worry if you don't yet know anything about one of these topics. You'll learn something about each of them when you read the article.

What I Know		
Underground Railroad	**Harriet Tubman**	**Thomas Garrett**

The main idea might be _____

_____

All Aboard with Thomas Garrett

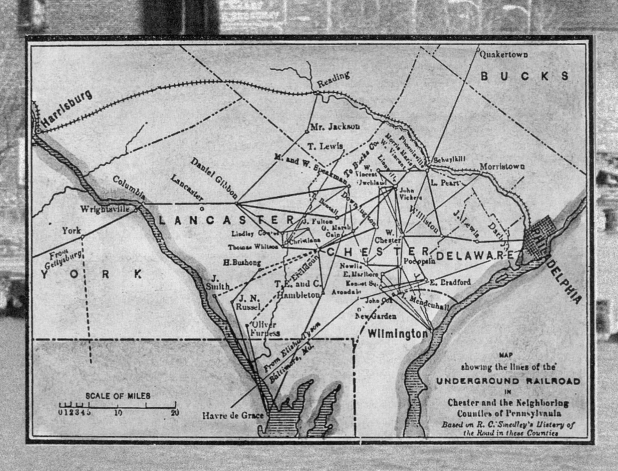

MAP
showing the lines of the
UNDERGROUND RAILROAD
IN
Chester and the Neighboring
Counties of Pennsylvania
Based on R. C. Smedley's History of
the Road in these Counties

Alice P. Miller

INTERPRET

Re-read lines 8–14. What
are the man and woman
doing? Underline the clues
in the text that tell you.

_____

_____

_____

_____

IDENTIFY

Circle the names of the two
people in the horse-drawn
carriage.

INFER

Why do you think Harriet
Tubman is dressed in
clothes borrowed from
Thomas Garrett's wife
(lines 18–19)?

_____

_____

_____

_____

_____

_____

_____

_____

WORDS TO OWN
prudent (pro͞o′dənt) *adj.:*
wise; sensible.

The elderly couple walked sedately down the stairs of the red
brick house, every detail of their costumes proclaiming their
respectability. The small lady was wearing an ankle-length gray
gown, a snowy-white lawn kerchief, and a pleated gray silk
bonnet, draped with a veil. The tall white-haired gentleman
wore the wide-brimmed beaver hat and the long black
waistcoat that was customary among Quakers.

When they reached the sidewalk, he assisted her into the
four-wheeled barouche[1] that stood at the curb. Then he
10 climbed into the barouche himself. The driver drove the horses
away at a leisurely pace. Not until they were beyond the city
limits did he allow the horses to prance along at a brisk pace
across the few miles that separated Wilmington, Delaware, from
the free state of Pennsylvania.

That tall white-haired gentleman was Thomas Garrett, a
white man who had for many years been breaking the law by
sheltering runaway slaves. And the little lady at his side was
runaway slave Harriet Tubman, clad in clothes donated by his
wife. On the preceding night Harriet had slept in a small room
20 secreted behind one wall of Garrett's shoe store, a room that
never remained unoccupied for very long. It was Harriet's first
visit to Garrett, but she would be returning many times in the
future.

Runaway slaves remained with Garrett for one night or two
or three until such time as Garrett considered it prudent to send
them along to the next station on the Underground Railroad.
He provided them with clothing and outfitted them with new
shoes from his shoe store. He fed them hearty meals and
dressed their wounds. He also forged passes for them so that
30 any slave stopped by a slave catcher would have evidence that
he or she was on a legitimate errand.

Some of the money he needed to cover the cost of his
hospitality came out of his own pocket, but he was not a rich
man. He could not have taken care of so many fugitives were it
not for donations made by fellow abolitionists in the North as

---

1. **barouche** (bə·ro͞osh′): type of horse-drawn carriage.

well as from supporters in foreign countries. There was never quite enough money, but no fugitive was ever turned away from his door. He would have gone without food himself before he would have refused food to a hungry slave.

40   Garrett, who was born in Upper Darby, Pennsylvania, in 1789, had been helping runaway slaves ever since 1822, when he rescued a young black woman who was trying to escape from her master. At that time he vowed to devote the rest of his life to helping fugitives, and he remained faithful to that vow.

Of all the stations on the Underground Railroad his was probably the most efficiently run and the one most frequently used. The fact that Wilmington was so close to Pennsylvania made it the most <u>hazardous</u> stop on the route. Slave catchers prowled the streets of Wilmington, on the alert for any
50   indication that a black person might be a runaway. They kept a sharp eye on all roads leading north from Wilmington.

For many years Garrett managed to get away with his illegal activities because he was a clever man and knew ways to avoid detection by the slave catchers. Sometimes he disguised a slave, as he had done with Harriet. Sometimes he dressed a man in a woman's clothing or a woman in a man's clothing or showed a young person how to appear like one bent over with age. Another reason for his success was that he had many friends who admired what he was doing and who could be trusted to
60   help him. They might, for example, conceal slaves under a wagonload of vegetables or in a secret compartment in a wagon.

The slave catchers were aware of what he was doing, but they had a hard time finding the kind of evidence that would stand up in court. At last, in 1848, he was sued by two Maryland slave owners who hoped to bring a stop to his activities by ruining him financially.

The suit was brought into the federal circuit court of New Castle under a 1793 federal law that allowed slave owners to
70   recover penalties from any person who harbored a runaway slave. The case was heard by Willard Hall, United States District

IDENTIFY

Underline facts you learned about Thomas Garrett in lines 32–44.

INTERPRET

Put into your own words the **main idea** of lines 52–62. Underline two **details** that support this main idea.

WORDS TO OWN
hazardous (hazʹər·dəs) *adj.*: dangerous; risky.

EVALUATE

Pause at line 75. Do you think the jurors were right to convict Thomas Garrett because he broke the law, or should they have let him go because he was doing the right thing? Give reasons for your response.

INTERPRET

What do lines 93–100 tell you about Thomas Garrett's **character**?

WORDS TO OWN
diligence (dil'ə·jəns) *n.:* steady effort.

Judge, and by Roger B. Taney, Chief Justice of the United States Supreme Court. Bringing in a verdict in favor of the slave owners, the jurors decided that the slave owners were entitled to $5,400 in fines.

Garrett didn't have anywhere near that much money, but he stood up and addressed the court and the spectators in these words:

"I have assisted fourteen hundred slaves in the past twenty-
80 five years on their way to the North. I now consider this penalty imposed upon me as a license for the remainder of my life. I am now past sixty and have not a dollar to my name, but be that as it may, if anyone knows of a poor slave who needs shelter and a breakfast, send him to me, as I now publicly pledge myself to double my diligence and never neglect an opportunity to assist a slave to obtain freedom, so help me God!"

As he continued to speak for more than an hour, some of the spectators hissed while others cheered. When he finished,
90 one juror leaped across the benches and pumped Garrett's hand. With tears in his eyes, he said, "I beg your forgiveness, Mr. Garrett."

After the trial Garrett's furniture was auctioned off to help pay the heavy fine. But he managed to borrow money from friends and eventually repaid those loans, rebuilt his business, and became prosperous. Meanwhile he went on sheltering slaves for many more years. By the time President Lincoln issued the Emancipation Proclamation[2] in 1863, Garrett's records showed that he had sheltered more than 2,700
100 runaways.

During those years he had many encounters with Harriet Tubman, as she kept returning to the South and coming back north with bands of slaves. Much of what we know about Harriet today is based on letters that he sent to her or wrote about her. A portion of one of those letters reads thus:

---

2. **Emancipation Proclamation:** presidential order abolishing slavery in the South.

"I may begin by saying, living as I have in a slave State, and the laws being very severe where any proof could be made of anyone aiding slaves on their way to freedom, I have not felt at liberty to keep any written word of Harriet's labors
110 as I otherwise could, and now would be glad to do; for in truth I never met with any person, of any color, who had more confidence in the voice of God, as spoken direct to her soul. . . . She felt no more fear of being arrested by her former master, or any other person, when in his immediate neighborhood, than she did in the State of New York or Canada, for she said she ventured only where God sent her, and her faith in the Supreme Power truly was great."

In April, 1870, the black people of Wilmington held a huge celebration upon the passage of the fifteenth amendment to the
120 Constitution of the United States. That amendment provided that the right of citizens to vote should not be denied or abridged by the United States or by any state on account of race, color, or previous condition of servitude.
Jubilant blacks drew Garrett through the streets in an open carriage on one side of which were inscribed the words "Our Moses."

INFER

Based on Thomas Garrett's letter to Harriet Tubman (lines 106–117), what do you think their relationship was like?

_____

_____

_____

INTERPRET

What do you think is the **main idea** of "All Aboard with Thomas Garrett"?

_____

_____

_____

_____

_____

_____

_____

_____

_____

_____

_____

WORDS TO OWN
servitude (sur′və·tood′) *n.*: condition of being under another person's control.
jubilant (joo′bə·lənt) *adj.*: joyful.

Get the Idea

Articles can have more than one **main idea.** You have probably noticed several in "All Aboard with Thomas Garrett." In the graphic organizer below, write what you think is the main idea of "All Aboard with Thomas Garrett." Then, fill in details that support that idea. Is this main idea the same one you predicted on page 196? If so, give yourself an extra pat on the back.

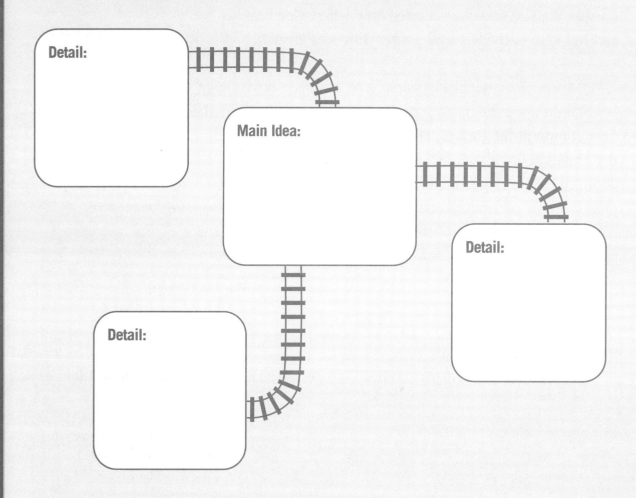

Detail:

Main Idea:

Detail:

Detail:

Reading Check

1. In what ways did Thomas Garrett help people fleeing slavery?

_____

2. Why was Thomas Garrett brought to trial?

_____

3. Why did African Americans call Thomas Garrett "Our Moses"?

_____

_____

Test Practice

Circle the correct answer.

1. All of these statements about Thomas Garrett are true *except* —

A he sheltered more than 2,700 runaways

B he was helped in his work by many friends

C he refused to pay fines levied against him in court

D he encountered Harriet Tubman on many occasions

2. According to the article, it was important that Garrett's stop on the Underground Railroad be efficient and well run because —

F slave catchers in Wilmington were particularly diligent

G Garrett didn't trust many of his friends

H Harriet Tubman would criticize the way Garrett ran his stop

J Garrett was a very rich man

3. Based on Garrett's letter about Harriet Tubman, you can **infer** that Garrett —

A was happy he couldn't write freely about Tubman's deeds

B admired Tubman's faith in God

C could not comprehend why Tubman worked so tirelessly

D did not think Tubman would be arrested in her lifetime

4. What is the **main idea** of this article?

F Harriet Tubman and Thomas Garrett were masters of disguise.

G Thomas Garrett once convinced a juror that he should not be fined.

H Thomas Garrett did all he could to help shelter runaways.

J Thomas Garrett loved riding the railroad.

Suit Helps Girl Enjoy Daylight

Features of Newspapers

Newspapers are written to share information with the general public, so they are designed to make that information easy to find. Here are some tips to help you find what you are looking for in a newspaper.

- Most newspapers are divided into **sections** for world and national news, local news, sports, arts and entertainment, business, and other subjects. Try to decide which section is most likely to have the information you want.

- The **headlines,** or titles, of news stories come in different sizes. The more important the story, the larger the headline. A good headline is attention-getting and clever.

- The **byline** is the name of the reporter who wrote the article. In this book, the headline and byline are on a separate page, but in a newspaper, they appear right above the text of the article.

- The **dateline** includes the name of the place where the reporter got the news, which is usually the same place where the story is happening. The dateline also often includes the date the reporter filed the story.

- The most important information is in the **lead,** the beginning of the article. In most news articles, the further you read, the less important the information. That way, the article can be cut from the bottom if it has to be shortened to make room for late-breaking news. News stories usually answer the *5W-How?* questions—*who? what? where? when? why? how?*—and many of these answers can be found in the lead.

Fill in which **section** *of the newspaper you think will have a story on —*

a playoff game _____

the presidential election _____

a school board meeting _____

movie listings _____

Suit Helps Girl Enjoy Daylight

Lise Fisher

IDENTIFY

Circle the **dateline** of this story. What does it tell you?

_____

_____

_____

IDENTIFY

What is the **lead** of this story? Underline the part of the text where you find out.

_____

_____

_____

_____

_____

_____

RETELL

Pause at line 30. List some of the things Logan could not do before she got her suit.

_____

_____

_____

_____

_____

_____

KEYSTONE HEIGHTS, Fla.—Tinted goggles and grayish green fabric covered the three-year-old's face while blocking sunlight from Saturday morning's hazy sky. The suit, however, couldn't hide her enthusiasm.

While other families record events like their children's first steps and words, Steve and Michele Williams will be marking down this day for their daughter, Logan. It was her first play day in the sunlight protected in a "Cool Suit" that blocks the sun's rays, and the event went better than the Williamses could 10 have imagined.

"It just opens up a whole lot of doors," said Logan's father. "The burden is off," a tearful Michele Williams said.

Doctors determined Logan had a rare genetic[1] disease— xeroderma pigmentosum, or XP, as it is known—when she was eighteen months old. For the fewer than one thousand XP patients worldwide, exposure to ultraviolet radiation[2] can lead to deadly skin cancers. The disease has no known cure.

Since the diagnosis, Logan has lived in a world of tinted windows and terror caused by the "bad light."

20 Light streaming in from a front door and bouncing off their refrigerator frightens the family. Getting Logan to a doctor's appointment has involved padding Logan with a helmet and clothes and covering the car's windows with plastic bags and blankets. She hasn't seen stores, and she marvels that they stock more than one box of cereal and a few toys. Barbara Pellechio, a teacher at Keystone Heights's McRae Elementary School, visits the girl two to three times a week at night because that's when Logan is awake. Like any young child, Logan is afraid of the dark even though it has been the only 30 time she can go outside and play.

The clothing is based on technology from NASA[3] and covers every inch of the little girl with tightly woven material to keep out the sun. Gloves outfitted with rough material for gripping hide her hands. An oversized shirt and pants that look and feel

---

1. **genetic** (jə·net′ik): passed on as a characteristic by one's parents.
2. **ultraviolet radiation:** invisible energy waves that are present in sunlight.
3. **NASA:** National Aeronautics and Space Administration, the U.S. government agency that conducts research in space.

like a soft sweat suit cinch at her wrists and ankles. A hood secured with goggles conceals her freckled face.

Everything Logan did Saturday was a milestone for Logan's parents and for more than twenty of the family's friends and relatives. They kept pulling up in cars, in trucks, and even in

40 the Keystone Heights fire engine.

Logan clutched purple and yellow flowers her parents bought and planted just for this day. She bounced on a trampoline with friends. Her hands found and clutched a lizard.

"This is probably the most special day of my life," said Alison Broadway, 33. The family friend was holding Logan when the girl spotted a butterfly. "I was holding her and she started squirming and screaming. . . . When they say miracles don't happen, they're wrong because one happened here today," said Broadway.

EVALUATE

The article says that Logan's suit is based on NASA technology, but a family friend calls the suit a miracle. Do you think the suit is a miracle or a technological advance? Explain your answer.

Newspaper Features Chart

Being able to recognize the features of a newspaper article helps you locate information and retell what you have read. Fill out the chart below with information from "Suit Helps Girl Enjoy Daylight."

Headline	
Byline	
Dateline	
Summary of Lead	

5W-How? Questions

Who?

What?

When?

Where?

Why?

How?

Reading Check

1. Why can't Logan go out in the sun?

_____

_____

2. When does Logan's teacher visit her? Why does she visit her at that time?

_____

_____

3. Describe Logan's "Cool Suit."

_____

_____

Test Practice

Circle the correct answer.

1. The **byline** tells you —

  A the most important information
  B who wrote the article
  C who made the "Cool Suit"
  D what the story is about

2. You could say that the "Cool Suit" is like a spacesuit because —

  F you can float when you wear it
  G it protects the person wearing it from a deadly environment
  H you need weeks of training before you can wear it
  J you have to wear an air tank with it

3. Which statement best sums up the point of the news story?

  A Logan has lived in fear of the sun.
  B Technology from NASA was used to make the "Cool Suit."
  C The "Cool Suit" is a miracle for Logan.
  D No cure has been found for XP.

4. In which section of the newspaper would you be *most* likely to find this article?

  F Health
  G Sports
  H Entertainment
  J World News

Separate but Never Equal

Compare and Contrast

People compare and contrast experiences to make sense of the world. We **compare** by noting ways in which things are similar, and we **contrast** by noting how they are different. The next time you're with your friends, notice how often they compare and contrast.

"José's party was like a rock concert."

"It was more like a zoo."

"Jesse's party was more fun."

"But José had better food."

Use the graphic organizer below to compare and contrast your school with another school you have visited, read about, or seen on TV or in the movies.

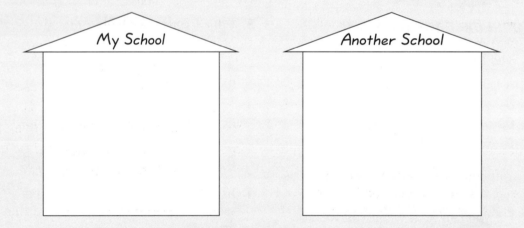

The article that follows is about segregation in the United States before 1954. Until then, segregation was legal as long as "separate but equal" facilities were provided for whites and African Americans. To help us understand what segregation was like, the writer compares life for blacks and for whites under segregation.

Every American should know about the two cases mentioned in this article: *Plessy* v. *Ferguson* and *Brown* v. *Board of Education of Topeka, Kansas.*

Separate
but Never Equal

Mara Rockliff

"separate but equal" facilities for blacks and whites was lawful.

Brown v. *Board of Education of Topeka, Kansas* is the name of a suit brought in 1951 by Oliver Brown on behalf of his daughter Linda. The Browns lived in Topeka, Kansas, where the schools were segregated, and Linda attended an all-black elementary school. Brown sued the Topeka Board of Education and lost the case.

Some months later Brown and the NAACP (National Association for the Advancement of Colored People) appealed to the U.S. Supreme Court, which combined their case with other school segregation cases from Virginia, South Carolina, and Delaware. In 1954, the Court ruled in favor of Brown. *Brown* v. *Board of Education* was one of the most important cases brought before the Supreme Court in the twentieth century.

Background

Legal cases are given names that usually indicate who is arguing against whom. *Plessy* v. *Ferguson* is the name of a case that involved someone named Plessy arguing against someone named Ferguson. The *v.* in the name stands for *versus,* a word from Latin that means "against." (It's like *vs.* in *Mets vs. Yankees* or *San Diego vs. Atlanta.*)

Homer Plessy was an African American man who, in 1892, was forced to leave a train car that was reserved for whites. In a Louisiana court he challenged the state law requiring separate train cars for blacks and whites. Ferguson was John H. Ferguson, the judge who heard the case and decided against Plessy. The case eventually reached the U.S. Supreme Court. There Plessy argued that the Louisiana law violated the U.S. Constitution.

Plessy lost his case in the Supreme Court: The majority held that requiring

INFER

Notice how John Lewis is described in line 10. In what way do you think his adult life was affected by his experiences as a boy?

_____

_____

_____

IDENTIFY

Underline what the Supreme Court allowed in its ruling in _Plessy_ v. _Ferguson._

_____

_____

COMPARE AND CONTRAST

When African Americans and whites rode buses in the 1940s, how were their experiences the same, and how were they different (lines 18–23)?

_____

_____

_____

_____

_____

_____

_____

When I was a boy, I would go downtown . . . , and I'd see the signs saying "White" and "Colored" on the water fountains. There'd be a beautiful, shining water fountain in one corner of the store marked "White," and in another corner was just a little spigot marked "Colored." I saw the signs saying "White Men," "Colored Men," and "White Women," "Colored Women." And at the theater we had to go upstairs to go to a movie. You bought your ticket at the same window that the white people did, but they could sit downstairs, and you had to go upstairs.

10   _—U.S. Congressman and civil rights leader John Lewis_

In 1896, in a famous case known as _Plessy_ v. _Ferguson,_ the U.S. Supreme Court ruled that states could enact laws separating people by skin color as long as the facilities for African Americans were equivalent to those for whites. This "separate but equal" decision stood for more than half a century, supporting a system of racial segregation in states throughout the South.

In reality, separate was never equal. Take buses, for example. The fare was the same for all passengers, regardless
20   of race. But if the "white section" at the front of the bus filled up, the invisible line separating it from the "colored section" simply moved back. Black people had to stand up so that white people could sit.

Consider shopping. An African American woman could buy the same dress as a white woman, but she wasn't allowed to try it on in the store—and if she found that it didn't fit, she couldn't return it. Or restaurants. Some white-owned restaurants filled orders for blacks only at their takeout window. Others wouldn't serve them at all.
30   Perhaps most separate, and most unequal, were the public schools. If you attended a "colored school," you might walk eight miles to school every morning, while buses full of white children drove past on their way to schools closer by. The schools attended by white children would be modern and well maintained, while yours would be old and run-down. White

students would have up-to-date books and materials, while you might be forced to share a twenty-year-old textbook with three other students.

In 1949, several African American parents sued their school
40 district over the inequalities between the local white elementary school and the school their children were forced to attend. Two years earlier the district had built a brand-new school for white students while leaving the black students' school in disrepair. Unlike the all-black school, the all-white school had an auditorium, a kindergarten, a part-time music teacher, a well-equipped playground, and a lunch program. The all-white school had a teacher and a separate room for each grade; the all-black school had only two teachers and two classrooms for all eight grades.

50 Finally, in 1954, the U.S. Supreme Court ruled in *Brown* v. *Board of Education* that segregated schools were by their very nature unequal. No longer would the highest court in the land support the myth of *Plessy* v. *Ferguson.* Separate could never be equal.

INFER

Re-read lines 30–49. Pretend you are an African American student in 1949, and describe your school day.

EVALUATE

Circle the Supreme Court ruling on *Brown* v. *Board of Education.* In your opinion, what makes this a landmark decision?

Comparison Chart

In the chart below, list characteristics of the education of African American children in 1949 as opposed to those of white children, as described in "Separate but Never Equal." In the middle part of the chart, list characteristics of education common to both white and black children in 1949. On the left and right parts of the chart, list characteristics unique to each category.

Education for Black Children	BOTH	Education for White Children

Reading Check

1. In the opening quote, John Lewis makes three **comparisons.** What are they?

_____

_____

2. Why did some African American parents sue their school district in 1949?

_____

_____

3. How long after 1949 did it take for the Supreme Court to rule that separate schools were unequal?

_____

_____

Test Practice

Circle the correct answer.

1. In *Brown* v. *Board of Education* the Supreme Court ruled that segregated schools are —

A similar

B legal

C unequal

D illegal

2. "Separate but Never Equal" works as a **title** for this article because the article —

F shows why the *Plessy* v. *Ferguson* ruling was unfair

G examines the conditions in public schools

H shows that things change over time

J justifies segregation

3. To learn more about the conditions described in this essay, you should —

A ask your principal

B talk to your history teacher

C read about conditions in northern schools

D study a map of the South

4. In which of these situations would reading a **compare-and-contrast** article be most helpful?

F You need to find out how life in China today differs from life in the United States.

G You need to do research on *Brown* v. *Board of Education*.

H You need to find out how many books Mildred Taylor has written.

J You want to learn how the Supreme Court works.

Wartime Mistakes, Peacetime Apologies

Taking Logical Notes

Research. The word alone is enough to make some people squirm and groan. But if you know how to take logical notes, doing research is no problem.

Get a stack of index cards, and follow these steps:

1. Read through the selection once to find the main ideas.
2. Make a card for each main idea.
3. Take notes in your own words, or use quotation marks around the author's words.

To get you started, there are two sample note cards below for lines 1–20 in "Wartime Mistakes, Peacetime Apologies." As you read the article, fill in the blanks on the cards. Then, make cards of your own for the rest of the article.

Yoshiko Imamoto

• On _____ (when?), FBI arrested her with no warning.

• 24-year U.S. resident

• had broken no laws

• life changed by _____ (what?)

• issued by _____ (who?)

Pearl Harbor

• 12/7/1941

• Japan attacked U.S.

• Japanese Americans felt _____ (how?).

• They were treated _____

_____ (how? by whom?).

Wartime Mistakes, Peacetime Apologies

Nancy Day

IDENTIFY

Circle the name of the president who issued Executive Order 9066. Underline the event that prompted the creation of the order.

EVALUATE

Why do you think that the United States felt Executive Order 9066 was necessary? Do you think imprisoning Japanese American citizens helped the war effort? Explain.

_____

_____

_____

_____

_____

IDENTIFY

Pause at line 26. Underline the effects of Executive Order 9066 on Japanese Americans after the war.

_____

_____

_____

IDENTIFY

Circle the full name of the organization that is abbreviated CWRIC. Underline the reasons that the CWRIC found Executive Order 9066 unjustified (lines 32–34).

On March 13, 1942, Yoshiko Imamoto opened her door to face three FBI agents. They let her pack a nightgown and a Bible, then took her to jail while they "checked into a few things." Imamoto had lived in America for twenty-four years. She was a teacher and had done nothing wrong. But a month earlier, President Franklin D. Roosevelt had issued Executive Order 9066, which drastically changed the lives of Imamoto and more than 120,000 other people of Japanese ancestry living in the United States.

10   When Japan bombed Pearl Harbor on December 7, 1941, Japanese Americans were caught in the middle. They felt like Americans but looked like the enemy. Neighbors and co-workers eyed them suspiciously. Then Executive Order 9066, issued on February 19, 1942, authorized the exclusion of "any or all persons" from any areas the military chose. The word "Japanese" was never used, but the order was designed to allow the military to force Japanese Americans living near the coast to leave their homes for the duration of the war. Some were allowed to move inland, but most, like Yoshiko Imamoto,
20 were herded into prisonlike camps.

     After the war, Japanese Americans tried to start over. They had lost their jobs, their property, and their pride. Some used the Japanese American Evacuation Claims Act of 1948 to get compensation[1] for property they had lost. But it was not until the late 1960s that cries for redress—compensation for all they had suffered—began to emerge.

     In 1976, Executive Order 9066 was officially ended by President Gerald Ford. Four years later, President Jimmy Carter signed a bill that created the Commission on Wartime
30 Relocation and Internment of Civilians (CWRIC) to investigate the relocation of Japanese Americans. The CWRIC concluded that Executive Order 9066 was "not justified by military necessity" but was the result of "race prejudice, war hysteria, and a failure of political leadership." In 1983, the commission recommended to Congress that each surviving Japanese

---

1. **compensation:** payment given to make up for a loss or injury.

American evacuee be given a payment of twenty thousand dollars and an apology.

A bill to authorize the payments was introduced in the House of Representatives in 1983 but met resistance. Intensive
40 lobbying[2] by Japanese Americans was met by arguments that the government had acted legally and appropriately at the time.

Meanwhile, three men who had long since served their jail sentences for refusing to comply with curfew[3] or relocation orders filed suit[4] to challenge the government's actions. The court ruled that the government had had no legal basis for detaining Japanese Americans.

The rulings increased pressure to provide redress. In 1988, Congress approved the final version of the redress bill, which became known as the Civil Liberties Act. It was signed by
50 President Ronald Reagan on August 10, 1988. Two years later, Congress funded the payments.

In 1990, at the age of ninety-three, Yoshiko Imamoto opened her door not to FBI agents, but to a small brown envelope containing a check for twenty thousand dollars and an apology from President George Bush. It had taken almost fifty years and the actions of four presidents, but the government had made redress and apologized for its mistakes.

---

2. lobbying: activity aimed at influencing public officials.
3. curfew (kʉr′fyo͞o′): Shortly before the relocation began, the head of the Western Defense Command, Lt. Gen. John DeWitt, set a curfew. Between 8:00 P.M. and 6:00 A.M. each day, "all persons of Japanese ancestry" had to remain indoors, off the streets.
4. filed suit: went to court in an attempt to recover something.

Time Line

A **time line** is a kind of chart that shows events in time order. In a time line, main events are listed from the beginning to the end. Fill out this time line with events from "Wartime Mistakes, Peacetime Apologies."

Time line

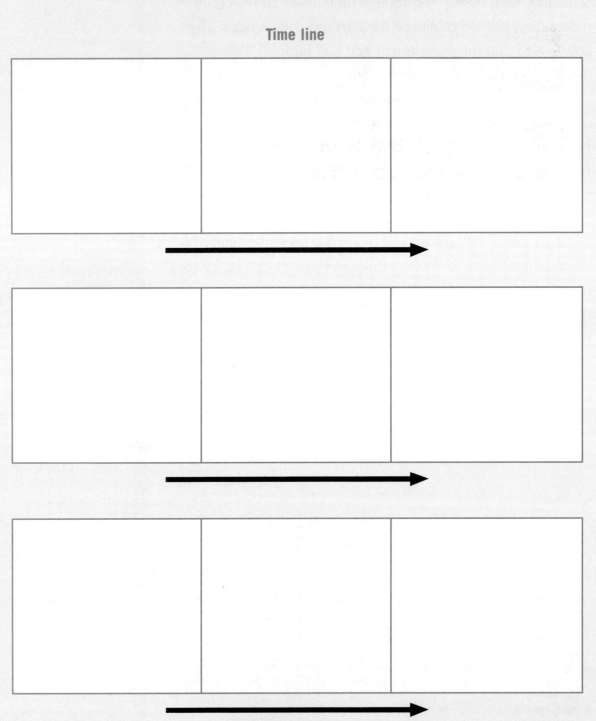

Reading Check

Use your note cards to answer these questions. Revise your note cards if they don't have enough information.

1. What powers did Executive Order 9066 give the military?

_____

2. What did the government finally do for interned Japanese Americans?

_____

_____

Test Practice

Circle the correct answer.

1. From information in the article, you can conclude that Yoshiko Imamoto came to the United States when she was —

A a young woman
B a mother with a young child
C a baby
D a child

2. Which sentence best **summarizes** Executive Order 9066?

F Military commanders must follow the instructions given by the secretary of war.
G When an area of any size is put under military control, all civilians in that area must be evacuated.
H The military may set aside certain areas and decide who enters, stays, or leaves those areas.
J Japanese Americans must leave California.

3. What is the **tone** of the letter the government sent with the payments?

A Friendly
B Angry
C Worried
D Apologetic

4. Discussion of a redress bill caused **conflict** between —

F Japanese Americans and people who felt that the government had done nothing wrong.
G Japanese American members of Congress and other elected officials
H people who had been evacuated and veterans of World War II
J Congress and the Supreme Court

5. Which of the following is a **main idea** that could be a heading on a note card?

A Yoshiko Imamoto arrested
B Japan attacked United States
C Compensation ordered
D Pearl Harbor

Getting Leftovers Back on the Table

Making Assertions

An **assertion** is a statement or claim. We make assertions all the time—
whenever we say something about someone or something.

"Selena is a good athlete."

"Joe is a nice guy."

An assertion is, or always should be, supported by evidence. Selena's
stellar performance on the field is evidence of her athletic ability. The
friendly way Joe treats people is evidence of his niceness.

When you make an assertion about a text, it should be supported by
evidence from the text. You should also be able to cite that evidence. Making
assertions about a text is easy if you follow these steps:

- Think about the facts in the text.
- Think about what those facts mean.
- Use those facts—evidence—to make an assertion, or statement, about
  the text.
- Check to make sure the evidence really supports your assumption.

Use the map below to make an assertion about your community. Then, in
the street below the park, support your assertion with evidence. An assertion
might be *Our town is in need of repairs.* Your evidence might be *The park
benches are broken. Many streetlights don't work. There are a lot of potholes.*
Now you try it.

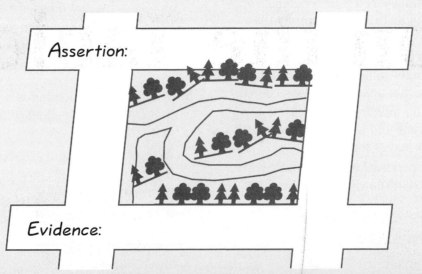

Assertion:

Evidence:

Getting Leftovers Back on the Table

Mara Rockliff

IDENTIFY

How much food goes to waste in the United States? Underline where you find the answer.

INTERPRET

Why do you think David succeeded in getting the food donated to charities when adults with the same idea did not?

When you're standing in line in the school cafeteria, do you ever wonder what happens to all the food that doesn't get served? Every day, giant bins behind the cafeterias—and supermarkets, restaurants, and bakeries—fill up with discarded food. As much as 20 percent of the food produced in the United States goes to waste. Yet every night millions of Americans go to sleep hungry.

Too big a problem for one kid to tackle? A sixth-grader named David Levitt didn't think so. He started small, in the
10 halls of his own Florida middle school. By the time he was in his first year of high school, his crusade against hunger had taken him all the way to the White House.

Getting Started

David's journey began the day he noticed how much food was thrown out in his school cafeteria. He stopped the principal in the hallway and asked why the school couldn't donate leftover lunches to local homeless shelters and soup kitchens.

The principal told him that several parents had had the same idea. School rules prohibited serving the same food twice,
20 however, so uneaten lunches had to be thrown away.

Overcoming Odds

David wasn't discouraged. He did research on a group in Kentucky that picked up leftovers from restaurants and donated them to charities. He used what he learned to draw up a plan for his own program. Then he presented it at a meeting of the county school board. The board approved David's plan—not just for his school, but for all ninety-two schools in the county. "It just took a kid to make them see this matters," David says.

Solving New Problems

30 The battle wasn't over yet. Conditions set by the state department of health had to be met. For example, donated food had to be packed in special containers—which the schools didn't have the money to buy. So David wrote to manufacturers and asked for donations. Soon cases of the containers arrived

at his doorstep, and David, now in seventh grade, was able to make his first delivery to a local food bank. "That," he says, "was satisfaction."

Success at Last

David went on to enlist the support of restaurants,
40 supermarkets, and caterers. After two years his program had brought a quarter of a million pounds of food to hungry people in his area. By the time he started high school, David and his older sister were at work on a proposal to be presented to their state legislature. Under the plan similar programs would be set up to bring leftover food to hungry people all over Florida.

That spring, David went to Washington, D.C., to receive an award for his efforts. As the First Lady presented him with his medal, he asked her, "What do you do with the White House leftovers?"

IDENTIFY

How did David solve the problem concerning special containers? Circle where you find the answer.

EVALUATE

David's success shows that teens can make a difference. Do you have ideas that might help your community? Write down one or more examples.

Assertion Web

After you finish reading the article "Getting Leftovers Back on the Table," you can make assertions about it. To make an assertion, think about what you learned from the essay. Ask yourself, *What statement or claim can I make about the information I read? Is there evidence in the essay to support this assertion?* Then, complete the graphic organizer below. Make an assertion, and support it with citations—quotations or mentions—of evidence from the essay.

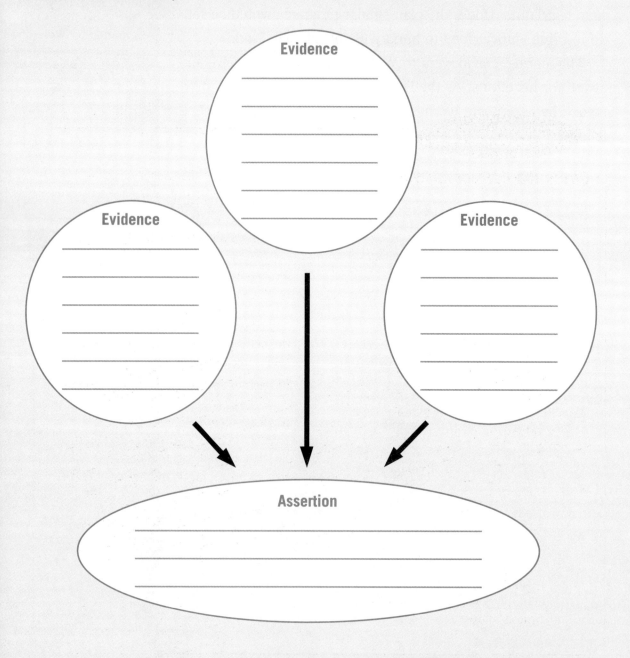

Evidence

Evidence

Evidence

Assertion

Reading Check

1. What plan did David present to the school board?

_____

_____

2. Describe two problems David faced in putting his plan into effect.

_____

_____

Test Practice

Circle the correct answer.

1. The information in this article supports the **assertion** that —

A it is impossible to solve the problem of hunger

B one person can make a big difference

C it is difficult to persuade a school board to take action

D researching other programs won't help you plan your own

2. Which of the following **facts** is *not* mentioned in the article?

F Twenty percent of food produced in the United States goes to waste.

G Millions of Americans go to sleep hungry.

H The Florida state health department has established rules for donating food.

J In some countries, hunger is an even bigger problem than in the United States.

3. We can reasonably **assert** that —

A David Levitt isn't easily discouraged

B things always go easy for David Levitt

C David Levitt is popular at school

D David Levitt gets good grades

4. After David's plan was approved by the school board, he did all of the following things *except* —

F persuade manufacturers to donate containers

G learn how to donate food in accordance with the state health department's guidelines

H ask restaurants and supermarkets for help

J send a proposal to Congress

One Child's Labor of Love

Evaluating Evidence

"Hey, our new basketball coach is great!" exclaims Tam.

"How do you know?" you ask.

"I just know. Take my word for it."

Tam has drawn a conclusion (our new coach is great!), and you want to know how he has reached his conclusion. By asking your question, you're trying to decide two things: First, does Tam have enough information to form a reliable conclusion? Second, does Tam have evidence to support his conclusion? Here's Tam's evidence: "I just know." This reply gives no evidence at all. Tam just says, "Take my word for it."

Since Tam's evidence doesn't convince you, you keep digging. "Not good enough, Tam. Tell me more."

"Her teams have won almost all of their games for the last five years."

That is certainly adequate and appropriate evidence for deciding whether a coach is good, but does a winning average automatically make a great coach?

"She showed me how to fix a problem I've been having with my jump shot. I've been struggling with that shot for a year, but she knew what I was doing wrong just from watching me play once."

This is certainly reliable evidence. It shows that the coach is knowledgeable.

Judging evidence is not hard. **Inappropriate evidence** makes you think, "What does that have to do with anything?" If you have to trust the person instead of relying on facts, it's **inadequate evidence.** Evidence is adequate when you've been given enough information to draw your own conclusion. What do you think? Is she a great coach or not?

Distinguishing Between Fact and Opinion

Appropriate evidence is based on facts. **Facts** are pieces of information that can be proved true. In the discussion about the coach, Tam cites facts about the coach's winning average. In contrast, **opinions** are personal beliefs or attitudes. Tam states one of those, "I just know" (definitely inappropriate evidence). A **valid opinion** is a belief or judgment supported by facts. Valid opinions can provide strong support for a conclusion. Be on the lookout for facts and valid opinions in "One Child's Labor of Love."

One Child's Labor of Love

THANK YOU FREE THE CHILDREN.

FROM
60 Minutes

THANK YOU
FREE THE
CHILDREN.

IDENTIFY

What was Craig Kielburger shocked to learn about slavery (lines 11–18)?

IDENTIFY

Underline the **facts** about Iqbal Masih that led Craig to start Free the Children (lines 19–28).

CBS, NEW YORK—Tuesday, October 5, 1999, 6:14 P.M.—When *60 Minutes* correspondent Ed Bradley first met Craig Kielburger three years ago, the 13-year-old possessed a passionate intolerance for child labor and slavery.

Now 16, Craig has met with some of the most important political and religious leaders of his time. And last year, he joined the ranks of John F. Kennedy, Harry Truman, Elie Wiesel, and Desmond Tutu as he took home the prestigious[1] Franklin and Eleanor Roosevelt Medal of Freedom. Bradley recently
10 revisited Craig to track his progress.

To understand how a teenager from Toronto became the inspiration for a 5,000-member organization called Free the Children, with chapters in 25 countries, consider what Craig had to say at age 13: "Basically, we're told slavery [was] abolished," Craig explained. "But it was really shocking, because . . . I was just reading through the different research that I got, and you find the worst type of slavery still exists today—slavery of children."

When Craig was age 12, he read a newspaper article about
20 a boy his age in Pakistan, Iqbal Masih. Iqbal's parents, like so many others, had offered their son's labor at age 4 in exchange for a small loan. Iqbal spent the next six years chained to a rug loom, working 12-hour days for pennies, until he finally escaped and joined a crusade against child labor. But after Iqbal won worldwide recognition, his life was cut short when, at age 12, he was shot dead in the streets of his village. No one has been convicted of the murder, and Craig vowed to keep his cause alive. . . .

Craig started a group called Free the Children. The board of
30 directors meet Saturdays in Craig's den, which has become the command center. They are in daily contact, by phone or fax, with a host of international human rights groups.

Having always done his homework to keep up on the issue, Craig soon felt that homework isn't enough. He had to meet the children he was trying to help. . . . This prompted him to take a

---

1. **prestigious** (pres·tij′əs): much admired and sought after.

trip to Asia—a trip his parents were wholeheartedly against. . . .
Craig's parents eventually found his cause so convincing that
they . . . bought his plane ticket to travel halfway around the
world. Chaperoned at each stop by local human rights advocates[2]
40 and armed with a video camera, Craig went from Bangladesh
to Thailand, and then to India, Nepal, and Pakistan.

"The perception that I had was that child labor is all in
the deep, dark back alleys, [where] no one can see it, beyond
public scrutiny.[3] But the truth is, it's practiced in the open,"
Craig says. . . .

"One shop that I went into, I met one 8-year-old girl . . .
[who] was just pulling apart syringes and needles, piece by
piece, and putting them in buckets for their plastics. She wore
no gloves, literally had no shoes. . . . All she was doing was
50 squatting on the ground, surrounded by a pile of needles. They
were from hospitals, from the street, from the garbage. We
asked her, 'Don't you worry about AIDS and other diseases like
that?' We got no response. She didn't know what they were." . . .

Craig spends a great deal of his time on the road, often
alone. He is part of an individualized program that allows him
to travel and keep up with his class work. . . . "I plan on going
all the way through my Ph.D., so I'm going to be in school
till I'm 40 or something," Craig says. "I hope to . . . study
international conflict mediation.[4] I've had the chance to travel
60 to Bosnia quite a bit . . . and areas of armed conflict . . . to
see what war does. I want to be involved in helping stop wars
before they begin." . . .

Craig has met his share of political leaders. . . . "It's great
meeting with them. . . . They're all incredibly interesting
people. I enjoyed meeting all of them, but they're still not
the people who impress me the most." . . .

So who does impress this teenager?

---

2. **advocates** (ad′və·kits): supporters; defenders.
3. **scrutiny** (skroot′'n·ē): close examination or study.
4. **mediation** (mē′dē·ā′shən): attempt to settle disputes by stepping in and trying
   to help.

INFER

Why might Craig's parents disapprove of his trip to Asia?

INTERPRET

The article quotes Craig as saying that child slavery is practiced in the open (line 44). Is this a **fact** or a **valid opinion**? Why?

INFER

Why do you think Craig is not so impressed by the world's political leaders?

EVALUATE

Craig suggests that if enslaved children were put in positions of power, the world would be a different place. What do you think?

"In Thailand, there was a young street girl, [to whom] I handed an orange. And she automatically took the orange,

70 and she peeled it, and she broke it, and she shared it with her friends," Craig says. "Or a child I saw in India. He was crippled, so his friends were carrying him from place to place so he wouldn't be left behind. And to this day I'm convinced that if you took these children and put them in those positions of power, we would see this world truly be a different place."

Evidence Chart

Writers of informational material make many **assertions**—statements or claims. They usually back their claims up with **evidence.** Sometimes, though, they have the evidence for a claim but don't present it due to lack of space. The evidence might be **facts** or **valid opinions**—opinions supported by facts. (Opinions that are not supported by facts don't count as evidence.)

The chart below lists some of the assertions made by the writer of the article and by Craig Kielburger. In the columns at the right, check whether evidence is presented or not and whether the evidence is fact or valid opinion.

Assertions	Evidence			
	yes	no	fact	valid opinion
by the writer				
• Craig has met with some of the most important political and religious leaders of his time.				
• Craig made a trip to Asia.				
• Craig spends a great deal of his time on the road.				
by Craig				
• Slavery still exists today—slavery of children.				
• The truth is that slavery is practiced in the open.				
• Political leaders are interesting but not the people who impress me most.				

Evidence Cards

The writer of this news report makes conclusions about Craig Kielburger, a teen who fights against child labor. Before you agree with those conclusions, you must be sure that the writer has provided enough supporting evidence. The cards below will help you evaluate the evidence. Read each conclusion. Then, list evidence from the article to see if there is enough to support each conclusion.

Conclusion I
Craig Kielburger is passionate about his belief that child labor and slavery cannot be tolerated.

Evidence

•

•

•

•

•

Conclusion II
Craig Kielburger refuses to let wrongs go unchallenged.

Evidence

•

•

•

•

•

Reading Check

1. What happened to Iqbal Masih after he escaped from slavery?

_____

_____

2. What does Craig think would make the world a better place?

_____

_____

Test Practice

Circle the correct answer.

1. What **theme** is addressed in "One Child's Labor of Love"?

  A Generous people are rewarded.

  B All children must be educated.

  C Good always triumphs over evil.

  D People should try to help those in need.

2. Which of the following statements is an **opinion**?

  F "I've had the chance to travel to Bosnia quite a bit . . . to see what war does."

  G "He was crippled, so his friends were carrying him from place to place so he wouldn't be left behind."

  H "I'm convinced that if you took these children and put them in those positions of power, we would see this world truly be a different place."

  J "I plan on going all the way through my Ph.D. . . ."

3. There is **adequate evidence** for the reader to conclude that Craig meets with political leaders to —

  A talk with the people who have impressed or inspired him most

  B complete an assignment for school

  C bring the issue of children's rights to their attention

  D have his picture taken with them

4. The author provides **adequate evidence** to support all of the following conclusions *except* —

  F Craig Kielburger cares deeply about the rights of children

  G Craig Kielburger is intolerant of child labor and slavery

  H one teenager's actions can make a big difference in the world

  J Craig Kielburger hopes to become famous and win awards

Uniform Style

Recognizing and Evaluating Evidence

Writers can cite many kinds of evidence to support a conclusion. When writers deal with emotionally charged issues—like requiring students to wear school uniforms—they usually bring out the heavy artillery: quotations, statistics, and case studies.

1. **Quotations** are likely to be comments from people who have something significant to say about the topic. **Direct quotations**—people's exact words—are easy to spot. They're always enclosed in quotation marks.

    According to a sixth-grader at Valley Academy, "Kids are proud of who they are instead of worrying about what they're wearing."

2. **Statistics** are information expressed as numbers (such as percentages or measurements). Sometimes statistics are presented in charts or graphs.

    One principal says that test scores went up 20 percent the first year kids wore uniforms.

3. **Case studies** are specific examples. Case studies may illustrate the point made in the conclusion.

    A recent study conducted in more than thirty public schools where uniforms are required shows that social and economic conflicts were greatly reduced.

When you read informational materials intended to persuade you to take a certain action or to think in a certain way, be sure to examine the kinds of support the writer has used. Ask yourself, "Does the evidence provide support for the conclusion? Would other kinds of support have worked better? Should the writer have presented *more* evidence—has the conclusion been supported only partially?" When you consider questions like these, you're evaluating the adequacy and appropriateness of the writer's evidence.

Uniform Style

Mara Rockliff

IDENTIFY

Experts—teachers and principals—are quoted for evidence in lines 6–23. Underline the **quotations,** and label them "direct" or "indirect."

EVALUATE

Do you agree that wearing uniforms makes students more serious (lines 13–18)? Why or why not?

_____

_____

_____

_____

_____

_____

_____

_____

_____

INTERPRET

What **conclusion** does the **direct quotation** in lines 28–30 support?

_____

_____

_____

_____

_____

_____

_____

*S*ome claim that it makes students harder working, less violent, and better behaved. Others protest that it takes away students' freedom to think for themselves.

A fiendish plot to control students through brain implants? No—it's the issue of public school students' wearing uniforms.

Why are more and more public schools in the United States considering uniforms? "It's the whole issue of setting a tone for the day," says Mary Marquez, an elementary school principal in Long Beach, California, the first school district in the nation
10 to make uniforms mandatory.[1] "When students are in their uniforms, they know they are going to school to learn, not going outside to play."

If sporting the latest fashions makes kids feel hip and cool, does wearing a school uniform make them feel more like serious students? Many teachers and principals say yes. They believe that uniforms motivate[2] their students to live up to higher standards and that they promote school spirit, discipline, and academic excellence.

But what about the right to individuality, creativity, self-
20 expression? That's what civil liberties experts are concerned about, and many students and parents agree. Some have even gone so far as to bring lawsuits against schools that won't let students wear what they like.

Still, many parents, tired of shelling out money month after month to buy trendy clothing for their children, are only too pleased to have uniforms settle the question once and for all. Many students also welcome an end to clothing competition. "I don't worry about what I wear in the morning," says twelve-year-old uniform wearer Hortencia Llanas. "I just slip on the
30 clothes." Students from wealthy families no longer show off their expensive clothes at school, and students who can't afford them no longer face ridicule for the way they dress. (Of course,

---

1. **mandatory** (man′də·tôr′ē): required.
2. **motivate** (mōt′ə·vāt′): cause someone to do something or act in a certain way; push or drive.

buying school uniforms can be hard on the pocketbook as well.
A number of schools have started programs to help parents pay
for them.)

Some of the statements made by supporters of uniforms
may seem exaggerated—for example, how could requiring
students to dress alike make public schools safer? But there are
logical arguments to back up this claim. Fights are less likely to
40 break out over a leather jacket or a $150 pair of sneakers if no
one is wearing such items to school. Those who don't belong
on school grounds stand out among students wearing school
uniforms.

In Long Beach, statistics tell the story: School crime went
down 36 percent after students began wearing uniforms.
Fighting dropped 51 percent and vandalism 18 percent. Other
districts that began requiring uniforms report similar
improvements.

In public school districts across the country, the jury is still
50 out on the question of school uniforms. But with so many
possible benefits, many ask: Why not give uniforms a try?

IDENTIFY

Underline two arguments in lines 36–43 that support the statement that uniforms make schools safer.

IDENTIFY

What **conclusion** do the **statistics** in lines 44–48 support?

_____

_____

_____

_____

EVALUATE

Do you think students should wear uniforms? Why or why not?

_____

_____

_____

_____

_____

_____

_____

_____

_____

Support Chart

When writers want to persuade us to accept their opinion about an issue, they must provide support for their **conclusions.** The writer of "Uniform Style" feels that there are many benefits to be gained from wearing school uniforms. Fill in each section of the organizer with details you found in the article.

Question: Should students wear uniforms?

Conclusion: Uniforms have benefits.

Supporting Evidence:

1. Statistics _____
_____
_____
_____
_____

2. Direct Quotations _____
_____
_____
_____
_____

3. Logic and Reasoning _____
_____
_____
_____
_____

Reading Check

1. What is civil liberties experts' concern about school uniforms?

_____

_____

2. Give three **statistics** cited by the writer in support of school uniforms.

_____

_____

Test Practice

Circle the correct answer.

1. Which statement best expresses the writer's **conclusion**?

   A Requiring students to wear uniforms solves all of their schools' problems.

   B Since uniforms offer many benefits, schools should give them a try.

   C School uniforms keep students from being creative.

   D School uniforms have proved to be a bad idea.

2. Why does the writer mention the concerns of civil liberties experts?

   F To prove that students who wear uniforms are less violent than students who wear street clothes to school

   G To remind readers that everyone should be concerned about students' test scores

   H To show that some people oppose school uniforms

   J To show how expensive kids' clothes are

3. Which of the following **conclusions** is supported in the article?

   A Students' ability to focus on their schoolwork improves when they aren't thinking about being fashionable.

   B Wearing uniforms makes kids feel hip and cool.

   C A family has no right to bring a lawsuit against a public school.

   D Schools that require students to wear uniforms should pay for them.

4. What **support** does the writer give for the idea that requiring students to wear uniforms instead of street clothes can prevent violence?

   F Statements by civil liberties experts

   G Statistics from Long Beach

   H A quotation from a school superintendent

   J A quotation from Hortencia Llanas

BECOMING A CRITICAL READER

Recognizing Persuasive Techniques
Recognizing Propaganda Techniques

Recognizing Persuasive Techniques

Persuasion is everywhere. Advertisements urge us to buy things; politicians ask for our votes; editorial writers try to influence our thinking on issues. **Persuasion** is the use of language or of visual images to get us to *believe* or *do* something. Skillful persuaders use a number of techniques to get us to see things their way.

IDENTIFY

What is **persuasion** used for?

Logical Appeals

Logic is correct reasoning. You're using logic when you put facts together and conclude that "if this is true, then that must be true." A logical persuasive argument is built on opinion
10 supported by **reasons** and **evidence.**

Whenever someone tries to persuade you, ask yourself, "*How is this person trying to convince me?*" Be alert to common kinds of fallacious, or faulty, reasoning. When you see the word *fallacious* (fə·lā′shəs), think of the word *false*. **Fallacious reasoning** is false reasoning. On the surface the person's arguments make sense, but if you look closely, you'll find flaws in the reasoning.

Fallacious Reasoning: Two Plus Two Isn't Three

Here are three kinds of fallacious reasoning:

1. Hasty generalizations. A **generalization** is a broad statement
20 that tells about something "in general." Valid generalizations are based on solid evidence. For example, someone who has experience with cats might say, "Most cats love milk." Valid generalizations, like that one, usually include **qualifying words**—*most, some, generally*. Qualifying words allow for exceptions to a generalization (here, cats that don't like milk).

A **hasty generalization** is one that is based on incomplete evidence.

IDENTIFY

Underline the text that explains the difference between a **valid generalization** and a **hasty generalization.**

HASTY GENERALIZATION
Jane Goes Overboard
30 Jane and I went to the Dinner Diner for lunch the other day. Jane ordered a cheeseburger, and it was horrible! She says that she'll never eat in a diner again.

EXPLANATION

Maybe the Dinner Diner's cheeseburgers do taste like shoe leather, but that doesn't mean *every* diner serves a bad cheeseburger. Jane is making a hasty generalization about *all* diners from a single bad experience.

40

I'M FINISHED WITH DINERS— THAT BURGER WAS **HORRIBLE**

2. Circular reasoning. Circular reasoning goes around and around without ever getting anywhere. It says the same thing over and over again, each time using slightly different words.

CIRCULAR REASONING

Too Long Is Too Long Is Too Long

We should cancel these play practices because they are too long. Sometimes they last three hours. We don't need to spend so much time practicing. Three-hour practices are too long.

50

EXPLANATION

This argument presents no reasons to back up the opinion. At first glance it seems to offer support, but if you look closely, you'll see that the same idea is repeated three times!

This man is not guilty, because he did not commit the crime. If he is not guilty, you cannot convict him, because he is innocent.

Circular reasoning.

3. Only-cause fallacy. In the **only-cause fallacy** a situation is seen as the result of only one cause. Situations often have many causes.

60

ONLY-CAUSE FALLACY

Todd Drops the Ball

Our team lost the game tonight because Todd didn't play well. Todd is usually our best player, but he missed lots of shots and didn't get many rebounds. The blame for this loss lies squarely on Todd's shoulders.

INTERPRET

Write your own example of **circular reasoning.**

EXPLANATION

70 Can you see the fallacy in this reasoning? Todd is only one player on a team of many, so his poor playing couldn't be the *only* reason his team lost. Maybe other players on the team didn't play well, either.

"We would have won if Todd had gotten that rebound in the first quarter."

Maybe the opposing team put their best defender on Todd. Maybe the winning team played a better game.

Recognizing Propaganda Techniques

Propaganda is a kind of persuasion designed to keep us from thinking for ourselves. Propaganda relies on appeals to our emotions rather than logical arguments and reasoning. Much propaganda consists of one-sided arguments.

Not all propaganda is bad, however. Most people would agree that a doctor who uses emotional appeals to discourage kids from smoking is using "good propaganda."

Here are several techniques used in propaganda. You'll probably recognize some of them.

10 **1. Bandwagon appeals.** A **bandwagon appeal** urges you to do something because everyone else is doing it. (The word *bandwagon* refers to a decorated wagon used in a parade. A bandwagon carried—yes—the band. Kids would often jump on the bandwagon for an exciting ride.) A person using a bandwagon appeal takes advantage of

20 our desire to be part of a group.

It's the "don't be the last person on your block to have one" technique, and it is often used by advertisers.

A BANDWAGON APPEAL

Eight out of ten people in your area have already signed up for this long-distance service. Time is running out, so hurry! Everyone knows what a bargain this is. Shouldn't you save money too?

30   EXPLANATION

The fact that "everyone is doing it" is not a convincing reason for *you* to do it (or to jump on the bandwagon).

2. **Use of stereotypes.** A **stereotype** is a fixed idea about all the members of a group, one that doesn't allow for individual differences. Stereotyping leads to prejudice—evaluating people on the basis of their membership in a group rather than on their individual characteristics.

USE OF A STEREOTYPE

You just can't trust politicians—they'll do anything to get

40   elected.

EXPLANATION

This sentence unfairly lumps all politicians together. As a group, politicians aren't always popular, but not all are untrustworthy.

3. **Name-calling. Name-calling** is using labels to arouse negative feelings toward someone instead of giving reasons and evidence to support an argument.

USE OF NAME-CALLING

Only a liberal tree-hugger would fail to see the importance

50   of building the new supermall. Who needs that rat-infested park, anyway? Let's pave it over!

EXPLANATION

No convincing reasons for building the mall are given. Instead, the person making this argument dismisses any opponents by calling them names.

4. **Snob appeal.** Advertisers use **snob appeal** when they associate their product with wealth, glamour, or membership

IDENTIFY

"People with green eyes are always jealous" is an example of which type of propaganda?

INTERPRET

Why is calling someone a name not a logical way to support an argument?

in a select society. The message they're sending is that using
their product sets you apart from the crowd.

60   USE OF SNOB APPEAL

The average person thinks that
any old hair-care product
will do. But you know better.
Ultra Turbo Hair is designed for
people who insist on quality—
people like you.

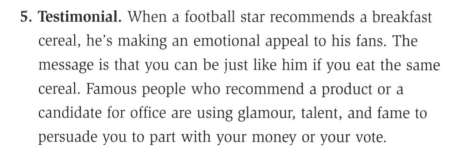

EXPLANATION

This advertisement makes an
appeal to people's desire to feel special. It offers no
70   information about the product itself.

5. Testimonial. When a football star recommends a breakfast
cereal, he's making an emotional appeal to his fans. The
message is that you can be just like him if you eat the same
cereal. Famous people who recommend a product or a
candidate for office are using glamour, talent, and fame to
persuade you to part with your money or your vote.

USE OF A TESTIMONIAL

Hello. I'm not
a politician,
but I play one
80   on television.
I'm here
today to urge
you to vote
for Richard
Richards as
governor of
our great
state.

90   EXPLANATION

In this situation a respected state senator or representative
would provide a more trustworthy testimonial than an
actor who plays a politician on TV.

INFER

How does the **snob appeal**
technique work?

_____

_____

_____

_____

_____

INTERPRET

Think of a product you use
and like. Then, list the
product and a person or
type of person who might
provide an effective
testimonial for that product.

_____

_____

_____

_____

_____

EVALUATE

Propaganda appeals can be
used for good and bad
purposes. Pick one of the
five types of propaganda
discussed in this article,
and describe when it should
or should not be used.

_____

_____

_____

Using Propaganda

Think of something you would like to convince your classmates about. It might be to buy or use a product (the fizzy-woodle you just invented), to join an activity (the Decorate the Halls committee), or to support a cause (collect food and clothing for the homeless), for example. Then, use each of the following types of **propaganda** to win your fellow students over.

1. bandwagon appeal: _____

_____

_____

_____

2. stereotype: _____

_____

_____

_____

3. name-calling: _____

_____

_____

_____

4. snob appeal: _____

_____

_____

_____

5. testimonial: _____

_____

_____

_____

Test Practice

DIRECTIONS: Match each item on the left with the type of fallacious reasoning or propaganda it defines or represents on the right. Write the letter of the correct answer on the line next to the number.

_____ **1.** a famous person's promotion of a product

_____ **2.** an argument that says the same thing over and over

_____ **3.** a statement that encourages you to do something because everyone else is doing it

_____ **4.** persuasion that appeals to people's desire to feel special

_____ **5.** an argument claiming that a situation is the result of a single cause

_____ **6.** a judgment about someone made solely on the basis of his or her membership in a group

_____ **7.** a conclusion based on incomplete evidence

_____ **8.** the use of labels to stir up negative feelings about someone

a. bandwagon appeal

b. stereotype

c. name-calling

d. snob appeal

e. testimonial

f. hasty generalization

g. circular reasoning

h. only-cause fallacy

Reading for Life

As you well know, you spend a lot of time reading every day. You read for school: math and science and history and English and . . . You read for fun: novels and magazines and mysteries and science fiction . . . On top of all your reading for school and pleasure, you also probably read a lot of documents. These documents supply some of the important information you need to live your life in our complicated modern world.

Public documents include information about organizations such as schools, government agencies, churches, and libraries. The announcement of the upcoming parent-teacher conference your teacher sends home with you is a public document. Other public documents are newspaper articles and listings, such as TV and movie schedules.

Consumer documents contain information about the products you buy. They include **product information,** which tells what the product will do; **coupons,** which offer special deals; **contracts,** which tell what services will and will not be provided; **warranties,** which tell what services you get if the product doesn't work; **instruction manuals,** which tell how to use the product; and **technical directions,** which give details on installing and assembling the product.

Workplace documents have two purposes. Those used for **communication** include memos, reports, and applications. Those used for **instruction** include employee manuals and user guides.

In the pages that follow, some of these documents have been used to help solve a problem: Should the city build a skateboard park? As you read, notice what kind of document each one is. Before you read, though, take a moment to list in the box below some of the documents you have already read.

Documents I've Read		
Public	**Consumer**	**Workplace**

READING FOR *Life*

Skateboard Park Documents

- Memorandum

- The City Beat

- Discount Coupon for S. B. Owner's Skate Bowl

- *excerpts from* Consumer Product Safety Commission Document 93

IDENTIFY

Underline the topic of this memorandum.

RETELL

Restate in your own words the need presented in section A.

_____

_____

_____

_____

_____

_____

_____

_____

_____

IDENTIFY

Re-read section B. What requirements does the city have to meet to avoid being sued by people who skate in the new park?

_____

_____

_____

_____

_____

MEMORANDUM

From: A. Longboard, Assistant Director of Parks and Recreation

To: J. Cool, Director of Parks and Recreation

Re: Establishment of a Permanent Skateboard Park

Critical Issues

A. Need. Ten percent of the families in this city, about seven thousand households, include at least one skateboarder. The city provides no designated space for skateboarding. Police reports show that citations for illegal skating are rising every month. This problem is particularly acute in downtown

10   areas, leading to complaints from businesses. The nearest public skateboard park is twenty miles to the east in Mogul, where illegal skating dropped sharply when its park opened last year.

B. Liability. California AB 1296 states that persons who skateboard on public property are expected to know that it is a potentially dangerous sport. They cannot sue the city, county, or state for their injuries as long as the city has passed an ordinance requiring

- helmet, kneepads, and elbow pads for all skaters in

20   the park

- clear and visible signs warning citizens of this requirement

- citations for skaters who violate the ordinance

Such an ordinance was enacted by our city council on July 15, 2000. Therefore, building a skateboard park would not pose a liability risk to the city as long as the above requirements are met.

C. Cost. Local groups have raised half the necessary $140,000. The Parks and Recreation Department's budget can fund the

30   other half. Costs will be minimal—only inspection for damage and yearly maintenance.

D. Location. The city already owns two sites:

- 1.3 acres of the park area between 180th Avenue and 360th Drive, bordered by Drab Street and Grinding Drive, two heavily used thoroughfares. On two sides of the park are neighborhood houses.

40

- 2.1 acres in the 15-acre sports park at Ramp and Spin avenues. This site is set back from heavily traveled roads but still offers excellent access and visibility from service roads within the park. It is also three tenths of a mile from the fire station and paramedic aid. There are no residential neighborhoods bordering the complex.

IDENTIFY

Is this memorandum a **public, consumer,** or **workplace document**?

_____

_____

_____

EVALUATE

If you were a member of this community, which location would you recommend? Why?

_____

_____

_____

_____

_____

_____

_____

_____

_____

_____

_____

_____

_____

_____

IDENTIFY

Is this newspaper article a **public, consumer,** or **workplace document**? Why?

_____

_____

_____

_____

_____

_____

INTERPRET

Pause at line 21. Why is D. T. Merchant in favor of a skateboarding park?

_____

_____

_____

_____

_____

_____

_____

The City Beat

N. Parker

A lively debate occurred at last Tuesday's packed city council meeting on the subject of whether to establish a skateboard park. Mayor Gridlock made a few opening remarks and then turned the microphone over to J. Cool, Director of Parks and Recreation. Mr. Cool read from portions of a report prepared by his staff, who had investigated the need for and the liability, risks, cost, and possible location of a park. Several members of the community spoke.

10 K. Skater said, "Skateboarding is a challenging sport. It's good for us. But right now we have no place to skate, and so kids are getting tickets for illegal skating. Lots of people say it's too dangerous, but that's not true. Kids get hurt in every sport, but you can make it a lot less dangerous for us if you give us a smooth place to practice. Still, we skaters have to be responsible and only take risks we can handle. That teaches us a lot."

D. T. Merchant remarked, "I am a store owner downtown. These skaters use our curbs and handrails as their personal skating ramps. They threaten pedestrians and scare people. If 20 we build them an alternative, I believe most will use it. Then the police can concentrate on the few who break the rules."

G. Homeowner had this to say: "Skaters are illiterate bums. They think safety gear means thick hair gel. They have no respect. They will disturb my neighborhood all night long with their subhuman noise. I would like to remind the city council—I pay taxes and I vote. A skateboard park? Not in my backyard!"

F. Parent: "My son is an outstanding citizen. He is respectful and well behaved. He also lives to skateboard. This city has placed my son at risk by failing to give him a safe place to skate. 30 If we were talking about building a basketball court, nobody would think twice before agreeing. I'm a voter too, and I expect the city council to be responsive to the needs of _all_ citizens."

Finally, S. B. Owner said, "I am the owner of the Skate Bowl. Skateboarding is not a fad. It is here to stay. You may not like the way some skaters act or look, but I know them all. They're great kids. Seems like most of the good folks here tonight are worried about safety. So here's what I propose: I will sell all safety gear in my store at 50 percent off. That's less than it costs me, folks. All that you parents have to do is fill out an emergency-information card for your skater and return it to me. I'll see that the information is entered in a database that paramedics, hospital workers, and police officers can access. I'll also make sure that everyone who comes to my store knows what the Consumer Product Safety Commission says: 'Kids who want to skate are going to skate. Let's help them skate safely.'"

Mr. Owner's proposal was met with a standing ovation. Plans to move ahead with the skateboard-park project will be formally put to a vote at next month's regular session.

IDENTIFY

What offer does S. B. Owner make in response to people's concerns about skating safety?

_____

_____

_____

_____

EVALUATE

Which speaker did you find most convincing? Why?

_____

_____

_____

_____

_____

_____

_____

_____

_____

_____

_____

DISCOUNT COUPON FOR

50%OFF   50%OFF

S. B. Owner's

SKATE BOWL

This coupon entitles bearer,

to **50 PERCENT OFF**

the regular list price on all helmets, kneepads, and elbow pads.

Discount does not extend to shoes, padded clothing, boards, trucks, stickers, or any other equipment. Discount does not include state or local sales tax. Discount is not good in combination with any other discount or coupon. Bearer must show photo identification, such as a school ID or a yearbook photograph.

excerpts from

Consumer Product Safety Commission
Document 93

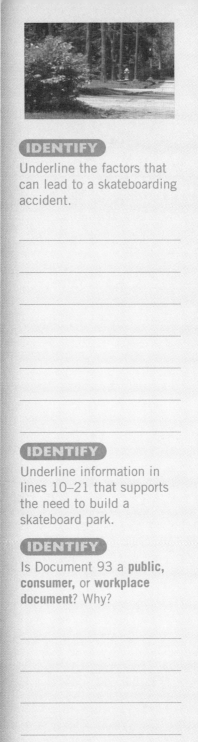

IDENTIFY
Underline the factors that can lead to a skateboarding accident.

Approximately 26,000 persons go to hospital emergency rooms each year for skateboard-related injuries. Several factors—lack of protective equipment, poor board maintenance, and irregular riding surfaces—are involved in these accidents.

Who gets injured. Six of every ten skateboard injuries happen to children under fifteen years of age. Skateboarders who have been skating for less than a week suffer one third of the injuries; riders with a year or more of experience have the next highest number of injuries.

10   Injuries to first-time skateboarders are, for the most part, caused by falls. Experienced riders suffer injuries mainly when they fall after their skateboards strike rocks and other irregularities in the riding surface, or when they attempt difficult stunts.

IDENTIFY
Underline information in lines 10–21 that supports the need to build a skateboard park.

IDENTIFY
Is Document 93 a **public, consumer,** or **workplace document**? Why?

Environmental hazards. Irregular surfaces account for more than half the skateboarding injuries caused by falls. Before riding, skateboarders should check the surface for holes, bumps, rocks, and debris. Areas set aside for skateboarding generally have smoother riding surfaces. Skateboarding in the 20 street can result in collisions with cars, causing serious injury or even death.

The skateboard. Before using their boards, riders should check them for hazards, such as loose, broken, or cracked parts; sharp edges; slippery top surfaces; and wheels with nicks and cracks. Serious defects should be corrected by a qualified repair person.

Protective gear. Protective gear—such as slip-resistant, closed shoes, helmets, and specially designed padding—may not fully protect skateboarders from fractures, but its use is recommended because such gear can reduce the number and 30 severity of injuries.

EVALUATE

Now that you've read a variety of **documents** on the subject, are you opposed to or in favor of building a skateboard park? Give two reasons why.

The protective gear currently on the market is not subject to federal performance standards, and so careful selection by consumers is necessary. In a helmet, look for proper fit and a chin strap; make sure the helmet does not block the rider's vision and hearing. Body padding should fit comfortably. If it is tight, it can restrict circulation and reduce the skater's ability to move freely. Loose-fitting padding, on the other hand, can slip off or slide out of position.

Source: U.S. Consumer Product Safety Commission, Washington, D.C. 20207.

Decision Tree

A decision tree shows the results that may arise from making one decision or another. Filling in this decision tree will help you decide if you are in favor of building a skateboard park. In each box, write at least one reason for making that particular choice.

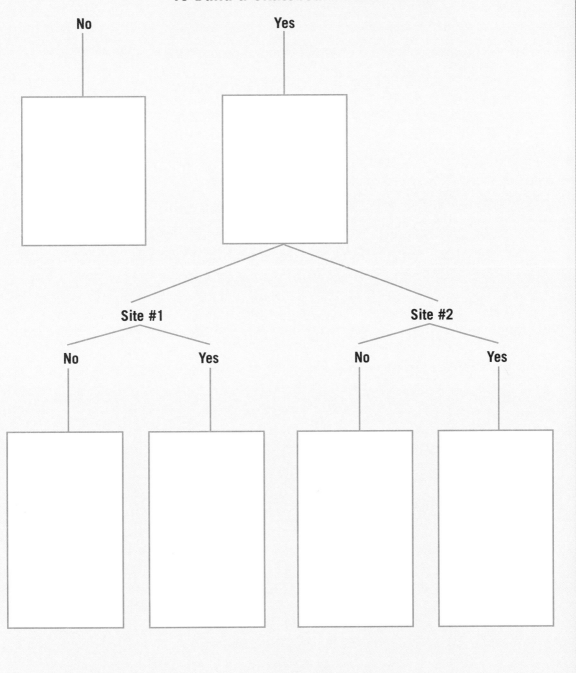

To Build a Skateboard Park—or Not

Reading Check

1. In the Memorandum, what reasons are given in support of building a skateboard park?

_____

_____

_____

2. What are the positive points of the second site proposed for the skateboard park?

_____

_____

_____

3. According to the CPSC Document 93, how does a skateboarder's age and experience affect the chance for injury?

_____

_____

_____

4. What should skateboarders look for when they buy protective clothing?

_____

_____

_____

Test Practice

Circle the correct answer.

1. The city could not get sued by a skateboarder who uses the park provided the city —

   A guarantees everyone's safety

   B builds the park in a residential neighborhood

   C passes an ordinance requiring that protective equipment be worn

   D regularly inspects the park for damage

2. Which opinion did F. Parent express at the council meeting concerning the skateboard park?

   F Skaters should be allowed to skate wherever they want.

   G Skaters already have plenty of safe places to skateboard.

   H A skateboard park is needed for the safety of our children.

   J A skateboard park would be intrusive and disruptive.

3. S. B. Owner's Skate Bowl coupon entitles the purchaser to 50 percent off the price of —

   A any single item in the store

   B a yearbook photo

   C a skateboard

   D selected safety gear

4. The Memorandum and the CPSC Document 93 are both alike in that they —

   F suggest locations for a skateboard park

   G recommend that skateboarders wear helmets

   H investigate the causes of skateboarding accidents

   J are written by the Director of Parks and Recreation

5. The Consumer Product Safety Commission suggests that —

   A skateboards should be checked for hazards

   B a skateboard park should be built immediately

   C local businesses should discount body padding

   D skateboarders can easily avoid injury

6. Which statement supports the idea that a skateboard park should be built?

   F Some residents dislike skateboarders.

   G Skateboard parks can cost taxpayers a lot of money.

   H An area set aside for skateboarding reduces injury.

   J Skateboarders should wear protective gear at all times.

Pet Adoption Application

Application Advice

One type of document you will use many times in your life is an **application form.** You usually have to fill one out when you want to adopt a pet; apply for a job, a driver's license, or a passport; join a club or team; or seek admission to a summer camp or a college. Application forms always ask for your name. They usually ask for your age, address, and phone number. What other information they require depends on what it is you are applying for.

Applications ask for important personal information about yourself, so they should be filled in very carefully. Here are some tips for filling out an application:

- Read the instructions before you start filling out the application. The instructions may tell you to print, to use a certain kind of pen or pencil, and to write in certain areas only.
- Don't leave any line blank. If a question doesn't apply to you, write *n/a,* which means "not applicable."
- Take your time, and write as neatly as you can.
- If the form requires a signature, be sure to sign and date it.
- After you fill out the application, read it through carefully to make sure you didn't miss anything.

Even though most pet adoption agencies allow only adults to adopt pets, for practice with applications, fill in the one on page 264. Be sure to follow all the tips listed above. They'll help you to do a good job.

PET ADOPTION
Application

IDENTIFY

Do you have to pay any money to adopt a pet? Put a check mark in the margin where you find this information.

INFER

What kind of information is asked for in the middle shaded area? Why do you think you are not supposed to write there?

_____

_____

_____

_____

_____

EVALUATE

Does this document request the information that you think is important to learn about someone who wants to adopt a pet? List some additional questions you think should be included.

_____

_____

_____

_____

_____

_____

INSTRUCTIONS: **Adopter,** print carefully in **WHITE AREAS ONLY**—do not write in shaded areas.

❑ Puppy ❑ Kitten ❑ Dog ❑ Cat

Pet Adoption Application

			1	Program	H T		Adoption Number
					D O	1	
Date / /	Single Adoption	Double Adoption	Age	MTA MTD	L R circle one	2	
					G		
Day	Time ❑ AM ❑ PM	Breed	Color	❑ Mr. ❑ Mrs. ❑ Ms. ❑ Miss ❑ Mr. & Mrs.
			Sex	❑ Adopter's Last Name First Name
Voluntary Contribution	Size: S___ M___ L___	Spay/ Neuter	
Cash	$	❑ Pure ❑ Mix	Vaccine Type	Street Address Apt. #
Check	$	Pet's Name	Vaccine Date	
D V M A circle one	$		Rabies Tag	City State/Zip Code
Credit A/R	($)	ASC Int. No.	Rabies Date	
Total Voluntary Contribution $ _____			Wormed	Home Phone Business Phone
X_____			Med. Given	NMR ❑ Tech. App.	( ) - ( ) -

Name of Reference	Address	City	State	Telephone	ID Source
				( ) -	❑ Yes ❑ No
				( )	D V ❑ Yes M A ❑ No
				( )	

1. WHOM IS THE PET FOR? Self____ Gift____ For whom?_____ Adopter's age:_____

2. IF YOU'RE SINGLE: Do you live alone? Yes____ No____ Do you live with family? Yes____ No____
   Do you work? Yes____ No____ What are your hours?_____

   IF YOU'RE MARRIED: Do you both work? Yes____ No____ Husband's hours:_____
   Wife's hours:_____ How many children at home?_____ Ages:_____, _____, _____
   Who will be responsible for the pet? Husband____ Wife____ Children____ Other_____

3. DO YOU: OWN ❑ RENT ❑ HOUSE ❑ APT. ❑ Floor #____ Elevator in the building? Yes____ No____
   (CHECK ONE)   (CHECK ONE)
   If renting, does your lease allow pets? Yes___ No___ Are you moving? Yes___ No___ When?_____
   Do you have use of a private yard? Yes___ No___ Is it fenced? Yes___ No___ Fence height:_____
   Where will your pet be kept?_____ / _____ Any allergy to pets? Yes___ No___
   DAYTIME   NIGHTTIME

4. DO YOU HAVE OTHER PETS NOW? Yes____ No____ Breed:_____
   Where did you get the pet?_____ How long have you had it?_____

   HAVE YOU EVER HAD A PET BEFORE? Yes____ No____ Breed:_____
   How long did you have the pet?_____ What happened to the pet?_____
   Have you ever adopted from this shelter? Yes___ No___ Where is the pet now?_____

5. YOUR OCCUPATION:_____ Business Phone: (   )_____
   Company:_____ Supervisor's Name:_____

VET'S NAME	CITY, STATE	ZIP CODE

Adopter's Signature:

Reading Check

1. A **reference** is a person who can provide information about you. Why would the adoption shelter want references for an adopter? _____

_____

2. Why is it important for the adoption shelter to know whether you rent or own your home? _____

_____

3. What information do you think the shelter is really looking for when it asks what pets you have now? _____

_____

Test Practice

Circle the correct answer.

1. Which of the following people would not be a suitable reference?

A A teacher
B A parent
C A classmate
D An aunt

2. The main thing the shelter wants to know about an applicant is —

F whether the applicant will feed the animal the right food
G whether the applicant plans to let the dog or cat run free through the neighborhood
H whether the applicant will always keep the pet's best interests in mind
J what kind of dog or cat the applicant wants

3. The abbreviation *n/a* stands for "not applicable." What does the term *not applicable* mean?

A None of your business
B Does not apply to me
C Not again
D No answer

4. The application asks for your veterinarian's name. What would be the best thing to do if you didn't already have a vet?

F Just leave the space blank.
G Write *n/a*.
H Ask the shelter to recommend one.
J Make up a name.

PART 3 STANDARDIZED TEST PRACTICE

DIRECTIONS

Read the story. Then, read each question that follows on page 269 and circle the letter of the best response.

The Path Through the Cemetery

Leonard Q. Ross

Ivan was a timid little man—so timid that the villagers called him "Pigeon" or mocked him with the title "Ivan the Terrible." Every night Ivan stopped in at the saloon which was on the edge of the village cemetery. Ivan never crossed the cemetery to get to his lonely shack on the other side. That path would save many minutes, but he had never taken it—not even in the full light of noon.

Late one winter's night, when bitter wind and snow beat against the saloon, the customers took up the familiar mockery. "Ivan's mother was scared by a canary when she carried him." "Ivan the Terrible—Ivan the Terribly Timid One."

Ivan's sickly protest only fed their taunts, and they jeered cruelly when the young Cossack lieutenant flung his horrid challenge at their quarry.

"You are a pigeon, Ivan. You'll walk all around the cemetery in this cold—but you dare not cross it."

Ivan murmured, "The cemetery is nothing to cross, Lieutenant. It is nothing but earth, like all the other earth."

The lieutenant cried, "A challenge, then! Cross the cemetery tonight, Ivan, and I'll give you five rubles—five gold rubles!"

Perhaps it was the vodka. Perhaps it was the temptation of the five gold rubles. No one ever knew why Ivan, moistening his lips, said suddenly: "Yes, Lieutenant, I'll cross the cemetery!"

The saloon echoed with their disbelief. The lieutenant winked to the men and unbuckled his saber. "Here, Ivan. When you get to the center of the cemetery, in front of the biggest tomb, stick the saber into the ground. In the morning we shall go there. And if the saber is in the ground—five gold rubles to you!"

Ivan took the saber. The men drank a toast: "To Ivan the Terrible!" They roared with laughter.

The wind howled around Ivan as he closed the door of the saloon behind him. The cold was knife-sharp. He buttoned his long coat and crossed the dirt road. He could hear the lieutenant's voice, louder than the rest, yelling after him, "Five rubles, pigeon! If you live!"

Ivan pushed the cemetery gate open. He walked fast. "Earth, just earth . . . like any other earth." But the darkness was a massive dread. "Five gold rubles . . ." The wind was cruel and the saber was like ice in his hands. Ivan shivered under the long, thick coat and broke into a limping run.

He recognized the large tomb. He must have sobbed—that was the sound that was drowned in the wind. And he knelt, cold and terrified, and drove the saber through the crust into the hard ground. With all his strength, he pushed it down to the hilt. It was done. The cemetery . . . the challenge . . . five gold rubles.

Ivan started to rise from his knees. But he could not move. Something held him.

Something gripped him in an unyielding and implacable hold. Ivan tugged and lurched and pulled—gasping in his panic, shaken by a monstrous fear. But something held Ivan. He cried out in terror, then made senseless gurgling noises.

They found Ivan, next morning, on the ground in front of the tomb that was in the center of the cemetery. He was frozen to death. The look on his face was not that of a frozen man, but of a man killed by some nameless horror. And the lieutenant's saber was in the ground where Ivan had pounded it—through the dragging folds of his long coat.

---

1. Ivan can best be described as —
   A brave
   B proud
   C fearful
   D sickly

2. Ivan's main **problem** is that he must —
   F carry the heavy saber
   G conquer his terror of the cemetery
   H fight the lieutenant
   J find the biggest tomb

3. When Ivan drives the saber into the frozen ground —
   A his heart gives out
   B he overcomes his fear
   C he sees a ghost
   D he pins his coat to the ground

4. By the **resolution** of the story, Ivan has —
   F claimed his five gold rubles
   G frozen to death
   H disappeared
   J been killed by the saber

5. The **setting** of this story creates an overall feeling of —
   A mockery
   B horror
   C peace
   D courage

6. Another good **title** for the story is —
   F "A Monstrous Fear"
   G "Ivan's Triumph"
   H "A Clever Soldier"
   J "The Lieutenant's Concern"

DIRECTIONS

Read the following selection. Then, read each question that follows on page 271 and circle the letter of the best response.

Little Mangy One

Lebanese folk tale,
retold by Inea Bushnaq

Once upon a time three little goats were grazing on the side of a stony hill. Their names were Siksik, Mikmik, and Jureybon, the Little Mangy One. Soon a hyena scented them and loped up. "Siksik!" called the hyena. "Yes sir!" answered the goat. "What are those points sticking out of your head?" "Those are my little horns, sir," said the goat. "What is that patch on your back?" continued the hyena. "That is my hair, sir," replied the goat. "Why are you shivering?" roared the hyena. "Because I am afraid of you, sir," said the goat. At this the hyena sprang and gobbled him right up. Next the hyena turned to Mikmik, who answered like his brother, and he too was quickly devoured.

Then the hyena approached Jureybon, the Little Mangy One. Before the hyena came within earshot, Jureybon began to snort. As the hyena drew nearer, Jureybon bellowed, "May a plague lay low your back, O cursed one! What have you come for?" "I wish to know what the two points on your head are," said the hyena. "Those? Why, those are my trusty sabers!" said the goat. "And the patch on your back, what is that?" said the hyena. "My sturdy shield, of course!" sneered the goat. "Then why are you shivering?" asked the hyena. "Shivering? I'm trembling with rage! I'm shaking with impatience, for I cannot wait to throttle you and squeeze your very soul till it starts out of your eye sockets!" snarled the goat, and began to advance on the hyena.

The hyena's heart stopped beating for an instant; then he turned and ran for his life. But Jureybon sprang after him over the rocks and gored him with his sharp little horns, slitting open his belly and freeing his two little brothers inside.

1. Unlike Siksik and Mikmik, Jureybon responds to the hyena by —

   A running away
   B refusing to talk to him
   C attacking him
   D answering all of his questions

2. The words Jureybon uses to describe his horns and the patch on his back suggest images of —

   F strength
   G anger
   H hunger
   J fear

3. What is the **conflict** in this story?

   A A hyena tries to eat three goats.
   B Three goats are arguing among themselves.
   C Three goats try to kill a hyena.
   D A hyena is trying to find his way home.

4. One of the **themes** of this story could be stated as —

   F never challenge a bully
   G cleverness can help the weak
   H be kind to strangers
   J there's strength in numbers

5. The first paragraph contains a context clue you can use to figure out the meaning of <u>devoured</u>. Which group of words helps you understand *devoured*?

   A "gobbled him right up"
   B "the hyena sprang"
   C "I am afraid of you"
   D "turned to Mikmik"

DIRECTIONS

Read the following two selections. Then, read each question that follows on pages 276–277 and circle the letter of the best response.

John Brown (1800–1859) was an abolitionist, someone working to end slavery in the United States. The first selection that follows is from Gwen Everett's biography of John Brown. Everett writes from the point of view of Brown's daughter Annie. In this selection, Annie recalls her father's fateful raid on a federal arsenal in Harpers Ferry, Virginia, in 1859. Brown had planned to march south with his "liberation army," freeing people from slavery, enlisting volunteers, and eventually bringing slavery to an end. He raided the arsenal in search of weapons.

from John Brown: One Man Against Slavery

Gwen Everett

We listened carefully to Father's reasons for wanting to end slavery.

None of us questioned his sincerity, for we knew he believed God created everyone equal, regardless of skin color. He taught us as his father had taught him: To own another person as property—like furniture or cattle—is a sin. When Father was twelve years old, he witnessed the cruel treatment of black men, women, and children held in bondage and he vowed, then and there, that one day he would put an end to the inhumanity.

"I once considered starting a school where free blacks could learn to read and write, since laws in the South forbid their education," he told us. "And, when we moved to North Elba, New York, we proved that black and white people could live together in peace and brotherhood."

"One person—one family—can make a difference," he said firmly. "Slavery won't end by itself. It is up to us to fight it."

Father called us by name: Mary, John, Jason, Owen, and Annie (me). He asked us to say a prayer and swear an oath that we, too, would work to end slavery forever. Then he told us his plan.

He would lead a small group of experienced fighting men into a state that allowed slavery. They would hide in the mountains and valleys during daylight. And, under the cover of night, members of his "liberation army" would sneak onto nearby plantations and help the slaves escape.

Freed slaves who wished to join Father's army would learn how to use rifles and pikes—spear-shaped weapons. Then, plantation by plantation, Father's liberation army would move deeper south—growing larger and stronger—eventually freeing all the slaves.

Father's idea sounded so simple. Yet my brothers and I knew this was a dangerous idea. It was illegal for black people to handle firearms and for whites to show them how. It was also against the law to steal someone else's property; and, in effect, Father was doing this by encouraging slaves to leave their masters.

The fateful night of Sunday, October 16, 1859, Father and eighteen of his men marched into Harpers Ferry. They succeeded in seizing the arsenal and several buildings without firing a single shot. By morning the townspeople discovered the raiders and began to fight back. Then a company of marines led by Lieutenant Colonel Robert E. Lee arrived to reinforce the local troops.

The fighting lasted almost two days. When it was over, Father was wounded and four townspeople and ten of Father's men were dead. Newspapers across the country reported every detail of the trial, which was held during the last two weeks of October in Charles Town, Virginia. On October 31, the jury took only forty-five minutes to reach its decision. They found Father guilty of treason against the Commonwealth of Virginia, conspiring with slaves to rebel, and murder.

On December 1, my mother visited him in jail, where they talked and prayed together for several hours. I wished I could have been there to tell Father how courageous I thought he was.

He was executed the next morning.

Father's raid did not end slavery. But historians said that it was one of the most important events leading to the Civil War, which began in April 1861. The war destroyed slavery forever in our country, but it also took 619,000 lives and ruined millions of dollars' worth of property. My father must have known this would come to pass, for the day he was hanged, he wrote: "I, John Brown, am now quite certain that the crimes of this guilty land will never be purged away but with Blood."

Years after Father's death, I still had sleepless nights. Sometimes I recalled our conversations. Other times I found comfort in the verse of a song that Union soldiers sang about Father when they marched into battle.

His sacrifice we share! Our sword will
victory crown!
For freedom and the right remember
old John Brown!
His soul is marching on.

Yes indeed, I think to myself, one man against slavery did make a difference.

In 1850, Congress passed the Fugitive Slave Law. This law required federal officials to arrest people fleeing slavery and return them to their "owners." Here, Harriet Tubman comes to the aid of a runaway who has been captured and is in danger of being returned to slavery.

from Harriet Tubman: Conductor on the Underground Railroad

Ann Petry

On April 27, 1860, [Harriet Tubman] was in Troy, New York. She had spent the night there and was going on to Boston to attend an antislavery meeting. That morning she was on her way to the railroad station. She walked along the street slowly. She never bothered to find out when a train was due; she simply sat in the station and waited until a train came which was going in the direction she desired.

It was cold in Troy even though it was the spring of the year. A northeast wind kept blowing the ruffle on her bonnet away from her face. She thought of Maryland and how green the trees would be. Here they were only lightly touched with green, not yet in full leaf. Suddenly she longed for a sight of the Eastern Shore with its coves and creeks, thought of the years that had elapsed since she first ran away from there.

She stopped walking to watch a crowd of people in front of the courthouse, a pushing, shoving, shouting crowd. She wondered what had happened. A fight? An accident? She went nearer, listened to the loud excited voices. "He got away." "He didn't." "They've got him handcuffed." Then there was an eruptive movement, people pushing forward, other people pushing back.

Harriet started working her way through the crowd, elbowing a man, nudging a woman. Now and then she asked a question. She learned that a runaway slave named Charles Nalle had been arrested and was being taken inside the courthouse to be tried.

When she finally got close enough to see the runaway's face, a handsome frightened face, his guards had forced him up the courthouse steps. They were trying to get through the door but people blocked the way.

She knew a kind of fury against the system, against the men who would force this man back into slavery when they themselves were free. The Lord did not intend that people should be slaves, she thought. Then without even thinking, she went up the steps, forced her way through the crowd, until she stood next to Nalle.

There was a small boy standing near her, mouth open, eyes wide with curiosity. She grabbed him by the collar and whispered to him fiercely, "You go out in the street and holler 'Fire, fire' as loud as you can."

The crowd kept increasing and she gave a nod of satisfaction. That little boy must have got out there in the street and must still be hollering that there's a fire. She bent over, making her shoulders droop, bending her back in the posture of an old woman. She pulled her sunbonnet way down, so that it shadowed her face. Just in time, too. One of the policemen said, "Old woman, you'll have to get out of here. You're liable to get knocked down when we take him through the door."

Harriet moved away from Nalle, mumbling to herself. She heard church bells ringing somewhere in the distance, and more and more people came running. The entire street was blocked. She edged back toward Nalle. Suddenly she shouted, "Don't let them take him! Don't let them take him!"

She attacked the nearest policeman so suddenly that she knocked him down. She wanted to laugh at the look of surprise on his face when he realized that the mumbling old woman who had stood so close to him had suddenly turned into a creature of vigor and violence. Grabbing Nalle by the arm, she pulled him along with her, forcing her way down the steps, ignoring the blows she received, not really feeling them, taking pleasure in the fact that in all these months of inactivity she had lost none of her strength.

When they reached the street, they were both knocked down. Harriet snatched off her bonnet and tied it on Nalle's head. When they stood up, it was impossible to pick him out of the crowd. People in the street cleared a path for them, helped hold back the police. As they turned off the main street, they met a man driving a horse and wagon. He reined in the horse. "What goes on here?" he asked.

Harriet, out of breath, hastily explained the situation. The man got out of the wagon. "Here," he said, "use my horse and wagon. I don't care if I ever get it back just so that man gets to safety."

Nalle was rapidly driven to Schenectady and from there he went on to the West—and safety.

1. The account called *John Brown: One Man Against Slavery* was written —

   A in the third person
   B in the first person
   C by Harriet Tubman
   D by John Brown himself

2. Which of the following statements would John Brown and Harriet Tubman be most likely to agree with?

   F One person fighting against slavery could make a difference.
   G The Fugitive Slave Law was fair and just.
   H Slavery could be ended without violence.
   J People should not involve family members in attempts to end slavery.

3. Which of the following sentences is an example of **first-person narration**?

   A "Harriet started working her way through the crowd. . . ."
   B "Years after Father's death, I still had sleepless nights."
   C "She knew a kind of fury against the system. . . ."
   D "People in the street cleared a path for them. . . ."

4. *Harriet Tubman: Conductor on the Underground Railroad* is —

   F a biography
   G an autobiography
   H an essay
   J a short story

5. Which of these titles seems most likely to be the title of an **autobiography**?

   A *The Civil War: 1861–1865*
   B *How I Gained My Freedom*
   C *Work Songs and Field Hollers*
   D *The Story of the Underground Railroad*

6. One difference between Ann Petry's account and Gwen Everett's account is that —

   F Gwen Everett writes in the first person
   G Ann Petry writes in the first person about someone she knew
   H Ann Petry has written an autobiography and Gwen Everett has written a biography
   J Gwen Everett did not know the person she wrote about

7. Which event completes the following sequence chart?

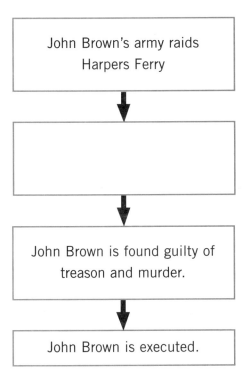

John Brown's army raids Harpers Ferry

↓

↓

John Brown is found guilty of treason and murder.

↓

John Brown is executed.

A John Brown vows to bring an end to slavery.

B John Brown recruits freed slaves into his army.

C John Brown is wounded in battle.

D John Brown fights in the Civil War.

8. In the excerpt from *John Brown: One Man Against Slavery,* who is **the speaker** of the lines "Slavery won't end by itself. It is up to us to fight it"?

F John Brown

G Annie Brown

H Gwen Everett

J Union soldiers

9. The **purpose** of the excerpt from *Harriet Tubman: Conductor on the Underground Railroad* is to —

A convince the reader that slavery was unjust

B inform the reader about one of Harriet Tubman's notable deeds

C give the reader background information about the Civil War

D encourage the reader to follow Harriet Tubman's example of bravery

10. From the readings, you can **infer** that both writers —

F interviewed Harriet Tubman

G worked to end slavery in their lifetime

H admire their subjects

J are related to John Brown

DIRECTIONS

Read the following poem. Then, read each question that follows on page 279 and circle the letter of the best response.

This poem describes a moment in the 1998 National Basketball Association Finals game between the Chicago Bulls and the Utah Jazz. The Bulls superstar Michael Jordan scored the winning shot with just 5.2 seconds left in the game. This victory brought the team their sixth NBA title. The game, which took place on June 14, 1998, in Salt Lake City, Utah, was thought to be Jordan's last. He retired from basketball a few months later, but returned to the NBA in 2001.

Forty-one Seconds on a Sunday in June, in Salt Lake City, Utah   *for Michael Jordan*
Quincy Troupe

rising up in time, michael jordan hangs like an icon,[1] suspended in space,
cocks his right arm, fires a jump shot for two, the title game on the line,
his eyes two radar screens screwed like nails into the mask of his face

bore in on the basket, gaze focused, a thing of beauty, no shadow, or trace,
5 no hint of fear, in this, his showplace, his ultimate place to shine,
rising up in time michael jordan hangs like an icon, suspended in space,

after he has moved from baseline to baseline, sideline to sideline, his coal-face
shining, wagging his tongue, he dribbles through chaos, snaking serpentine,[2]
his eyes two radar screens screwed like nails into the mask of his face,

10 he bolts a flash up the court, takes off, floats in for two more in this race
for glory, it is his time, what he was put on earth for, he can see the headline,
rising up in time, michael jordan hangs like an icon, suspended in space,

inside his imagination, he feels the moment he will embrace, knows his place
is written here, inside this quickening pace of nerves, he will define,
15 his eyes two radar screens screwed like nails into the mask of his face,

---

1. **icon** (ī′kän′) *n.:* image; also, person or thing regarded with great respect and admiration.
2. **serpentine** (sur′pən·tīn′) *adj.* used as *adv.:* in a snakelike way.

inside this moment he will rule on his own terms, quick as a cat he interfaces[3]

time, victory & glory, as he crosses over his dribble he is king of this shrine,[4]

rising up in time, michael jordan hangs like an icon, suspended in space,

his eyes two radar screens screwed like nails into the mask of his face

---

3. **interfaces** *v.*: brings together; joins.
4. **shrine** *n.*: place held in high honor because of its association with an event, a person, or a holy figure.

---

1. Which of the following phrases from the poem contains a **simile**?

   A "he bolts a flash up the court"
   B "fires a jump shot for two, the title game on the line"
   C "he feels the moment he will embrace"
   D "rising up in time, michael jordan hangs like an icon"

2. "Quick as a cat" (line 16) is an example of —

   F metaphor
   G simile
   H personification
   J alliteration

3. Which of the following statements describes the poem's structure?

   A The first and third lines of each stanza rhyme.
   B Each stanza begins with the same line.
   C Each line has the same number of words.
   D The first and second lines of each stanza rhyme.

4. Which of the following phrases is repeated four times in the poem?

   F "he bolts a flash up the court, floats in for two more in this race"
   G "he bolts a flash up the court, takes off, floats in for two more in this race"
   H "michael jordan hangs like an icon, suspended in space"
   J "it is his time, what he was put on earth for, he can see the headline"

5. Which word best describes the speaker's **tone** in this poem?

   A Dazed
   B Admiring
   C Loving
   D Envious

6. Which of the following phrases is an example of alliteration?

   F "inside this quickening pace of nerves"
   G "suspended in space"
   H "the title game on the line"
   J "he bolts a flash up the court"

DIRECTIONS

Read the Web page. Then, read each question that follows on page 281 and circle the letter of the best response.

FEATURES | HOME | SEARCH | FEEDBACK | SITE MAP | NASA

WELCOME! Solar System Exploration is one of four space science themes for the Office of Space Science at the National Aeronautics and Space Administration (NASA). This Web site is your launching pad to find out more about the programs and people in them.

FEATURES

WHY EXPLORE OUR SOLAR SYSTEM?   THE PLANETS

A HISTORY OF EXPLORATION   THE PEOPLE

SCIENCE GOALS –

NEWS –

MISSIONS –

TECHNOLOGY –

RESEARCH –

EDUCATION –

WHAT'S NEW? **EXTRA!** *Mars 2001 Odyssey is on its way to Mars!*

LATE BREAKING

Perseid Dawn
The best time to see this year's Perseid meteor shower is just before dawn on August 12, 2000.

New Asteroid Target Chosen for Japanese-U.S. Mission
The MUSES-C project has announced that the asteroid target of the project and the launch date have been changed.

Hubble Discovers Missing Pieces of Comet Linear
The Hubble telescope discovered a small armada of "minicomets" left behind from what some scientists had prematurely thought was a total disintegration of the explosive comet LINEAR.
More News . . .

LATEST IMAGES

The Color of Regolith

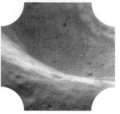

On June 14, 2000, NEAR Shoemaker trained its camera on Eros' large-diameter crater for a series of color pictures intended to measure the properties of regolith inside the asteroid's craters.

RESEARCH ANNC.

CLICK HERE to find out about upcoming research opportunities in the NASA Office of Space Science.

RECENT ADDITIONS

17 MAY 2000
SSE main page has a new look!

17 MAY 2000
The history timeline has been updated.

| Internal | NASA Office of Space Science |

Curator: A. M. Sohus
Webmaster: J. Tenisci
Last Updated: 9 August 2000

1. The source of this home page is —

   A NASA (the National Aeronautics and Space Administration)
   B a group of amateur astronomers
   C the MUSES-C project
   D Solar System Exploration

2. This page was last updated on —

   F June 14, 2000
   G May 17, 2000
   H August 12, 2000
   J August 9, 2000

3. If you wanted to find out about the scientists who work at NASA, which feature would you go to?

   A A History of Exploration
   B The Planets
   C The People
   D Education

4. If you wanted to find out about research opportunities at NASA, what would you click on?

   F Recent Additions
   G Research Annc.
   H Latest Images
   J Late Breaking

5. If you wanted to find out about water on Mars, what would you click on?

   A The Planets
   B Latest Images
   C Recent Additions
   D A History of Exploration

6. Suppose you've read "Hubble Discovers Missing Pieces of Comet Linear." To read more about the Hubble telescope, you should click on —

   F "The Color of Regolith"
   G "The People"
   H "Recent Additions"
   J "More News"

7. Which of the following topics are listed in the contents of this Web page?

   A "Missions" and "Education"
   B "Feedback" and "Site Map"
   C "The Planets" and "The People"
   D "Welcome!" and "Features"

DIRECTIONS

Read the informational article. Then, read each question that follows on page 283 and circle the letter of the best response.

Celebrating the Quinceañera

Mara Rockliff

You stand at the back of the church between your parents and godparents, your knees shaking. You feel special, and a bit awkward, in your first formal dress and your tiara. Your honor court has walked up the aisle ahead of you: fourteen girls in pastel dresses, fourteen boys in tuxedos. With you and your escort there are fifteen couples—one for each year of your life. The long months of planning and preparation have finally ended. Your quinceañera has begun.

The quinceañera (kēn′sā·ä·nye′rə, from the Spanish words *quince,* "fifteen," and *años,* "years") is a rite of passage celebrated by Mexicans and Mexican Americans. People believe that the tradition can be traced back to the Aztec culture, in which girls commonly married at the age of fifteen. Today a girl's quinceañera marks her coming-of-age. It means that she is ready to take on adult privileges and responsibilities.

The most important part of your quinceañera is the *misa de acción de gracias,* the thanksgiving Mass. You slowly walk up the aisle to the front of the church. You kneel, placing a bouquet of fifteen roses on the altar to thank the Virgin Mary for bringing you to this important day. A birthstone ring glitters on your finger, and a religious medal hangs from your neck, inscribed with your name and today's date—special gifts from adult relatives or friends of the family. The priest will bless your medal during the Mass.

Next comes a sermon, followed by prayers and readings from the Bible. You recite your speech, and the service ends. Then the photographer rushes over, and you pose for an endless series of photographs with your family and friends.

But the quinceañera celebration has just begun, for the fiesta is still to come. You enter to the sound of music, a traditional mariachi band or a DJ playing current hits. You dance in turn with your father, your grandfathers, your escort. You and your honor court perform a group dance that you have rehearsed. Then everyone joins in the dancing.

You're almost too excited to eat, but the food is wonderful. There's your favorite—chicken in mole sauce, made from chilies and unsweetened chocolate.

The tables are covered with everything from tamales and corn soup to an elaborately decorated cake.

Later, as everyone watches, your father removes the flat shoes you have worn all day and replaces them with a pair of high heels. In your parents' eyes you are no longer a child. They'll treat you differently from now on, and they'll expect you to act more like an adult as well.

Among your many gifts, one stands out: the last doll. It's not a toy for you to play with, of course; it's a symbol of the childhood you're leaving behind. If you have a younger sister, you might present it to her. You look around at the people who have watched you grow up. You see tears in many eyes. The quinceañera is a tradition many centuries old, but for you it will happen only once.

---

1. A **summary** of this article would —
   A criticize aspects of the celebration
   B cover the most important points
   C discuss the quality of the writing
   D focus on one part of the article

2. In an **outline** of this article, all of these might be details under a main heading *except* —
   F girl dances with father and grandfathers
   G honor court performs dance
   H DJ or mariachi band plays music
   J what happens at the party

3. If you quoted a phrase or sentence from this article on a note card, you would put the writer's words —
   A in quotation marks
   B in capital letters
   C in parentheses
   D in a footnote

4. Which sentence best states the **main idea** of this article?
   F The food is the best part of the quinceañera.
   G The quinceañera happens only once in a girl's lifetime.
   H The quinceañera is a girl's rite of passage into adulthood.
   J Girls who celebrate their quinceañera usually do not appreciate what it represents.

5. If you were taking notes for a **summary** of this article, what event would you cite in the blank below?

   You go to thanksgiving Mass.

   _____

   Your medal is blessed.
   You give a speech.
   A Father gives you high heels.
   B You receive a symbolic doll.
   C You enjoy a wonderful feast.
   D You place roses on the altar.

DIRECTIONS

Read the following passages. Then, read each question that follows on page 285 and circle the letter of the best response.

Pet Heroes

We got Max from a group that traps wild kittens and tames them. When Max came to us, he was scrawny and little. Now he's a broad-shouldered, sun-yellow cat, the biggest cat in the 'hood. Max is my hero because he's a gentle giant with a soft meow. Yet he's kept some of his wild ways. He runs from everybody except me and my parents. He insists on his freedom to roam outside, especially on moonlit nights. He won't eat cat food unless he's really, really hungry. He prefers the mice and rats he catches on his own. Max knows we don't want him to catch birds, so he just watches them. He's kind to other cats—as long as they show him respect. He hates being pounced on. He loves curling up next to the sweet-smelling lavender plants in our yard, jumping from high places, cuddling at night, and getting stroked and scratched while giving me a cat massage with his big paws. I used to worry when he took off for a few days, but he always comes back. Max is my golden boy. He has a little voice but a big heart.

—Lynn

Rita is a small, shaggy, sandy-brown fluff ball. She's what some people call a mix—some poodle, some terrier, and a bit of something else. Rita is my hero because she's my hearing-ear dog. A woman from a place that trains dogs for deaf people found Rita in an animal shelter. Rita had been there for weeks, and nobody had claimed her. She went through five months of training. Then I got lucky. I was chosen to be the one who got to take her home.

I get along well by using American Sign Language, but having Rita tell me when she hears sounds like the ringing of an alarm clock or a telephone makes me feel even more independent. I love Rita. She is my special friend.

—Alex and Rita

Before I got Mopsy, I didn't know a bunny could be so much fun. Mopsy likes to play jokes on our cat. She creeps up behind him and nibbles his tail. She follows me around like a hopping shadow. Sometimes, to get attention, she jumps straight up in the air. Then, when she gets tired, she flops down and takes a power nap. Mopsy loves to play, and she's never mean. My mom says that Mopsy must have learned her playful ways from her mother, who was a classroom rabbit.

Once a week we take Mopsy to visit my great-grandfather at his nursing home. He and his friends love to see her. Mopsy gets to sit on their laps and on their beds. She is quiet and never bites. That's why she's my hero.

—Michael

1. Which **title** fits all three passages?
   A "Giving Humans a Helping Hand"
   B "My Pet Is My Hero"
   C "Courageous Critters"
   D "Keeping Animals Safe"

2. Which of the following **main ideas** is found in all three passages?
   F To be considered a hero, an animal must show great courage.
   G Animals make better use of their time than humans do.
   H People can learn a great deal from their animal friends.
   J People should spend more time with their pets.

3. All of the following titles describe articles that probably deal with topics related to these readings except—
   A "Tips on Caring for Your Dog"
   B "Can Pets Make People Happy?"
   C "My Iguana Is a Good Friend"
   D "When Rover Made My Day"

4. What word *best* describes the **tone** of all three passages?
   F sarcastic
   G critical
   H sincere
   J mocking

5. Which of the following statements about pets is *not* a **fact**?
   A Cats make better pets than dogs.
   B Dogs can be trained to help deaf people.
   C Some cats like to hunt for their own food.
   D Mopsy visits a nursing home every week.

DIRECTIONS

Read the article. Then, read each question that follows on page 287 and circle the letter of the best response.

Too Much TV Can Equal Too Much Weight

by Jamie Rodgers, 12 years old
Children's Express

In 1970, only 10 percent of kids in America were overweight. In the 1980s, it was 30 percent, and in the 1990s, it was 60 percent. Studies show that obesity is linked to watching TV and using the Internet.

Children's Express interviewed two professors from Johns Hopkins University School of Medicine about the link. Ross Andersen, M.D., is with the weight management center, and Carlos Crespo, M.D., is an assistant professor of health and fitness.

"Dr. Crespo and I have published a study that appeared in the *Journal of the American Medical Association*. We looked at how fat kids were in relation to the number of hours of television they watch per day," said Andersen. "We found that kids who are low TV watchers were much leaner. The kids who were the fattest were those who watched a lot of TV. We defined a lot as four or more hours per day. Roughly, one in three kids in America is watching four or more hours per day. I would estimate sitting in front of a computer would be just as great a risk factor for being overweight."

Andersen and Crespo say the blame is not just on the parents. Sometimes it's a lack of places to play.

"[It's a] lack of facilities, services for the children to be able to go out and play basketball or go to a swimming pool. The community should have open spaces and safe spaces for girls and boys to be active," said Crespo.

"The thing is not that it's bad to watch TV; it's just that you need to have a balance. There [is] a certain number of hours in the day you're supposed to sleep, do your homework, . . . [and] go to school, and then there is a certain [number] of hours that you're free to do whatever you want. If you spend that time watching TV, then you spend less time doing physical activity.". . .

"Kids and parents need to look for opportunities to remain physically active. So instead of sitting down to watch *Who Wants to Be a Millionaire*, it may be that the whole family could get up and go for a walk.". . .

1. What percentage of American children were overweight during the 1990s?

   A 10

   B 20

   C 40

   D 60

2. Studies show that obesity is linked to watching TV and —

   F going for walks

   G doing homework

   H using the Internet

   J taking long naps

3. Which of the following statements is *not* true?

   A The author uses quotations to support her conclusions.

   B The author uses statistics to support her conclusions.

   C The author uses experts' opinions to support her conclusions.

   D The author does not provide adequate support for her conclusions.

4. The doctors define "a lot of TV" as —

   F one or more hours per day

   G two or more hours per day

   H three or more hours per day

   J four or more hours per day

5. Andersen and Crespo place part of the blame for overweight in children on —

   A lack of playgrounds

   B poor health education

   C lack of medical attention

   D fast foods

6. The doctors believe that children and parents should —

   F prepare meals together

   G remain physically active

   H watch TV together

   J surf the Internet

7. The *best* statement of the writer's **conclusion** is that —

   A the whole family should go on a diet

   B obesity in children is linked to watching TV

   C parents must take blame for children's obesity

   D we need to stop watching TV

DIRECTIONS

Read the article. Then, read each question that follows on page 289 and circle the letter of the best response.

His Gift to Girls

A taxi driver funds a school in India.

Ritu Upadhyay

Hundreds of little girls in the tiny Indian village of Doobher Kishanpur wake up and go to school each day. Sure, in America girls do the same thing. But in Doobher Kishanpur (doo′ bur kish′ən·poor), it's nearly a miracle. Thanks to a generous cab driver, many of these students are the first girls in their family to read and write.

Om Dutta Sharma has spent the past 20 years driving a yellow taxicab in New York City for 80 hours a week. After saving all his extra cash, Sharma used it to open the Ram Kali School for Girls in 1997. The school is named for his mother, who—like many poor women in India—never learned to read or write.

Before the school opened, the girls in this village had no chance to learn. Their parents, who are very poor, could not afford to send them to schools in the neighboring towns where the boys study.

An Unlikely Hero

Sharma, 65, came to the U.S. 25 years ago with one goal: to make money. A trained lawyer in India, Sharma was frustrated to learn that he would not be able to practice law in the U.S. unless he went back to school. As he stood on the street, cars whizzing by, the idea of driving a taxi struck him: "I love to drive, so why not get paid?"

Sharma never wanted money for himself. He felt he had a debt to repay to the poor farming community where he grew up. "If I can help somebody be on the right path, then the purpose of living is achieved," says Sharma.

By American standards, Sharma's salary is not much. But in India, it goes a

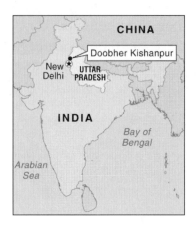

long way. Each month his dollars pay four teachers ($58 each), a local pharmacist ($100) for medicine, and a physician ($100) to keep all the schoolchildren healthy. He also donates the earnings from a mango grove he inherited in India to the school. That pays for the students' books and school uniforms.

A Driver's Work Is Never Done

Sharma says he will retire only when he has enough money to open up four more schools, as well as free health clinics. For now, he's happy saving his money and meeting passengers. "I learn so much when they open up their hearts and minds to me."

1. Om Dutta Sharma wanted to give something back to the village where he grew up. What did he do?

   A He came to the United States and worked as a taxi driver.
   B He opened a school for boys in a neighboring town.
   C He came to the United States to study law.
   D He opened a school for girls in Doobher Kishanpur.

2. The information in the article supports the **assertion** that —

   F all children in India attend school
   G not all children in India attend school
   H all schools in India are financed by the government
   J in India, boys and girls attend classes together

3. Which statement is an **opinion**?

   A Om Dutta Sharma pays the salaries of four teachers.
   B Sharma pays for the girls' books and uniforms.
   C Sharma's mother never learned to read or write.
   D Sharma wouldn't have liked being a lawyer in the United States.

4. Which **assertion** would Sharma probably agree with?

   F Few children deserve an education.
   G Helping people gives meaning to life.
   H It's important to leave the past behind you.
   J Success is measured by the kind of job you have.

5. We can reasonably **assert** that this article was written to —

   A persuade people to like Sharma
   B show the value of education
   C explain the benefits of driving a cab
   D show that it doesn't take millions to make a difference

DIRECTIONS

Read the following essay. Then, read each question that follows on page 291 and circle the letter of the best response.

from All I Really Need to Know I Learned in Kindergarten

Robert Fulghum

This is my neighbor. Nice lady. Coming out her front door, on her way to work and in her "looking good" mode. She's locking the door now and picking up her daily luggage: purse, lunch bag, gym bag for aerobics, and the garbage bucket to take out. She turns, sees me, gives me the big, smiling Hello, and takes three steps across her front porch. And goes "AAAAAAAAGGGGGGGGGHHHHHHHHH!!!!" *(That's a direct quote.)* At about the level of a fire engine at full cry. Spider web! She has walked full force into a spider web. And the pressing question, of course: Just where is the spider *now*?

She flings her baggage in all directions. And at the same time does a high-kick, jitter-bug sort of dance—like a mating stork in crazed heat. Clutches at her face and hair and goes "AAAAAAAGGGGG-

GGHHHHHHHHHH!!!!!" at a new level of intensity. Tries opening the front door without unlocking it. Tries again. Breaks key in the lock. Runs around the house headed for the back door. Doppler effect[1] of "AAAAAGGGHHHHaaggh . . ."

Now a different view of this scene. Here is the spider. Rather ordinary, medium gray, middle-aged lady spider. She's been up since before dawn working on her web, and all is well. Nice day, no wind, dew point just right to keep things sticky. She's out checking the moorings and thinking about the little gnats she'd like for breakfast. Feeling good. Ready for action. All of a sudden everything breaks loose—earthquake, tornado, volcano. The web is torn loose and is wrapped around a frenzied moving haystack, and a huge piece of raw-but-painted meat is making a sound the spider never heard before: "AAAAAAA-GGGGGGGGGHHHHHHHHHH!!!!!!" It's too big to wrap up and eat later, and it's moving too much to hold down. Jump for it? Hang on and hope? Dig in?

Human being. She has caught a human being. And the pressing question is, of course: Where is it going, and what will it do when it gets there?

---

1. **Doppler effect:** change in the pitch of a sound, produced when the source of the sound moves toward or away from the listener.

The neighbor lady thinks the spider is about the size of a lobster and has big rubber lips and poisonous fangs. The neighbor lady will probably strip to the skin and take a full shower and shampoo just to make sure it's gone—and then put on a whole new outfit to make certain she is not inhabited.

The spider? Well, if she survives all this, she will really have something to talk about—the one that got away that was THIS BIG. "And you should have seen the JAWS on the thing!"

---

1. What does the writer **compare** and **contrast** in this essay?

    A A jitterbug and a stork
    B People and spiders
    C A spider web and a front porch
    D Breakfast foods

2. What **pattern** does the writer use to organize his essay?

    F Block method
    G Point-by-point method
    H Chronological order
    J Cause-and-effect pattern

3. Both the human and the spider start out feeling —

    A scared
    B hungry
    C good
    D sleepy

4. The human and the spider are both —

    F very old
    G male
    H very young
    J female

5. The spider —

    A thinks of the human as a piece of raw but painted meat
    B thinks of the human as a friend
    C wants to go in and shower
    D bites the human

6. The human —

    F thinks of the spider as a piece of raw but painted meat
    G thinks of the spider as having rubber lips and poisonous fangs
    H doesn't think anything of the spider at all
    J thinks the spider is cute

7. After the encounter the human will —

    A take a shower and put on a new outfit
    B kill the spider
    C call the exterminator
    D let the spider rebuild her web

8. After the encounter the spider will —

    F crawl into a hole and die
    G talk about the one that got away
    H repair her web
    J go after the human

DIRECTIONS

Read the following application form. Then, read each question that follows on page 293 and circle the letter of the best response.

Natural History Museum Volunteer Application

1. Name: _____

Address: _____ City, State, Zip code: _____

Home telephone: _____ E-mail: _____

Social Security number: _____ Age: ❑ Under 18 ❑ Over 18

2. Education School most recently attended: _____

3. Employment If a résumé is available, please submit it along with your application. (Please check *Past* or *Present*.)

❑ Past ❑ Present Volunteer Work: _____

Special skills or training: _____

Computer skills: _____

Fluency in other languages (please specify): _____

4. Is there a specific department or program at the museum in which you would like to work if a volunteer job is available? _____

Why do you want to volunteer at the Natural History Museum? _____

_____

5. Availability Please check the times you are available to volunteer.

	Mon.	Tues.	Wed.	Thurs.	Fri.	Sat.	Sun.
9.00 A.M–1:00 P.M.							
1.00 P.M.–5:00 P.M.							
5.00 P.M.–8:30 P.M.	███	███	███	███			███

When can you start? _____

A minimum commitment of one year is required. Can you meet this requirement? ____

I have read and am in possession of a copy of the "Volunteer Regulations and Procedures."

Signature _____ Date _____

1. In what section should you indicate that you speak more than one language?

   A 1
   B 2
   C 3
   D 4

2. The purpose of section 5 is to find out —

   F what hours you're available to work
   G what work experience you have
   H where you live
   J what your educational background is

3. For what department is the museum hiring?

   A Tours
   B Research
   C Sales
   D The application doesn't say.

4. Which of the following statements belongs in section 4?

   F I can design Web sites.
   G I've always been interested in dinosaurs.
   H I can start working immediately.
   J I am a skilled scuba diver.

5. For how long must you agree to work if you take the job?

   A Six months
   B One year
   C Two years
   D Three months

ACKNOWLEDGMENTS

For permission to reprint copyrighted material, grateful acknowledgment is made to the following sources:

Atheneum Books for Young Readers, an imprint of Simon & Schuster Children's Publishing Division: "The Bracelet" by Yoshiko Uchida from *The Scribner Anthology for Young People*, edited by Anne Diven. Copyright © 1976 by Yoshiko Uchida.

Susan Bergholz Literary Services, New York: "Eleven" from *Woman Hollering Creek* by Sandra Cisneros. Copyright © 1991 by Sandra Cisneros. Published by Vintage Books, a division of Random House, Inc., New York, and originally in hardcover by Random House, Inc. All rights reserved.

CBS News Archives: From "One Child's Labor of Love" from *60 Minutes II*, October 5, 1999. Copyright © 1999 by CBS Inc.

Children's Express Foundation, Inc.: From "Too Much TV Can Equal Too Much Weight" by Jamie Rodgers from *Children's Express*, accessed September 22, 2000, at http://www.cenews.org/news/200007obesetv.htm. Copyright © 2000 by Children's Express Foundation.

Clarion Books/Houghton Mifflin Company: "The Mysterious Mr. Lincoln" from *Lincoln: A Photobiography* by Russell Freedman. Copyright © 1987 by Russell Freedman. All rights reserved.

Cobblestone Publishing Company, 30 Grove Street, Suite C, Peterborough, NH 03458.: "Wartime Mistakes, Peacetime Apologies" by Nancy Day Sakaduski from *Cobblestone: Japanese Americans*, April 1996. Copyright © 1996 by Cobblestone Publishing Company. All rights reserved.

Coffee House Press: "Forty-one Seconds on a Sunday in June, in Salt Lake City, Utah" from *Choruses* by Quincy Troupe. Copyright © 1999 by Quincy Troupe.

Ruth Cohen for Lensey Namioka: "The All-American Slurp" by Lensey Namioka. Copyright © 1987 by Lensey Namioka. All rights reserved.

Don Congdon Associates, Inc.: "All Summer in a Day" by Ray Bradbury. Copyright © 1954 and renewed © 1982 by Ray Bradbury.

Gwen Everett: From *John Brown: One Man Against Slavery* by Gwen Everett. Text copyright © 1993 by Gwen Everett.

The Gainesville Sun: "Suit Helps Girl Enjoy Daylight" by Lise Fisher from *The Gainesville Sun*, January 31, 1999. Copyright © 1999 by The Gainesville Sun.

Greenwillow Books, a division of HarperCollins Publishers, Inc.: "Ankylosaurus" from *Tyrannosaurus Was a Beast* by Jack Prelutsky. Copyright © 1988 by Jack Prelutsky.

Grolier Publishing Company, a division of Scholastic Inc.: From "Nilou" from *Newcomers to America: Stories of Today's Young Immigrants* by Judith E. Greenberg. Copyright © 1996 by Judith E. Greenberg.

HarperCollins Publishers: "Zlateh the Goat" from *Zlateh the Goat and Other Stories* by Isaac Bashevis Singer, illustrated by Maurice Sendak. Text copyright © 1966 by Isaac Bashevis Singer.

Houghton Mifflin Company: "Medusa's Head" from *Greek Myths* by Olivia Coolidge. Copyright © 1949 and renewed © 1977 by Olivia E. Coolidge. All rights reserved.

Jet Propulsion Laboratory, California Institute of Technology: From *Solar System Exploration* Web site, accessed August 10, 2000, at http://sse.jpl.nasa.gov. Copyright © 2000 by the Jet Propulsion Laboratory, California Institute of Technology.

Alice P. Miller: "All Aboard with Thomas Garrett" by Alice P. Miller from *Cobblestone*, vol. 2, no. 2, February 1981. Copyright © 1981 by Alice P. Miller.

North Shore Animal League, Port Washington, New York: North Shore Animal League Pet Adoption Application. Copyright © 2000 by North Shore Animal League.

Pantheon Books, a division of Random House, Inc.: "Little Mangy One" from *Arab Folktales* by Inea Bushnaq. Copyright © 1986 by Inea Bushnaq.

People Weekly: From "Brave Hearts" (retitled "Trial by Fire") from *People Weekly*. Copyright © 1997 by Time Inc.

Random House, Inc.: Excerpt (retitled "Brother") from *I Know Why the Caged Bird Sings* by Maya Angelou. Copyright © 1969 and renewed © 1997 by Maya Angelou.

Random House Children's Books, a division of Random House, Inc.: "Just Once" by Thomas J. Dygard from *Ultimate Sports* by Donald R. Gallo. Copyright © 1995 by Thomas Dygard.

Russell & Volkening as agents for Ann Petry: "A Glory over Everything" from *Harriet Tubman: Conductor on the Underground Railroad* by Ann Petry. Copyright © 1955 and renewed © 1983 by Ann Petry.

The Saturday Review: "The Path Through the Cemetery" by Leonard Q. Ross from *Saturday Review of Literature*, November 29, 1941. Copyright © 1941 by General Media International, Inc.

Scholastic Inc.: "Ta-Na-E-Ka" by Mary Whitebird from *Scholastic Voice*, December 13, 1973. Copyright © 1973 by Scholastic Inc.

Simon & Schuster Books for Young Readers, an imprint of Simon & Schuster Children's Publishing Division: Excerpt (retitled "Storm") from *Woodsong* by Gary Paulsen. Copyright © 1990 by Gary Paulsen.

Gina Spadafori: "Animal Instincts" by Gina Spadafori from *Pets.com, The Magazine for Pets and Their Humans*, vol. 1, issue 4, June 2000. Copyright © 2000 by Gina Spadafori.

Time Inc.: "His Gift to Girls" by Ritu Upadhyay from *Time for Kids*, vol. 5, no. 16, February 4, 2000. Copyright © 2000 by Time Inc.

Laurence S. Untermeyer on behalf of the Estate of Louis Untermeyer, Norma Anchin Untermeyer, c/o Professional Publishing Services Company: "The Dog of Pompeii" from *The Donkey of God* by Louis Untermeyer. Copyright © 1932 by Harcourt Brace & Company.

Villard Books, a division of Random House, Inc.: From *All I Really Need to Know I Learned in Kindergarten* by Robert L. Fulghum. Copyright © 1986, 1988 by Robert L. Fulghum.

PHOTO CREDITS

Abbreviations used: (tl) top left, (tc) top center, (tr) top right, (l) left, (lc) left center, (c) center, (rc) right center, (r) right, (bl) bottom left, (bc) bottom center, (br) bottom right, (bkgd) background.
Page 3, Getty Images/Stone; 15, (c) Courtesy of The San Diego Museum of Man, San Diego, California, (bkgd), Image Copyright ©2003 Photodisc Inc.; 29, Nancy Davis/HRW Illustration; 43, (br), Image Copyright ©2003 Photodisc Inc., (bkgd), Dr. E.R. Degginger; 53, *Boy by the Sea* (1995) by Jonathan Green, Naples, Florida. Oil on canvas (18"x17"). Photograph by Tim Stamm; 59, (tr), National Archives, Photo No. 111-B-6135, (c), The Granger Collection, New York; 67, Brian Callanan/HRW Illustration; 81, Lester Lefkowitz/ Getty Images/FPG International; 87, (c), Peter Bollinger/HRW Illustration, (bkgd), Image Copyright ©2003 Photodisc Inc.; 91, Image Copyright ©2003 Photodisc Inc.; 101, Image Copyright ©2003 Photodisc Inc.; 113, Image Copyright ©2003 Photodisc Inc.; 119, Chang Park/HRW Illustration; 291, Joel Spector/HRW Illustration; 144, Museo Archeologico, Syracuse, Sicily, Italy. Scala/Art Resource, New York; 159, Suzanne Duranceau/HRW Illustration; 169, Kansas State Historical Society; 175, (c), Michael Newman/PhotoEdit, (bkgd), Image Copyright ©2003 Photodisc Inc.; 181, (c), Harstock, (bkgd), Image Copyright ©2003 Photodisc Inc.; 184, (c), Index Stock Imagery, (bkgd), Image Copyright ©2003 Photodisc Inc.; 193, (lc),(rc), The Granger Collection, New York, (bkgd), Image Copyright ©2003 Photodisc Inc; 199, (br), The Granger Collection, New York, (bkgd), Tony Freeman/ PhotoEdit; 207, (br), © Jon Fletcher/The Gainesville Sun, (bkgd), Image Copyright ©2003 Photodisc Inc.; 213, (tl), Courtesy of the Library of Congress, (br), Ohio Historical Society; 219, (tl),(l),(bl),(bkgd), Courtesy of the Library of Congress; 225, (tr), PictureQuest, (bkgd), Image Copyright ©2003 Photodisc Inc.; 231, (lc),(c),(rc), Courtesy of Free the Children, (bkgd), Image Copyright ©2003 Photodisc Inc.; 239, (l), Mary Kate Denny/PhotoEdit, (r), Robin L. Sachs/ PhotoEdit; 244, Image Copyright ©2003 Photodisc Inc.; 253, Image Copyright ©2003 Photodisc Inc.; 261, Image Copyright ©2003 Photodisc Inc.

AUTHOR AND TITLE INDEX